The spectacular career of Gustav Adolf by no means established Sweden as a great power. In the four years after his death such a development became increasingly improbable. At Westphalia in 1648 the improbable became a fact; but the momentum of Swedish imperial expansion did not culminate until 1658, when Charles X imposed peace upon a prostrate Denmark.

The core of this volume of four essays, by the doyen of historians of Sweden, lies in the two studies of the man who bestrode the summit. One, an examination of Charles X's domestic policies and constitutional significance; the other, a discussion of the objectives of his foreign policy. Both are matters of controversy, and these studies attempt to assess the debate. Flanking these essays are, on the one hand, a study of Oxenstierna's magnificent failure in Germany between 1633 and 1636; and on the other, an examination of the great controversy surrounding the death of Charles XII: a controversy which became perhaps the most baffling – and certainly the most protracted – that Swedish historiography can show.

FROM OXENSTIERNA TO CHARLES XII

Four studies

FROM OXENSTIERNA TO CHARLES XII

Four studies

MICHAEL ROBERTS

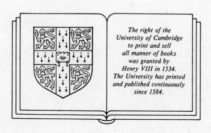

The right of the
University of Cambridge
to print and sell
all manner of books
was granted by
Henry VIII in 1534.
The University has printed
and published continuously
since 1584.

CAMBRIDGE UNIVERSITY PRESS

CAMBRIDGE
NEW YORK   PORT CHESTER
MELBOURNE   SYDNEY

Published by the Press Syndicate of the University of Cambridge
The Pitt Building, Trumpington Street, Cambridge CB2 1RP
40 West 20th Street, New York, NY 10011–4211, USA
10 Stamford Road, Oakleigh, Melbourne 3166, Australia

© Cambridge University Press 1991

First published 1991

Printed in Great Britain at the University Press, Cambridge
Phototypeset by Wyvern Typesetting Ltd, Bristol

British Library Cataloguing in Publication Data
Roberts, Michael, *1908–*
From Oxenstierna to Charles XII: four studies.
1. Sweden, 1523–1818
1. Title
948.502

Library of Congress cataloguing-in-publication data
Roberts, Michael, 1908–
From Oxenstierna to Charles XII: four studies
Michael Roberts.
p. cm.
ISBN 0 521 40014 7
1. Sweden–History–Charles X Gustavus, 1654–1660. 2. Sweden –
History – Charles XI, 1660–1697. 3. Sweden – History – Charles XII,
1697–1718. 4. Charles X Gustav, King of Sweden, 1622–1660.
5. Oxenstierna, Axel, greve, 1583–1654. 6. Charles XII, King of
Sweden, 1682–1718. I. Title.
DL721.B63   1991
948.5′03–dc20   90–1901 CIP

ISBN 0 521 40014 7 hardback

for

Paul F. Nix

Contents

Introduction

The four pieces which go to make up this book were written at different times and with different purposes in mind. No common theme pervades them; no link binds one to another. Each addresses a specific topic which happened at the time to interest me, and which it seemed to me had some interest in the general context of the period; and on each of them information in English was not easy to come by. The first of them originally appeared in *Scandia*, the third and fourth in *Karolinska Förbundets Årsbok*, and I am grateful to the editors of these journals for their kind permission to reprint them.

The first, that on Axel Oxenstierna's career in Germany from 1632 to 1636, was provoked by the publication in 1978 of what (alas!) seems destined, at least for the foreseeable future, to be the final volume of the great series of Oxenstierna's letters and state-papers which began to appear in 1888. Its publication passed, apparently, unnoticed: no Swedish historical journal remarked it. That seemed to me a regrettable omission. And so, after waiting a year or two, I resolved to attempt to repair it. I was in any case under an obligation to the Leverhulme Trust to produce a study of this period; and that volume which appeared in 1978 filled an important gap, making what had seemed to be a formidable enterprise a good deal easier. It was now possible to follow in great detail Swedish policy in Germany during the whole of this tangled period; and the story of the great Chancellor's fortunes and misfortunes shed much-needed light upon an aspect of the Thirty Years' War to which (with a couple of conspicuous exceptions)[1] little attention had been given since the days of Georg Irmer, Moritz Ritter, and Johannes Kretzschmar.

If then the essay on Oxenstierna began as something of a celebration, the two studies of Charles X represent the outcome of a pro-

---

[1] I refer to Sverker Arnoldsson's *Svensk-fransk krigs- och fredspolitik i Tyskland 1634–1636* (Göteborg 1937), and to Sigmund Goetze's important dissertation, *Die Politik des schwedischen Reichskanzlers Axel Oxenstierna gegenüber Kaiser und Reich* (Kiel 1971). But in this respect the situation has altered considerably since 1978.

I

tracted attempt to come to terms with that paradoxical and under-rated monarch. When I was an undergraduate striving to get the hang of the seventeenth century, the only literature on Charles X seemed to be a solid chapter in the old *Cambridge Modern History*, and Emile Haumant's *La Guerre du Nord*. Half a century later the situation had scarcely altered, unless the enquirer happened to command a reading knowledge of Swedish or Polish. The result was a view of the king (generally accepted by most English historians) which was a travesty, or at least a caricature. Charles X was dismissed as a brutal and bellicose character, a conscienceless aggressor, an imperialist of the most deplorable type, who dragged his exhausted country into unnecessary wars, and was rescued from the consequences of his folly by the diplomacy of France. There is, of course, more than a grain of truth in this judgment. But in regard to foreign policy it more or less ignores a difficult question: whether after Westphalia territorial expansion was, or was not, an inevitable precondition for Sweden's survival as a great power; and the further question whether the programme of peaceful economic imperialism envisaged by Oxenstierna in 1650 was not perhaps a feasible alternative to wars of conquest, at all events in the short run. These are questions still debated by Swedish historians, and the answer to them is still not self-evident. Moreover, excessive preoccupation with Charles's wars has too often led non-Swedish historians to miss the remarkable range of his gifts and achievements: as a diplomat who in 1650 did more than any other statesman to round off the Westphalian settlement; as an administrator of marked ability; as a king who took the business of kingship with unrelaxing seriousness; as a consummate tactician in domestic affairs, no less than on the battlefield. As Stellan Dahlgren has demonstrated, the *reduktion* of 1655 was essentially his personal work, the outcome of his minute and expert calculations; and the more famous *reduktion* of Charles XI was firmly based on the work of his father. Charles XI was able to impose it on the high nobility at a moment when it was discredited and demoralised; Charles X, more subtle, far more intelligent, much more fruitfully laborious, manoeuvred the high nobility and the Council into accepting his *reduktion* at a moment when their strength had not yet been seriously impaired, and when their self-confidence was still high. Not only that: he was able to carry them with him in entering upon a war which the three lower Estates would certainly have preferred to avoid. To his aggressions they were in fact a party; and whatever blame attaches to his foreign policy must be shared (at least to begin with) by his Council. Charles XI's solution to Sweden's predicament – peace, renunciation of expansion, the balance of power, independence of foreign subsidies – was a programme whose feasibility was at least dubious in his father's day. After 1675 absolutism had become conceivable; after 1680 it became almost popular; and Charles XI felt it to be essential to the programmes he had in mind. But was it conceivable or possible to Charles X? Did he seek to establish it? Once again we are confronted with a question still debated. So it seemed to me that it might be a useful service to attempt two short studies, having these controversies in mind: one on Charles's foreign policy; one on the constitutional situation during his reign.

The fourth essay, like its two predecessors, deals with a controversy. No ordinary controversy, confined to professional historians: this was the most far-spreading, at times the most passionate, and certainly the most protracted controversy in all Swedish history. The first shot in it was fired as early as 1719; the last, not until 1950. It concerned the circumstances of Charles XII's death in the trenches before Fredrikshald, and the issue appeared to be deceptively simple: did he fall by enemy action, and thus meet a death appropriate to a hero? Or was it a case of murder; and if murder, with what motive, and by what hand? These questions evoked deep and sometimes partisan feelings; and the answer to them might be influenced by such considerations as the lingering hope of reversing the verdict of the Peace of Nystad; or, as the Age of Liberty drew to its conclusion, by revulsion against its politicians, and detestation of its founders. But there was no getting away from the fact that Charles's death was of decisive importance in the history of his country. Absolutism collapsed overnight; the constitution of 1721 established the virtual sovereignty of the Estates; for two generations thereafter Sweden was ruled (and sometimes misruled) by the most representative and effective parliamentary institutions that contemporary Europe could show. Government by the consent of the governed, which the political nation learned and practised during the Age of Liberty, struck such deep roots into the national consciousness that it could never afterwards be eradicated. Thus in the long view what mattered was not Charles's life but his death; and when men disputed the manner of it they were not arguing about an event of trivial or transient importance. Moreover, to most Swedes, even though some of them might in retrospect disapprove of Charles's obstinate refusal to compromise, and almost all repudiated his absolutism, he nevertheless remained a national hero, and the suggestion that he might have been murdered by one of his subjects (or even with the connivance of his sister) was abhorrent. Yet throughout the eighteenth century curious anecdotes, family traditions, gossip retailed at second- or third-hand, kept that suggestion very much alive; and they were given unmerited support by the farcically perfunctory exhumation of 1746: to such effect that the text-books of the early nineteenth century accepted murder as a historical fact.

Serious historiography began with Voltaire, though he was mainly concerned to vindicate the innocence of one of his countrymen. Jöran Nordberg's life of Charles XII, published in 1740, was a commissioned semi-official biography from which dangerous thoughts had been discreetly removed before publication. For the rest of the century there was really nothing. The most eminent historians of the time – Olof von Dalin, Sven LagerBring, Jonas Hallenberg – devoted themselves to other matters: to the demythologizing of Sweden's early history, in the case of the first two; to a great life of Gustav Adolf, in the case of Hallenberg; and all three left their major works unfinished. And this applies also in all respects to Erik Gustaf Geijer early in the next century. Not until the appearance of the Danish historian Paludan-Müller's examination of the problem in 1846 did it begin to interest the professional historians. Paludan-Müller was concerned primarily to demolish the fantastic constructions of Per Wieselgren, which represented the *reductio ad absurdum* of typical eighteenth-century attributions of guilt to this person or that; but it had the important effect of enlisting the interest of Anders Fryxell, a brilliant narrator, if a rather slap-dash historian, whose forty-six volumes enjoyed wide popularity. It was at the insistence of Fryxell, among others, that the exhumation of 1859 was carried out, this time with at least some attempt to give the appearance of scientific procedure; and its categorical verdict of accidental death seemed to relieve the Swedish people of a burden of guilt of which it had long been sensible. Provided, of course, that that verdict stood up to scrutiny; and there were those who felt (rightly) that it did not.

Thereafter historiographical fashions came and went, not least in regard to Charles XII. In the relatively liberal climate of the later nineteenth century, historians had, in general, taken a negative view of him: in the first two decades of the twentieth they were much more indulgent. The trend of this 'New School' was towards a general rehabilitation; and it engendered a feeling that yet another exhumation was necessary: an exhumation furnished this time with all the apparatus and expertise that modern science could provide. After all, with the bicentenary of the king's death imminent, it seemed that a decent piety demanded that the tenebrous circumstances surrounding it be cleared up.

But the exhumation of 1917, so far from dissipating all doubts, proved to be the forerunner of two decades in which Swedish historians concerned themselves with the problem as they had never done before. They were in any case in the process of dividing into two camps, arrayed against each other on many a 'dark and bloody ground'. Some of their battles appeared, at that time, to be over fundamentals; but those of them who were revisionists did not fail to notice that Charles's death offered a suitable opportunity for a skirmish, and they did not fail to avail themselves of it. They found themselves by no means alone, though some of their allies were irregulars: despite the exculpatory verdict of 1917, the twenties saw a marked revival of the murder-theory; and the publicity which was given to it produced in the thirties a corresponding reaction among conservative historians, and especially in military circles. Each side in this combat had learned one thing from 1917: that it was essential to have recourse to the widest possible range of expertise. They found the experts very ready to oblige. But the effect of importing these reinforcements was unfortunately to make the issue so technical and so complex that few historians were now competent to command the whole field; though this by no means deterred them from carrying on the battle: in the dark year 1940 it reached a climax of acrimony.

Thereafter some of the steam went out of it, as the historians came to realise that this had become too hard a matter for them; by the end of the forties the paroxysm had passed; by the mid-fifties the exhausted disputants were content to admit that there was not much point in wrangling further over a problem which they could not solve.

This essay, then, so far from being a contribution to the controversy, is designed rather to celebrate its obsequies. Some gesture of the kind seemed called for, since for several years the false trails and alternative suspects had exerted upon me the compulsive fascination of a detective story. But now it was over – over with the last page torn out – and I need puzzle myself no longer to provide a credible solution to the mystery. But if I could not solve it I could at least commemorate it.

I

Oxenstierna in Germany, 1633–1636

I

In 1888 the Royal Swedish Academy of Letters, History and Antiquities embarked upon the great task of publishing the writings and correspondence of Axel Oxenstierna. In that year there appeared simultaneously the first volume of the First Series, containing his own letters and state papers, and also of the Second Series, devoted to letters addressed to him.[1] Of the Second Series, which is ordered by correspondents rather than on a chronological basis, twelve volumes have so far appeared; of the First Series, fifteen, covering his output down to the moment when in July 1636 he quitted Germany for ever: the last of them to be published (volume XII), which had long formed an awkward gap in the collection, came in 1978, just ninety years after the start of the enterprise. Though it would be an exaggeration to say that what we now have is no more than the tip of the iceberg, it is certainly true that much material still awaits publication: after all, the great Chancellor's active political life did not close until his death in 1654; and though correspondence in the Second Series does in many cases extend beyond 1636, many very important correspondents are as yet unrepresented in it.

What we have, then, is a magnificent but unfortunately uncompleted historical monument which at present seems unlikely to be carried further. The year 1636 is certainly a natural place to suspend operations, if they must be suspended at all; but it is unfortunate that the cessation of publication leaves the historian who may wish to investigate Oxenstierna's later career almost totally stranded.[2] For as with the sources, so with the literature. It is a truly astonishing fact

---

[1] *Axel Oxenstiernas skrifter och brevvexling*, I and II Series (Stockholm 1888–1978) (cited hereafter as *AOSB*).

[2] At the beginning of the last century, however, there appeared *Bref ifrån Svea-Rikes Canceller Grefve Axel Oxenstierna till Grefve Johan Oxenstierna . . . åren 1642–1649* ed. Carl C. Gjörwell (Stockholm 1810, 1819).

that there exists no full life of Oxenstierna in any language. The contrast with Richelieu, or with Wallenstein (to look no further) is striking. There is, indeed, a good study of his youth and early career by Willhelm Tham; and there is Nils Ahnlund's splendid biography which takes the story down to Lützen.[3] But otherwise there is literally nothing. Ahnlund's book is a heroic torso, a great historian's masterpiece; but how should we feel if French historiography could show no study of Richelieu which progressed beyond the Day of Dupes? The comparison is not unfair; for when we close Ahnlund's book he leaves us on the threshold of the most strenuous and dramatic period in his subject's life: the period in which his eminence in Europe attained its brief climax; and, after that, the period when he was in all but name the effective ruler of his country. When Oxenstierna's partnership with Gustav Adolf was dissolved in the mists of Lützen, there lay ahead of him in the immediate future a tangled thicket of experience, still imperfectly investigated by the historian,[4] and not at all by the biographer.

All the more reason, then, to celebrate the completion of the publication of his papers from 1633 to 1636 – the years when the thicket is densest, and the wait-a-bit thorns most deterrent to the explorer. And though there can be no question, within the necessarily limited dimensions of an essay, of embarking upon a detailed narrative of his policies, the eight thick volumes on this period now available make it possible at least to get some idea of the nature of the problems which confronted him, the difficulties with which he had to struggle, and his personal reactions to the pressures upon him.

If we should be tempted to judge those policies by their results, it is difficult to deny that by the summer of 1636 they had failed at all points. The League of Heilbronn was broken and dead; Protestant Germany was rallying to the terms of the Peace of Prague; the old enemy Denmark had once again obtained, in Bremen, a lodgment in north Germany; the conquests in Prussia had been restored to Poland, the tolls at the Prussian ports had been lost; the Rhineland and Alsace had perforce been abandoned to the tutelage of France; the grandiose Swedish pretensions to compensation – territorial or monetary – had been whittled away to nothing; the 'security' which Gustav Adolf had been seeking now seemed beyond hope of attainment. In 1633 Oxenstierna had commanded a prestige in Europe such as no subject before him had enjoyed: a position unparalleled,

---

[3] Wilhelm Tham, *Axel Oxenstierna, hans ungdom och verksamhet intill år 1612* (Stockholm 1935); Nils Ahnlund, *Axel Oxenstierna intill Gustav Adolfs död* (Stockholm 1940).
[4] The best and most recent work is the excellent dissertation by Sigmund Goetze, *Die Politik des schwedischen Reichskanzlers Axel Oxenstierna gegenüber Kaiser und Reich* (Kiel 1971).

perhaps, before that of Wellington after Waterloo. Armed with plenipotentiary powers which were almost regal, treating petty princes as his equals, he stood covered before kings,[5] and it seemed neither unreasonable nor presumptuous that he should entertain the idea of having himself made Elector of Mainz: the only question was whether such an elevation was necessary or expedient. Two years later the picture had changed dramatically. By the spring of 1635 his authority was collapsing; central Germany was as good as lost, and in order to reach the coast from Worms he had no option but to make a long detour through France and Holland, bearing with him the booty from a scene of action to which he would never return. A few months later, and the picture was darker still. In August 1635 he found himself the prisoner of his own mutinous officers; driven, in desperate bargaining, to buy them off with promises impossible to fulfil, secretly sending to the Emperor appeals for peace which were answered only by the imprisonment of his envoy. By the end of the year he sat solitary, impotent, embittered, in Stralsund, a weary and disillusioned Canute vainly bidding the tide of German patriotism to retreat, powerless any longer to control the course of events; his forces reduced to one small precarious army, his options limited to a choice between accepting such terms as John George might be prepared to give him, or submitting himself to the fetters of a French alliance.

It is only when we look more closely at the circumstances encompassing this disastrous record that we can understand, not only how the situation came about, but also – more important for our present purposes – the magnitude of the task, and the quality of the man who confronted it. Oxenstierna's record of failure does not damage his reputation: it illustrates it. This is the heroic period of his career; though at the same time it is the most inglorious.

II

What was required of him, on the morrow of Lützen, has only to be stated for its impossibility to become obvious. He must now not only conduct his country's foreign policy, not only manage the finances of war; but also assume the responsibilities and discharge the functions of a commander-in-chief: he was doomed to be Gustav Adolf, no less than Axel Oxenstierna. It was a load no man could

---

[5] As he reminded his colleagues on his return home: *Svenska Riksrådets Protokoll* (Handlingar rörande Skandinaviens Historia, 3rd Series) (Stockholm 1878–), VI. 401 (cited hereafter as *RRP*).

carry. Already, in July 1632, he had written to his brother of the crushing burden of work which even then fell upon him:

God is my witness that I am simply not able to do it, and am so harassed *varietate rerum*, so beset *mole negotiorum*, so burdened *difficultatibus*, so surrounded *periculis*, that often I know not what I do . . . I am quite weary of life, and allow all my duty to fall into arrears . . . For as to devotion and good-will, they are still what they always were; but my strength and my capacity diminish.[6]

But he underrated both the one and the other. What was imposed on him in 1632 was as nothing to the burdens of 1633–6.

At the beginning of 1633 the government in Stockholm sent him his commission.[7] It gave him powers greater than were entrusted to any Swedish subject before or since; greater than he desired, greater (as he was later to remark) than was prudent.[8] He was now in supreme control of all Sweden's interests in Germany. It was his business to conduct the intricate diplomacy necessary to sustain the war-effort. He was the director and supervisor of the extensive administrative apparatus which had been set up in Germany in the wake of the Swedish conquests: it fell to him, for instance, to organise the postal system, to fix tolls on rivers, to regulate trade and fairs, to establish a new ecclesiastical organisation for the occupied lands, to see to the provision of scholarships for deserving students out of ecclesiastical revenues.[9] The work was often of an incredibly minute particularity: amid the great issues of war and peace he had to find time personally to specify exactly how much wine, how much meat, how much bread, must be provided from the archdiocese of Mainz, what taxes should be paid by householders, craftsmen, and stock-farmers, and how the salt trade was to be regulated.[10] He was the head of a whole new civil service, German in personnel, half-Swedish in nomenclature. But on top of all this he was also, of course, the director of military operations. He must determine strategy; he must allocate available resources to this army or that; arrange for and control recruiting, taking care that the military enterprisers did not cheat the Swedish crown. He must settle bitter delimitation disputes in regard to the assignment of quarters; compose the often violent jealousies between generals, for which disputes over quarters provided an inexhaustible store of inflammable material; he must flatter the vanity, appease the pride, and curb the

---

[6] *AOSB* I.VII, 509 (to Gabriel Gustafsson Oxenstierna, 25 July 1632). (Dates are throughout Old Style.)

[7] *RRP* III. 12 (11 January 1633).

[8] *AOSB* I.XIV.389; *RRP* VI. 400–1.

[9] *AOSB* I.XI.244, for scholarships in the diocese of Magdeburg.

[10] *AOSB* I.X.183–6.

disintegrating ambitions of commanders who were also near-sovereign princes. The task of ensuring the proper functioning of the vital apparatus of 'contributions' was in itself a full-time occupation. Every day confronted him with the question of how the armies were to be paid, and by whom. How persuade financiers, in Hamburg or Amsterdam, or among German adventurers doing well out of the war, to make the necessary loans? How coax the enterprisers to shoulder, for just a little longer, the cost of keeping their troops in a state of no more than simmering mutiny? How reconcile the fundamental principle that war must pay for itself, with the no less fundamental principle that the economic life of Germany must be preserved in sufficient health to permit the financial bloodletting without which the war could not go on?[11] One main object of the creation of the League of Heilbronn was precisely in order to provide a steady income of men and money. But the object was not achieved; the League members were chronically in arrears. The cumbrous machinery of the League itself, with its *consilium formatum* under Oxenstierna's presidency, added another burden: that of wrestling with the 'slowness, and vain discourses, and untimely meannesses' which he later blamed for the League's collapse.[12]

As if this were not enough, he found himself saddled with an infinity of responsibilities and problems which had little or nothing to do with the affairs of Germany, though they constituted a substantial addition to the sum of his labours. He still kept in his hands the management of the 'licenses' – those tolls which Sweden levied at the Baltic ports which were in her occupation – for he rightly believed that his long experience made him better fitted for the work than anybody else, and that the agents he appointed would function more efficiently under his direction than under that of any conceivable successor. But if he clung to this responsibility by his own choice, the government at home heaped upon him tasks of the most miscellaneous, and sometimes of the most vexatious, kind. At not infrequent intervals he was called upon to transmit to Stockholm, by the hand of Lars Grubbe or some other trusted emissary,[13] vast memoranda covering the whole field of domestic concerns. He was, of course, incomparably the most experienced member of the Council, and it was perhaps natural that his colleagues should rely heavily on his advice. But the practical effect at times was that in addition to all else he was virtually forced into the position of acting as prime minister *in absentia*. It must be admitted that he by no means

---

[11] On this, see e.g., *AOSB* I.IX. 89 (to Gustav Horn, 26 June 1633).
[12] *AOSB* I.XII. 472 (to Gabriel Gustafsson Oxenstierna, 19 September 1634).
[13] For Grubbe, see P. G. Berggren, *Lars Grubbe, hans lif och verksamhet* (Karlstad 1898).

always waited to be asked his opinion; and though on such occasions he might apologise for giving it unsolicited, that was no more than a courteous epistolary gesture.[14] He did not merely acquiesce in a domestic pre-eminence which was thrust upon him; he assumed it almost as a right. If he was *not* consulted, and particularly if his advice was not taken, or was not acted upon sufficiently effectively, his colleagues in Stockholm could expect to be told, in letters of great pungency, that he resented it; and on occasion were plainly informed that they had made asses of themselves.[15]

One of the most important of these domestic tasks was the drafting of the Form of Government which became law in 1634. It was soon afterwards supplemented, at the request of the Regents, by the comprehensive instruction for provincial governors (*landshövdingar*) and other local officials. These were matters of major importance; and they fell properly within the ambit of his office as Chancellor. But there were other matters where the relevance was not so obvious. It was to Oxenstierna, for instance, that the Regents turned for a detailed determination of the wage-scales for civil servants; it was to him likewise that they applied for a ruling on the question of their own official emoluments.[16] On the best types of taxation, on the easing or maintenance of the fiscal burdens, on the framing of budgets, on the correct minting policy to be followed, he sent precise and lengthy recommendations which he undoubtedly assumed would be attended to – as, in fact, they usually were. At the Regents' request he drew up for them a schedule of rates for tolls and duties in Sweden and Finland:[17] one might almost suppose that the office of Treasurer was by some accident vacant, and that its functions too had been transferred to Oxenstierna's shoulders. A great mass of correspondence, of increasing acrimony, dealt with the production and marketing of copper, and the folly of the government in putting its trust in the wrong agents.[18] At the end of 1635, with his German world collapsing all round him, he sent them home from Stralsund proposals for the development of Stockholm as a centre of population and trade, together with the first idea for the establishment

<hr/>

[14] 'I know that I act presumptuously in thus giving my views unasked, but . . . ': *AOSB* I.IX.357 (7 September 1633).

[15] E.g. *AOSB* I.XII.649, where he blames the government for being too soft with Riga, tells them that they should have consulted with him first, and adds: 'Such proceedings make me weary of my life, and remove much of the hope for the country which I might otherwise have had' (to Gabriel Gustafsson Oxenstierna, 1 November 1634).

[16] *AOSB* I.XI.382 (to Gabriel Gustafsson Oxenstierna, 6 March 1634); *ibid.* 741 (Memorial for Lars Grubbe, 20 May 1634).

[17] *AOSB* I.XI.188 (2 February 1634).

[18] See, e.g., *AOSB* I.X.438; and, for the government's defence, *Handlingar rörande Skandinaviens Historia* (Stockholm 1842–) (cited hereafter *HSH*) 25. 141–51.

of a loan-bank there.[19] His theological learning, as well as his experience of the problem in Gustav Adolf's time, made him the natural man to consult in regard to the revived plan for the establishment of a *consistorium generale*:[20] later developments would make plain how much they needed his firm hand in dealing with such formidable ecclesiastics as Bishop Rudbeckius of Västerås. Oxenstierna's unwavering conviction that Sweden's safety demanded the keeping of a strong navy produced reiterated exhortations which revealed an astonishing intimacy with naval affairs. Indeed, his mastery of the subject made the Admiral, Karl Karlsson Gyllenhielm, look like an ineffective and negligent amateur: when it came to drawing up the naval estimates Gyllenhielm was very ready to avoid this tiresome duty by simply presenting to the Council the draft estimates which Oxenstierna had taken care to send over to him.[21] But he was not only the universal, omniscient, all-competent minister – Richelieu, Bullion, Sublet de Noyers, all rolled into one – he was also very much the Elder Statesman, entitled by his length of service and his unique relationship with Gustav Adolf to be informed, to advise, and to warn. From Frankfurt or Mainz he sent home weighty admonitions, warnings against peer-creation, warnings against the pursuit of private advantage, or the abuse of noble privileges; and when the Estates met he despatched to them quasi-royal allocutions exhorting them to unity and the necessary sacrifices.[22] Before the *riksdag* of 1634 he drew up not only the Proposition which was to be laid before them, but also (by way of avoiding untoward accidents) the Resolution which the Estates were to take upon it when the Diet ended. Gustav Adolf himself had rarely gone as far as this.[23]

The correspondence with Stockholm displays a range of precise information and a tenacity of memory for relevant detail which are almost incredible: the cumulative effect is overwhelming. In the midst of raging mutiny or military disaster he was able to write, calmly, copiously, and with authority, upon matters as diverse and often as technical as gun-founding, mining, fortifications, types of naval vessels, fisheries, tithe, the guilds, roads and bridges, canals, town privileges and town government, ecclesiastical policies and preferments . . . there seems no end to the list. Five years after he had

---

[19] *AOSB* I.XIV.291 (to Gabriel Gustafsson Oxenstierna, 30 November 1635).

[20] *HSH* 30. 100–1. For the question of a *consistorium generale*, see M. Roberts, *Gustavus Adolphus. A History of Sweden 1611–1632* (1953). I. 405–12.

[21] *RRP* v. 345 (24 November 1635).

[22] *AOSB* I.XII.95–102.

[23] *HSH* 29. 237. Though admittedly he acted at the invitation of the Regents. And cf. p. 92, below.

left Prussia to join Gustav Adolf in Germany he still had clearly imprinted on his memory, in minute detail, the location and strength of defensive works and garrisons in that province.[24]

But it was not only with matters of state – matters which, in many cases, it might have been expected that the Regents should deal with themselves – that he concerned himself, or was made to concern himself. Letters on comparative trivialities abound, in response to commissions or solicitations from home. Nothing, it seemed, however petty, was deemed to fall outside his duty; no call upon his time was forborne by his colleagues. He must see to the selection and despatch of Rhine wine for the Court; he must order the cloth for Gustav Adolf's funeral, must advise the government on which regalia were to be placed in the coffin, must select a suitable necklace for Queen Christina. His views were sought – and were given in great detail – on the proper furnishing for the Council chamber in Stockholm castle.[25] At rare intervals he managed to find time to devote to his family concerns: detailed directions for managing the family estates; the ordering, supervision and inspection of the pearl-embroidery for his son Johan's wedding outfit; necessary measures for the care of the estates of his son-in-law, Gustav Horn, after Horn was taken prisoner at Nördlingen.[26] There seemed to be a general presumption that he was sufficiently at leisure to keep a fatherly eye on any young relative of himself or his colleagues who might be shipped out to Germany to make a career for himself; even his political enemy, Johan Skytte, did not scruple to add to the Chancellor's labours by commending his son to his care. One gets the impression that in Stockholm they regarded him as a kind of commissionaire.

Thus the first and not least important thing to remember in judging Oxenstierna's record in Germany is the sheer overwhelming burden of work which was heaped upon him. Often he felt that it was more than he could bear. But though he might lament the paucity of secretarial assistance, might complain that he had no one to whom he could delegate, might appeal (in vain) for the sending of a trusty coadjutor from home, somehow or other everything was attended to, every commission executed. In 1633 he was already a man past middle age, as age went in those days – he was born in 1583 – but though soon after his return home he began to complain of the weight of years and its attendant disorders, his constitution was sound enough to give him another eighteen years of vigorous

[24] *AOSB* I.XIII.346–8.
[25] For some examples of all this, see *AOSB* I.XI.661; XII.319, 342; XIII.508.
[26] *AOSB* I.XV.239; XIV.295, 309; XV.22; XIII.390, 393.

activity after that. Certainly his years in Germany revealed a mental stamina capable of enduring severe strains with a fortitude which was only very rarely shaken: he was the fortunate possessor of the Wellingtonian gift of sleep.

Not the least of his troubles was simply his remoteness from Stockholm. In summer it might take a month for a letter to reach him, in winter much longer; and in times of military adversity communications were often hazardous. The inevitable consequence was that the Chancellor and his colleagues could not satisfactorily co-ordinate policy. On critical issues, such as the question what *satisfactio* Sweden might be prepared to accept, they repeatedly found themselves out of step: in the interval between the despatch of a letter and the receipt of the reply to it the situation might change in such a way as to make the reply irrelevant; and at times the directives from Stockholm had a wild unreality which must have caused Oxenstierna to throw up his hands in despair.[27] Another consequence was that the home government's reference to him of purely domestic problems might arrive in Germany at the most inopportune moments. For this the Regents were not, of course, responsible: they might well have postponed their enquiries to a more convenient season if they could have foreseen in what circumstances those enquiries would arrive. Thus it happened that their commission to draw up a code of instructions for *landshövdingar* and the local administration fell upon him in the middle of the crisis produced by the disaster at Nördlingen; thus it was that at the moment when he was the prisoner of his officers in Magdeburg he found himself also required to answer in detail a long questionnaire on the policy to be pursued on a great number of not very urgent domestic issues.[28]

The difficulty was of course felt on both sides. For the Regents had perforce to conduct certain aspects of Sweden's foreign policy themselves: they could not always wait for Oxenstierna's advice, nor were they always in a position to follow it when it arrived. This was the case, for instance, in regard to relations with Russia, and the question whether Sweden should risk an alliance with the Tsar while Russia was still fighting the Poles. It was the case too in some respects in

---

[27] A good example of this is the tangled and self-contradictory directive of 12 October 1635 which reached Oxenstierna in Stralsund on 29 November, and which contained (among other solutions) the idea that he might somehow persuade the Protestant states of Germany to make *another* peace with the Emperor in place of the Peace of Prague: (*HSH.* 37. 75–90); or Gabriel Gustafsson's hasty suggestion (in a postscript!) that it might be 'a good thing' to conclude an alliance with John George and other Protestants provided they would defend the Baltic coast 'and keep us safe from the Emperor' – this on 11 June 1635, with the Peace of Prague already made! *AOSB* II.III.364.

[28] *AOSB* I.XII.503–18 (14 August 1635).

regard to Denmark: they had to respond to Danish *démarches* in Stockholm according to their own judgment; and on the question of whether to accept Kristian IV's son as successor to John Frederick of Bremen their instinctive hostility to Denmark only slowly retreated before the realities of the situation in Germany. Above all, this was the case in regard to Poland. Oxenstierna had been negotiating with the Poles, off and on, for half his political lifetime, and rightly believed that he knew more about the best way to manage them than anybody else: 'I have dealt with Polish affairs so long that I know them like the Lord's Prayer'.[29] But though the Regents did in fact take care to ask for his advice, and though Oxenstierna was not slow to give it, the responsibility for this crucial settlement fell not on himself as Chancellor, but on the inexperienced, divided, and pessimistic government in Stockholm; and they proved unable to hold their negotiators to the ultimate line of concession which had been agreed upon.[30] The resulting truce of Stuhmsdorf, with its surrender not only of Swedish holdings in Prussia but also of the 'licenses' at the Prussian ports, moved Oxenstierna to a tremendous outburst of anger. It was not only that he disapproved of the terms obtained; what angered him still more was what he considered to be the incompetence of the Swedish negotiators (as he contemptuously remarked, not one of them – except his son Johan – was capable of speaking Latin),[31] the leaking of Sweden's limit of concession to the French ambassador who was acting as mediator, and the failure to notify him officially of the terms until two months after they had been settled. He vented his resentment in intemperate (and in part indefensible) letters which deeply wounded his colleagues.[32] They felt, and they had reason to feel, that in his insistence on his own policies he brushed aside considerations which seemed to them impossible to ignore: the exhaustion of the country, the recalcitrant temper of the Estates,[33] the sheer impossibility (as they saw it) of carrying on a war against the Poles in addition to what for many of

---

[29] *AOSB* I.XIV.92.

[30] The fullest account of the government's Polish policy is Herbert Rettig, *Die Stellung der Regierung und des Reichstages Schwedens zur polnischen Frage, April 1634 bis November 1636* (Halle 1916).

[31] *AOSB* I.XII.272.

[32] See, e.g., *AOSB* I.XIII.22, 339–43, 350, 353; XIV.91–6; II.III.379. If he had not lost his temper he would hardly have ventured the statement that the chances of successful war against Poland were now better than in the memory of man: *AOSB* I.XII.341; or told his son that he had 'dishonoured my name': *AOSB* I.XIII.350. The truth was that he did not consider there was any Swede fit to conduct a negotiation of this kind except himself: *ibid*. 446. He may well have been right, but it would have been better not to say so.

[33] 'I have lived through nine *riksdagar* or more in his late Majesty's time', wrote Gabriel Gustafsson, 'and never seen the Peasants as wild as now.' *AOSB* II.III.339 (19 July 1634).

them had now become the pointless struggle in Germany. It was no very satisfactory answer to their problems to be told that things had been much worse in 1611.[34]

Oxenstierna for his part came increasingly to feel that he had to deal with a government which exaggerated its difficulties, a government which was nerveless, which could not always be depended upon to stand firm. And his diagnosis, prejudiced and selfregarding as it was, was in its fundamentals correct. The Regency was indeed a weak government. Until the acceptance of the Form of Government in 1634 their constitutional authority was by no means clearly defined; and even afterwards they lacked the capacity for leadership and the evident determination which the situation demanded. It was Oxenstierna's firm opinion that the Regents ought to settle upon their policy before canvassing it with the Council, and still more before opening it to the *riksdag*;[35] but in his view they neglected this necessary element of government. They did not enforce discipline upon themselves or their colleagues: on their own confession far too much time was devoted to dealing with private business. Johan Skytte and Gabriel Bengtsson Oxenstierna came back from their provincial governorships unsummoned, to pursue (it was suspected) private political ambitions of their own.[36] The Regents were constantly apprehensive of the incalculable antics of Gustav Adolf's widow, and not less so of the designs of John Casimir of the Palatinate to stake out his son's claim to the succession (in which apprehensions Oxenstierna entirely agreed with them); and there was always the nagging fear of what might happen if Christina should die. There were moments when it seemed that she might:[37] the news of her alarming illness filled the cup of Oxenstierna's troubles during the mutiny at Magdeburg. And if they felt themselves insecure politically, they were weak also in other respects. Too many of them were ageing men, with not much vigour remaining.

Oxenstierna's main standby and support was his brother Gabriel

---

[34] 'I can well remember the times when we had neither officers, men, money, artillery, ammunition, ships, or any other necessity, were under pressure on all sides and had the enemy all over the country – an enemy much more powerful than now, and with such a hatred and evil intention towards us as any they can now have, yet although it was his late Majesty who corrected these faults, still he was at the beginning of his reign: young, and equally inexperienced in government and war, and supported by none, or very few . . . it is no very new thing for a crown to be in a position of owing money in difficult times': *AOSB* I.XIII.11 (5 January 1635).

[35] *AOSB* I.VIII.233 (13 February 1633).

[36] *AOSB* II.III.314 (Gabriel Gustafsson to Axel Oxenstierna, 27 December 1633).

[37] In June 1635 she was seriously ill with what Dr Robertson called '*in generale vocabulo exantemata* or *moebellos, germanice steenpoggen*'': *RRP* IV.132; and again a year later: *RRP*. v. 86. Oxenstierna suggested fewer medicines and a proper diet: *AOSB* I.XIII.506.

Gustafsson, who combined efficiency, a great capacity for work, and general popularity;[38] but he was undeniably inclined to take a gloomy view of things. From time to time he transmitted depressing bulletins from the governmental sick-room. Karl Karlsson Gyllenhielm, we learn, is grown very feeble, and suffers from asthma (he contrived, all the same, to survive for well over another decade, and to emerge as a leader of opposition in the forties); Per Sparre, too, is mostly sick; Gabriel Bengtsson suffers from some unspecified ailment, especially in his head; Gabriel Gustafsson himself is laid up with running eyes, and much troubled by the stone. The effects upon the conduct of business were very serious. There was also, in general, a chronic shortage of secretarial staff; no one, it seemed, was capable of writing a letter in German. Characteristically, their response to this predicament was to implore Oxenstierna to do something about it.[39]

A situation already bad was made much worse by absenteeism, slackness, and incompetence. The lengthy absences of Åke Tott and Clas Christersson Horn meant that for four weeks (in the middle of a war) no business could be transacted in the College of War, since there was no one at hand who was authorised to transact it. The investigation into the working of the collegial system which was undertaken in 1636 revealed that this was by no means an exceptional situation.[40] The Admiralty seems to have been conspicuously ill-ordered: the Admiral 'lamented' that he had not been able to be there for much of the time.[41] There were occasions at the beginning of 1636 when Gabriel Gustafsson found himself the only member of the government present in the Council.[42] Of his relative Gabriel Bengtsson, whom he had pushed into the office of Treasurer, he later remarked that he had proved incompetent, and drily added that: 'Affairs in the Treasury have a tendency to be rarely accurate.'[43] The Marshal, Jakob de la Gardie – never celebrated as an enterprising commander – raised all sorts of difficulties about taking up his command in Prussia, and was generally considered to have no stomach for fighting a battle; the Admiral politely excused himself, 'for many

---

[38] Christina later described him as 'un homme qui avait des talens agréables au peuple. Il étoit affable, honnête, aimé, de la Noblesse et du peuple. Il étoit éloquant à la mode du Pais mais d'une éloquence naturelle sans étude, n'ayant qu'une légère teinture du Latin': J.W. Arckenholtz, *Mémoires concernant Christine Reine de Suède* (Amsterdam and Leipzig 1751–60), III. 44.

[39] *HSH* 29. 237.

[40] *RRP* VI. 9, 43, 112.

[41] *RRP* VI. 154. There is much useful light on the chaos in the Admiralty in Ulf Sjödell, *Riksråd och kungliga råd. Rådskarriären 1602–1718* (Lund 1975).

[42] *RRP* VI. 1, 3, 5.

[43] *AOSB* II.III.356, 359.

reasons', from commanding the fleet.[44] Everywhere, it seemed, it was the same story: 'Here is great confusion and disorder', wrote Gabriel Gustafsson, 'and some of *ipsa capita collegiorum* do not do their work properly . . . The Chancery College, where most public business ought to be initiated and carried on, neither does nor can do an effective job.'[45]

It was perhaps not surprising that a government so constituted should not have been a government united. Their open disagreements reached such a pitch in the Council that Per Banér remarked that it was 'more a wrangling- than a council-chamber'.[46] And though it might be difficult to trace clear and stable political alignments among its members, there was usually a faction among them which was hostile to Oxenstierna. He was well aware of it, both from his own knowledge and from the reports which his brother sent to him. The anti-Oxenstierna group included, at one time or another, Karl Karlsson Gyllenhielm, Per Banér, Per Brahe, and above all Oxenstierna's old enemy Johan Skytte.[47] Outwardly they continued for a time to pay lip-service to the doctrine that Oxenstierna was indispensable in Germany; but that did not deter them from a serious attempt to displace him. The opportunity presented itself when it became necessary to appoint a new High Steward. Gabriel Gustafsson believed that Skytte wanted the Chancellor's office for himself; and whether this was so or not, the attempt was certainly made to kick Oxenstierna upstairs into the Stewardship, and so render the Chancellorship vacant. It is interesting, if profitless, to speculate what the effect upon the history of Germany might have been if they had succeeded. The voting was alarmingly close; but in the end the Stewardship went to Gabriel Gustafsson, by ten votes to seven;[48] and the opportunity was taken to thrust another member of the clan – the incompetent Gabriel Bengtsson Oxenstierna – into the office of Treasurer. After which the Chancellor could feel a little more confident of having the government behind him. But only a little; for Gabriel Gustafsson, as he himself confessed, was too junior to impose his authority. Party-divisions continued; and they were accompanied by – and perhaps provided the explanation for – a distressing tendency to break confidence. Important information was leaked – to John Casimir, to the Queen Mother, and thence to her

[44] *RRP* v. 83.

[45] *AOSB* II.III.360, 400. And Johan Oxenstierna wrote to his father: 'of all the Colleges there is none so wretched as the Chancery . . . P Banér has not been here for four months': C.T. Odhner, *Sveriges inre historia under Drottning Christinas förmyndare* (Stockholm 1865), p. 59.

[46] *RRP* v. 77–8.

[47] *AOSB* I.VIII.266.

[48] *AOSB* II.III.329; *RRP* IV. 126.

relations in Brandenburg; and it was a leak of this kind – this time to the French ambassador, d'Avaugour – which undermined Sweden's negotiating position during the conferences which preceded the truce of Stuhmsdorf: in a very unedifying Council debate Karl Karlsson Gyllenhielm, Jakob de la Gardie, and Johan Skytte all protested, a shade too eagerly, that they were not responsible.[49]

In view of all this it is scarcely surprising that by the end of 1635 Gabriel Gustafsson could note that his brother had become a good deal less open with his colleagues at home: he complained, indeed, that they no longer trusted him.[50] This may well be true of some of them; for there were those who persuaded themselves that he was the main, and perhaps the only, obstacle to a peace. From as early as August 1634 Per Banér and Skytte were intriguing to have him recalled.[51] On 30 October 1635 de la Gardie told the Council that he was 'afraid that the Chancellor and the French ambassador [St Chamont] had jointly resolved to persist in the war, and that thereby the country would be put in a still worse predicament', to which 'Herr Johan Skytte said that he had often feared the same thing himself'.[52] It was an ominous sign that Johan Adler Salvius, who had hitherto been one of Oxenstierna's clients and *protégés*, but was now beginning to trim his sails to the wind and to entertain ambitions to succeed him in Germany, should have permitted himself the acid comment that although Oxenstierna 'to avoid an affront' might have determined to die in Germany, that would not be particularly help- ful, and they would have to make peace just the same.[53]

In justice to the Regents it must be remembered that though under the impact of the disasters in Germany their confidence in the Chancellor might for a time be shaken, they had in the past given him very wide discretion, strong moral support, and warm encour- agement and approbation. They had been magnanimous in their endorsement of the idea that he might aspire to the Electorate of

---

[49] *RRP* v. 230–2.

[50] *AOSB* II.III.396 (Gabriel Gustafsson to Oxenstierna, 1 January 1636). Oxenstierna wrote on 29 August 1635: 'I gather that at home, and perhaps in our *collegium*, are some who begin to censure our *consilia* and what we do, and still have to do, out here . . . Our difficulties and problems, alas, are now greater than we can bear. If on top of all this we are now to run the danger of being persecuted at home, you may easily imagine . . . what effect it will have on our courage and our will to endure': *AOSB* I.XIII.594, 599. And again, defending his censure of the Stuhmsdorf negotiations, 'They complain of me to the Regents, and that's not enough; they complain of me to the Regents and the Council, and that's not enough; to the Estates of the realm, and even *that's* not enough; so they print my letters. I shall answer them, and gladly undergo what the law imposes': *AOSB* I.XIV.92 (to Gabriel Gustafsson, 27 September 1635). Fortunately he thought better of it.

[51] Goetze, *Die Politik des schwedischen Reichskanzlers Axel Oxenstierna*, p. 131.

[52] *RRP* v. 250–1.

[53] *RRP* v. 195.

Mainz; on receiving the news of Nördlingen they had sent him the cheering thought that after all this was the first battle Sweden had lost for four years; they had conveyed a real appreciation of the enormous burden of work which lay upon him – even if their actions did not always bear out that assurance.[54] The very fact that they delegated so much to him which they ought to have been able to tackle themselves was a sign of their confidence, as well as of their deficiencies. And if in practice they displayed a lack of imaginative understanding of his difficulties, he on his side was not altogether in a position to cast a stone. The problems which faced them at home were real problems, and Oxenstierna did not endear himself to his colleagues by simply shrugging them off as difficulties which only required *mascula consilia* to be surmounted. There must have been times when his barely concealed contempt for their incapacity, his assumption that he knew better than they did, his exercising of a liberty to lecture, were resented;[55] and his intemperate censure of Per Brahe and Jakob de la Gardie for their conduct of the Stuhmsdorf negotiations was resented very bitterly. But the bitterness was reciprocal. In the autumn of 1635, in private letters to his brother, Oxenstierna permitted himself a succession of quite unusual temperamental outbursts:

The burden is intolerable, but my love of my country prevents me from being sorry for myself [!]. Others do nothing but cry that their needs must be supplied, and they give no thought to me and the rest of us here, who daily stand in danger of being betrayed, slain, captured. I will not and shall not stand it any longer, but they may appoint someone else in my place who can manage things better, and who will appreciate what a nice time I and some others have been having. And so I ask you to present my compliments to the Regents and Council, and put them in mind to send someone else to replace me in the autumn – someone who can make as good a peace as they have made in Prussia.[56]

The threat was not seriously meant, of course: the savage irony of the final clause shows that. If he returned home, who was there to succeed him? In the early months of 1636 he could see only one candidate, Sten Bielke, the governor of Pomerania. But Sten Bielke was bedridden half the time, and on occasion so ill that he could not write his name.[57] However great Oxenstierna's exasperation, however strong his resentment, he was still the necessary man, and

[54] *RRP* IV. 92; *HSH* 26. 164–5; 32. 208.

[55] Oxenstierna's confidential agent, Peder Smalz, reported in January 1636 that Åke Axelsson Natt och Dag complained that Oxenstierna 'always assumes that he knows more than anybody else; and that he is only interested in getting money for the war in Germany, without bothering himself about how it is to be got': Sverker Arnoldsson, *Poeter och Pirater* (Stockholm 1958), p. 34.

[56] *AOSB* I.XIV.94, 265.

[57] *AOSB* II.III.478 (Per Brahe to Oxenstierna, 8 October 1634).

he knew it; and he would quit Germany only when he could do no more good by staying. And when that time came he would have occupation enough in putting affairs at home in good order.

III

It was against this troubled domestic background that he had to execute his commission in Germany. Here the problems, the difficulties, the harassments, were of a different order. He had to direct the war-effort, co-ordinate the foreign policy, preside over the counsels, of a collection of allies divided among themselves both upon the objects to be aimed at and upon the means to pursue them. However great the authority which derived from Sweden's position as head of the evangelical party in Germany, he could only rarely permit himself the imperious tone which Gustav Adolf had so often assumed, and still less the outbursts of choler with which he had vented his indignation upon Laodicean allies, froward French diplomats, or insubordinate commanders: where the king would have simply ordered, the Chancellor must seek to persuade and convince. The great majority of the generals in his armies (like their troops) were not Swedish subjects; they owed him no unconditional obedience. In the three years after Lützen the only native Swedish generals who were really fitted to command an army were Gustav Horn and Johan Banér; and after Horn was taken prisoner at Nördlingen Banér had no compatriot of much capacity until Lennart Torstensson arrived in Pomerania from Prussia at the end of 1635. In this situation Oxenstierna was very much at the mercy of German Protestant princes in the Swedish service, or of allies with their own armies who wished to go their own way. Even the most faithful of them, William V of Hesse-Cassel, required tactful handling; George of Brunswick-Lüneburg aspired to fight his own war, for specific personal and dynastic ends; William of Saxe-Weimar had broken with Oxenstierna in December 1632, and his 'fantastic proceedings' were considered by him to be one cause of the collapse of Sweden's political position after Nördlingen.[58] It was obviously essential to keep on good terms with William's brother Bernard, who had assumed the command at Lützen after Gustav Adolf's death, regarded himself as the king's natural military heir and successor, and felt himself entitled to be recognised as *generalissimo* of all the armies of Sweden and her allies. But Oxenstierna would not willingly entrust the supreme command to one who was not a Swedish subject, least of all when

[58] Gustaf Björling, *Johan Banér* (Stockholm 1910), ii. 73; *AOSB* i.ix.631 (to Johan Banér, 28 October 1634).

there was such a rival in the field as Gustav Horn – who happened, incidentally, to be Oxenstierna's son-in-law. Relations between Horn and Bernard were in any case not good, and Horn bluntly threatened to throw up his command if Bernard were appointed above his head.[59] The only occasion on which they fought a battle shoulder to shoulder was on the fatal day of Nördlingen, and the feud between them lived on in Swedish propaganda and historiography, which blamed Bernard's rashness and ambition as the cause of the disaster.[60] However that may be, Nördlingen at least settled the issue of the command, and in March 1635 Bernard was put at the head of all the forces of the four Circles of Upper Germany.[61] Johan Banér did indeed retain his independent command in the Upper Saxon Circle, and would be the agent of Swedish recovery after 1635; but here again there were personal difficulties. For Oxenstierna, while justly appreciating Banér's quality as a fighting general, found him temperamentally uncongenial, and complained of his 'insolent, presumptuous and ambitious spirit'.[62] Banér, for his part, chafed under Oxenstierna's military directives, and plainly regarded him as an amateur strategist who had better refrain from meddling in matters that he did not understand.

There was some truth in this; but Oxenstierna, for cogent reasons, was not prepared if he could help it to allow the control of military operations to fall into other hands. Politics and war were too closely interrelated for such an arrangement to be tolerable, or even practicable; there must be no *generalissimo* – not Bernard, in the first instance, and not Banér afterwards. As Director he must direct, and must be felt to direct, if any sort of coherence was to be maintained; his stubborn clinging to the Directorship, and his insistence that it should be a reality, was not (as Björling once wrote) 'pedantic punctiliousness', nor a jealousy of rivals, it was sound common sense.[63] Nevertheless, it obviously entailed serious disadvantages. To insist on conducting operations at a distance, especially in the slow and uncertain state of communications in Germany, was a recipe for military misfortune; and inevitably it led to friction with the generals on the spot. Conspicuously so with Johan Banér, whose strategic

[59] Lars Tingsten, *Huvuddragen av Sveriges Politik och Krigföring i Tyskland efter Gustav II Adolfs död till och med sommaren 1635* (Stockholm 1930), pp. 65, 120.

[60] *AOSB* I.xii.390; Göran Rystad, *Vem vållade Nördlingenkatastrofen 1634? En studie i propaganda* (Lund 1959); Arne Stade, 'Gustaf Horn och Nördlingenkatastrofen 1634'. *Historisk tidskrift* (1965); and in general Göran Rystad, *Kriegsnachrichten und Propaganda während des dreissigjährigen Krieges* (Lund 1960).

[61] His commission (written by himself) is in *AOSB* I.xiii.162.

[62] *AOSB* I.xv.329 (to Gabriel Gustafsson, 29 March 1636).

[63] Björling, *Johan Banér*, ii. 340. Björling's harsh criticisms of Oxenstierna's handling of Banér are much softened in Birger Steckzén's *Johan Banér* (Stockholm 1939).

appreciations clashed with Oxenstierna's, and whose difficulties and handicaps were too often simply brushed aside.

But Banér on his side failed to take into account the fact that Oxenstierna was always operating under constraints of a different sort: constraints which forced him at times to sacrifice the best military solution to political considerations. Those constraints could result in what from a soldier's point of view were undoubted errors of judgment: for instance, the persistence in the months after Lützen in maintaining four or five armies scattered over Germany, instead of the concentration for which Banér pleaded;[64] or the disastrous appointment of the incompetent von Thurn to command in Silesia, which arose from Oxenstierna's ineradicable distrust of Hans Georg von Arnim; or his stubborn refusal to burden Pomerania with 'contributions' – a policy which was dictated by his determination to avoid, at almost any cost, the alienation of the Pomeranian Estates, but which produced in the autumn of 1633 a situation in which no effective resistance could be offered to Wallenstein's dramatic advance from Silesia.[65] But political considerations might also entail important military advantages – as for instance when at the end of 1635 Oxenstierna forced Banér to detach troops to Westphalia. For it was *militarily* important to keep George of Lüneberg in line, and still more so to rescue Sweden's only ally, William V of Hesse. The great victory by a concentrated force which Banér hoped for, even if it had been decisive (and the days of decisive victories in this war were over, if they had ever existed), would arguably have been more than offset by the loss of William V. And so, when Oxenstierna 'wrecked' Banér's Saxon offensive in January 1636 by responding to William's desperate appeals and sending reinforcements to the Weser instead of to the Saale he may well have been justified.[66]

It is true that already in 1633 Oxenstierna's preference was for a defensive strategy. But this, though perhaps the reaction of an amateur and a layman, was perfectly feasible provided the contributions were systematically organised and regularly paid, which unfortunately they were not. And it is worth while remembering that Horn, too, was for a defensive strategy, on purely military grounds. There were certainly occasions on which Oxenstierna's strategic judgement was justified by the event: as for instance his disapproval of the joint advance upon Regensburg in 1634, which

[64] Steckzén, *Johan Banér*, p. 143.

[65] See Roland Nordlund, 'Kontribution eller satisfaktion. Pommern och de svenska krigsfinanserna 1633', *Historisk tidskrift* (1974).

[66] See Björling's trenchant criticisms in *Johan Banér*, II. 251, 339; and Banér's letter to Oxenstierna, 3 November 1635, in *AOSB* II.VI.243–5.

ended in disaster at Nördlingen; and conspicuously so in regard to his order to Bernard to attack Regensburg in the autumn of 1633 – an order which stopped Wallenstein's irresistible advance upon Pomerania in its tracks, and which led (incidentally) directly to Wallenstein's downfall.[67] And his refusal to allow Banér to quarter his troops in the coastlands, bitterly as it was resented at the time, was after all later endorsed by Banér himself, when he declared that the coastlands must be spared, as Sweden's last reserve in an emergency.[68] Still, it may be granted that Oxenstierna was too prone to split his forces in order to keep every line of approach covered, and that he had a general disposition to think in terms of diversions which did not always divert; and there are many occasions on which Banér's irritation and frustration are entirely understandable. Yet, somehow or other, they contrived to maintain reasonable relations, and to work together. Banér, whatever his feelings, nearly always obeyed orders; and Oxenstierna came to see that some latitude should be allowed to his commander: in the last six months of his stay in Germany he was increasingly leaving decisions to Banér's discretion.

The waywardness and insubordination of the German officers, and the unceasing and often desperate need to find the money to pay the armies, combined to produce a policy designed to meet both these difficulties: the policy of appeasing the ambitious and the discontented, and at the same time writing off indebtedness, by the granting of donations.[69] The device had been used extensively in Gustav Adolf's lifetime, and it was used still more extensively after his death: the volumes of Oxenstierna's correspondence for 1633–6 contain lists of scores of such donations: and the applications for them (from at home, as well as from Germany)[70] continued even after Sweden's military position had become so precarious that a donation could be of very dubious value. These donations were grants of land, for the most part in enemy areas already in Swedish occupation, or in areas which it might reasonably be expected would soon become so – a speculation on the part of the grantee which often proved a disastrous miscalculation. They were to be held on semi-feudal tenure, reserving the rights of the Swedish overlord, and rendering dues or

[67] For Oxenstierna's relations with Wallenstein, into which it is not possible to enter here, see Pekka Suvanto, *Die deutsche Politik Oxenstiernas und Wallenstein* (Helsinki 1979).

[68] Björling, *Johan Banér*, II. 256, 440.

[69] Roland Nordlund, 'Krig genom ombud. De svenska krigsfinanserna och Heilbronnförbundet 1633', in Hans Landberg et al., *Det kontinentala krigets ekonomi. Studier i krigsfinansiering under svensk stormaktstid.* (Uppsala 1971).

[70] The undeserving Åke Tott, whose application was turned down in 1633, had the nerve to renew it in August 1635: *AOSB* I.IX.139; XIII.441.

services to the Swedish crown.[71] The device had the disadvantage that the grantees tended to exploit their grants ruthlessly while they still sat secure in them: a result by no means to Oxenstierna's liking, but (as he remarked) 'we have to put up with it if we don't want to make enemies of them'.[72] Those who invested in donations might be the necessary props of war, but he had a very poor opinion of them in general:

The princes and the officers here have no concern for the public interest, beyond mere words; but in truth each seeks his private advantage – how those who have ecclesiastical lands in their territories may grab them; others, how they may get their hands on abbeys, convents, estates, and anything that is going. Princes, counts, lords, towns, nobles and others demand great fiefs according to their importance; and if one refuses them they are disgusted and think a great wrong has been done them. They became accustomed to it in his late Majesty's time, so that a great part of the conquered land has been granted away, and for practically all, promises made and grants prepared . . . [73]

Like Gustav Adolf before him, Oxenstierna assumed it to be the evident duty of German Protestant princes to give hearty support to a cause which was not simply that of Sweden, but – even more – their own cause too; and like him he was contemptuous of those who postponed that cause to private short-sighted advantage. On the constancy and fidelity of the allies whose efforts he was trying to co-ordinate he placed little or no reliance: already in February 1633 he proceeded on the assumption that as soon as they felt that they could do without Swedish aid they would not hesitate to leave him in the lurch. That moment, indeed, never came; but what came instead was the mass desertion which followed the Peace of Prague.

These broken reeds – princes, as Oxenstierna in exasperation remarked, with 'centuries of nonsense in their heads'[74] – were the Estates which formed the League of Heilbronn, together with a handful of other Estates outside it whom he tried to coax into joining it: Estates of the Upper and Lower Saxon Circles, and above all George William of Brandenburg, on whose fidelity he hoped to the last – with increasing improbability – that he could rely. No rational hope of this sort could be entertained of the greatest Protestant prince in Germany: the Elector John George of Saxony. Though at the beginning of 1633 Oxenstierna could write of the Elector's 'heroic resolution' to fight on, and though for the next two years he was painfully careful to treat him with courtesy and consideration – with notable self-restraint he refrained absolutely from recrimination after

---

[71] The principle was very clearly laid down by the Regents: *HSH* 26. 143 (17 August 1633).
[72] *AOSB* I.XI.178.
[73] *AOSB* I.VIII.673.
[74] *AOSB* I.VIII.334.

the disaster at Steinau – it was simply not possible to maintain good relations indefinitely. It was not only that each was by temperament thoroughly uncongenial to the other: Oxenstierna dismissed the Elector as 'an insignificant tosspot', and was contemptuous of his beer-befogged, vacillating policies;[75] John George angrily described Oxenstierna as 'ein Plackscheisser'.[76] The difficulty went much deeper. After Lützen John George regarded himself as once more the leader and natural head of German Protestantism; and he could not forgive Oxenstierna's success in asserting Sweden's right to dispute that claim. He was outraged by what he considered to be his presumptuous semi-regal pretensions, and was profoundly suspicious of his designs: was it not obvious that he wished to make himself 'absolute master and *dictatorem perpetuum* in Germany'? Had he not usurped an imperial prerogative by purporting to restore the Palatines to their Electorate? Were not his policies a contrivance to prolong the war, while the Elector's consistently aimed at peace?[77] John George had concluded his alliance with Gustav Adolf reluctantly, and only when Tilly's soldiery invaded his lands; he felt himself to have since then been committed to a role alien to the imperialist traditions of his house; and he would welcome any opportunity to reconstruct a 'Third Party' in Germany which might be the instrument for negotiating a general peace for the *Reich*. The most estimable trait in his character was his strong German patriotism; and the goal of his policy, for as far ahead as his dim vision could look, was to clear Germany of the foreigner. The League of Heilbronn to him was a quite unacceptable violation of the constitution of the Empire: it was monstrous that it should have been brought into being upon the initiative of a foreign subject, and be dependent for its continuance upon a foreign power.[78]

From the Swedish point of view it was no doubt satisfactory that the Elector's hatred of foreign meddlers should extend also to the French: the attempts of Richelieu and his agents to turn him into a French client and launch him as the leader of anti-Habsburg Germany in opposition to Oxenstierna were hopeless from the beginning, even if Oxenstierna had not forestalled them by organising the

---

[75] *AOSB* I.xv.332. 'With them [the Saxons] there is no lack of long *orationes* and *dubitandi rationes* and much ceremony; but I have never yet heard anything *reale* there, and if one tries to negotiate *realiter* one is considered to be acting *imperiose*', *AOSB* I.viii.6. For the vacillations of Saxon policy, see *Svenska Residentens Lars Nilsson Tungels efterlämnade papper* (Historiska Handlingar, 22. 1–2) (Stockholm 1907–9), *passim*; for the Elector's bibulous proclivities, *ibid.*, 195–6.

[76] Goetze, *Die Politik des schwedischen Reichskanzlers Axel Oxenstierna*, p. 103.

[77] *Lars Tungels . . . papper*, pp. 94, 104, 118–19, 140, 210 and 250.

[78] *Lars Tungels . . . papper*, 97, 155, 213.

League of Heilbronn. But it was disturbing that John George's opposition to foreign intervention did not, apparently, extend to Denmark, nor prevent the conclusion of a marriage between his daughter and Kristian IV's son. Behind this apparent exception to his principles lay the hope of using Kristian's reiterated proffers of mediation to obtain a peace: proffers which Oxenstierna regarded with alarm, and which he spent some ingenuity in evading. Still worse were the truces which the Elector (or his general, Arnim) concluded with Wallenstein, and the alarming negotiations with the imperialists to which they gave rise. When John George at last reached agreement with the Emperor by the Preliminaries of Pirna in 1634, and consented to their embodiment (and substantial amendment) in the Peace of Prague of 1635, Oxenstierna could feel that Saxon policy had reached its logical conclusion. And that conclusion turned the Elector into Sweden's active enemy, and Oxenstierna's bitterest foe: an enmity which was personal, for John George now saw in him the last remaining obstacle to the general German peace at which he aimed; and there was truth in his claim that it was Oxenstierna, and not Sweden, that he was fighting.[79]

Menaced thus on his north-eastern flank by a wholly unreliable ally and rival, Oxenstierna was similarly threatened in the west by the ambitions of another dubious friend: France. Richelieu was not prepared, if he could help it, to tolerate a Swedish domination of Germany, any more than John George was. He had done his best to prevent the formation of the League of Heilbronn; and when he was worsted in that, pursued a policy designed simultaneously to undermine Oxenstierna's authority within the League, to create by subsidies and bribes to Protestant princes a French party in Germany, and yet to use Sweden's direction of the war-effort to avert the necessity for France's direct intervention. He had some success: it was Swedish forces that chastised Charles of Lorraine, Swedish forces that took Philippsburg, Sweden that was left to bar the way to Spanish troops moving north from Italy. In Alsace, on the Rhine, Sweden and France confronted each other in a tangled relationship in which suspicion was never far removed from outright hostility. And when, after Nördlingen, the League of Heilbronn began to collapse, Richelieu reaped the due reward of this policy in the shape of the transference of that useless and bankrupt asset to France. The realities of the Franco-Swedish relationship were made startlingly clear when in December 1634 the Cardinal ordered Feuquières to contrive the kidnapping of Oxenstierna and Bernard of Saxe-Weimar. He

---

[79] *RRP* v. 170, 351.

changed his mind before any attempt could be made to put this plan into execution – if these two were removed, who else had sufficient authority to do France's business? – and in the event the course of affairs would push Sweden and France into renewed co-operation, and eventually into reluctant alliance; but Oxenstierna, if he had known of the designs upon his person, would have been confirmed in the conviction – which he had held since 1629, and would retain for the rest of the war – that France was a slippery and untrustworthy associate whose only recommendation was the subsidies which she might be induced to pay.[80]

IV

When we have taken into account the burdens, the difficulties, and the vexations which Oxenstierna had to endure we have, after all, still done no more than detail a long list of mitigating circumstances. In themselves they provide no satisfactory explanation of the course of events in Germany in the years 1633–6. The collapse of the authority which Oxenstierna inherited from Gustav Adolf was no doubt in part attributable to military disaster. But this is not the whole explanation. For the collapse was political no less than military. It could be interpreted as the damning verdict upon a policy; and for that policy Oxenstierna seemed to be responsible. And to understand what happened we need to know what that policy was.

At the beginning of 1633 the Chancellor and his colleagues at home were in broad agreement as to what Sweden's objectives must now be. Their aim was peace. Already in 1632, in the high tide of Gustav Adolf's victories, there had been some members of the Council who did not hesitate to say that Sweden's objectives had been attained, that there was no point in continuing the war, that their main concern now must be to get out of it on terms which would give the maximum return for the efforts which Sweden had made on behalf of the Protestant cause.[81] Neither the Council nor

---

[80] Sverker Arnoldsson, *Svensk-fransk krigs- och fredspolitik i Tyskland* (Göteborg 1937), p. 97, for this episode and for Franco-Swedish relations generally; see also Erik Falk, *Sverige och Frankrike 1632–4* (Stockholm 1911), and the good survey in D. P. O'Connell, *Richelieu* (1968), pp. 280–330.

[81] Thus Claes Fleming argued: 'when thus the Protestants can balance the Catholics it is to be presumed (with God's help) that the end of the war has been attained. But if the war be prolonged, it is to be feared that our friends could become our enemies, and – some from jealousy, some from war-weariness – take a line which might not only damage us but all our co-religionists.' Gabriel Gustafsson Oxenstierna argued that they could now make peace 'with reputation. If we go on, war will beget war, and so we shall have *bellum in perpetuum*.' Jakob de la Gardie demanded proof from Scripture that Sweden was fighting a war for religion: if so,

Oxenstierna had ever shown much enthusiasm for those plans for the alteration of the constitutional situation in Germany which had latterly suggested themselves to Gustav Adolf; and certainly they had none now. Their political horizons had undergone a sharp contraction; their concern was no longer with the fate of Germany but with the advantage of Sweden. They were, indeed, still prepared to think that the restoration of Germany to what it had been in 1618 was a Swedish interest: as Per Banér observed, Sweden's safety depended 'a good deal' on the restitution of the German Protestant states to their former condition.[82] But when they spoke of restoration, they did so with reservations so large as to qualify the idea very considerably. For if they had their way, the map of Germany would bear a very different appearance from that which it had presented fifteen years ago. They wanted *satisfactio*, that is, the transference into Swedish hands by way of 'recompense and debt of gratitude' of large areas of north Germany: in particular, of the lands lying on the Baltic coast. It was to prevent these lands from falling into hostile hands that Gustav Adolf had launched his expedition; and their retention was still considered essential on strategic grounds: they were, after all, the bulwarks which protected Sweden from invasion.[83] But in 1633 this by no means exhausted Sweden's territorial appetite. Both Oxenstierna and the government were thinking of acquisitions – Bremen-Verden, or Magdeburg and Halberstadt or other north German bishoprics, or even Mainz – which had no immediate relevance to any defensive strategy. *Satisfactio*, indeed, tended to merge into another fundamental war aim: *assecuratio*; by which was meant some sort of guarantee that Sweden would never again be exposed to the kind of danger which had seemed to threaten her as a result of the successes of the Habsburgs at the close of the 1620s: the danger of an imperial domination of the *Reich*. There were two conceivable means of obtaining such a guarantee, and they were not mutually exclusive. One was a strong Swedish foothold in Germany, and the admission of Sweden to the imperial Diet in virtue of her membership of one or more Circles of the Empire. The other, which had been a main preoccupation of Gustav Adolf at the close of his life, was the creation of some association of German states under Swedish leadership which could be counted upon to act as a breakwater against any resurgence of Habsburg power. Three things, then: the coastlands, *satisfactio*, *assecuratio* – without these they could hardly risk making

---

why was she not also fighting France and the Pope?: *RRP* II. 144–7, 157 (12 March, 14 April 1632).

[82] *RRP* III. 248.

[83] And also offered the best naval bases for keeping an eye on Poland and Denmark.

the peace they were seeking. And there was one other consideration on which they insisted; for they were agreed that if and when Sweden extricated herself from the German imbroglio, it must be 'with reputation'. The day was not far off when some of them, at all events, would be ready in their desperation to abandon everything else, if only that could be preserved.

A programme of this nature had not been easy to realise when Gustav Adolf was alive; and it became very much less so now that he was dead. It might even be altogether impossible, if it became too obvious that they were determined on peace. Nevertheless, a significant step in that direction was taken early in 1633, when Oxenstierna (with the full approval of the government in Stockholm) organised the withdrawal of all purely Swedish troops from central to north Germany.[84] The operation was conducted in strict secrecy in order not to upset the German allies, and it seems to have been carried out without exciting suspicion. But the implications were plain. Henceforward, as Oxenstierna put it, Sweden must simply 'lend her name' to the war-effort of her allies. It was still essential to maintain her position as the acknowledged leader of the resistance to the Emperor, for if she were to allow that position to fall into other hands her prospects of adequate *satisfactio* would be jeopardised; but henceforward the burden of war must be transferred as far as possible to German shoulders. The war, he wrote, must be waged

caute and *prudenter* . . . so that it is ours only in name, though we proclaim and protest to the whole world that we are resolved, with the allies, and with the help of God, to prosecute it; but with a secret determination that we shall be at no expense because of it, either in men or money, except what must unavoidably be borne in regard to the Baltic coast . . . since in the long run no reliance is to be placed on these people and the alliances which have been made with them. I have had ample experience of the fact that they will tolerate us only as long as they feel that they need our help, but when the danger they are in is over there will not be one of them who will give us the smallest thanks for all our trouble and expense.[85]

Behind this programme lay not only Oxenstierna's disillusionment with the German Estates but also his concern for the defence of Sweden itself. In August 1633 he defined his policy as being, first, to prevent Sweden's being attacked or disturbed at home; and secondly, to secure a reasonable *satisfactio*.[86] The order was not insignificant. At a time when only the life of a sickly child stood between Władysław IV

---

[84] Nordlund, 'Kontribution eller satisfaktion', pp. 325–30. The Stockholm government even instructed him, if necessary, to destroy all Swedish-held positions in central Germany: *HSH* 24. 274–5 (15 December 1632).

[85] *AOSB* I.VIII.162 (4 February 1633): cf. *AOSB* I.XII.324–5 (Memorial for Johan Oxenstierna, 28 August 1634).

[86] *AOSB* I.IX.227.

and the Swedish crown, Oxenstierna saw the greatest threat to his country as coming not from Germany, but from Polish intrigues and (when the truce ran out) Polish hostility.[87] 'The Polish war', he wrote, 'is *our* war ; win or lose, it is our gain or loss. This German war, I don't know what it is, only that we pour out blood here *pro reputatione*, and have naught but ingratitude to expect.'[88] There was also, of course, the perennial danger from Denmark; but about that he was less concerned: Kristian IV's obvious hope of meddling in Germany had at least the advantage of directing Danish attention southwards.[89] The real importance of the German war, then, was as a diversion: its function was to provide a target at which Sweden's enemies might 'shoot their arrows', so that they might have no leisure to attack her nearer home.[90] It gave Sweden a breathing-space which she might use to rally her forces and perfect her defences against any future assault. Thus the first military priority, at any rate before Nördlingen, was the home front. The navy must be kept up to full strength: on it depended Sweden's safety. The fortresses must be kept well supplied; the government must stockpile arms and ammunition, and he volunteered to assist them in stockpiling salt also.[91] In short, 'we must let this German business be left to the Germans, who will be the only people to get any good of it (if there is any), and therefore not spend any more men or money here, but rather try by all means to wriggle out of it'.[92] It is true that when that sentence was written, at the beginning of 1635, circumstances had greatly changed for the worse; but it accords well enough with his whole policy from 1633 onwards.

The formation of the League of Heilbronn on 13 April 1633 appeared to be a major diplomatic success. It reaffirmed Sweden's leadership of Protestant Germany. It represented a defeat for Richelieu, for John George, for Kristian IV. And it seemed to go a long way towards meeting Sweden's prerequisites for peace.

In the first place, it provided something which looked like a solid *assecuratio*. For though the articles of confederation took care to make it clear that the League was not directed against the Emperor or the imperial constitution, they did bind its members to go on fighting until 'German liberties, and observance of the principles and constitution of the *Reich*, be once more put upon a stable footing'; and

[87] *AOSB* I.VIII.152, 216, 234.
[88] *AOSB* I.XII.633 (to Johan Banér. 28 October 1634).
[89] All the same, he urged the government to take all necessary precautions: *AOSB* I.VIII.609.
[90] *AOSB* I.VIII.609 (to Sten Bielke, 8 May 1633).
[91] *AOSB* I.XI.741.
[92] *AOSB* I.XIII.27 (7 January 1635).

that meant, in fact, until those liberties and principles had been accepted by a repentant Emperor. It was thus (on paper) a safeguard against any return to the position of 1629. The League was committed to the restoration of Germany to the condition in which it had been at the outbreak of war; and that commitment was reinforced by the treaty which Oxenstierna concluded on the following day with the representatives of the Palatinate house, whereby he pledged himself to restore the Elector to Bohemia, and in return obtained the Palatines' acceptance of his Directorate, and a promise that they would not 'depend' on any other king, prince or Estate. But the League not only took care of *assecuratio* and restitution; it also laid a basis for *satisfactio* – not, indeed, with any precision, but at least in the shape of a general engagement to fight on until Sweden had obtained what was referred to as a 'proper' compensation. Moreover, it opened the way to the prosecution of Oxenstierna's policy of shifting the burden of war to the shoulders of the Germans: the four Circles of Upper Germany bound themselves to raise the forces necessary for carrying on the war, and *also* to provide the financial and other support necessary to their maintenance; and an annexure to the agreement spelled out in detail the obligations of each member, fixed procedures against those falling into arrear, arranged for the establishment of magazines, and prescribed just what administrative staff would be required; and these forces, these administrators, were to be bound, not only to the League, but to the crown of Sweden. Finally, the League appointed Oxenstierna its Director, with effective control not only of all military operations (on which he had a veto) but also of finance. And they did this, as they were careful to point out, not out of respect for the crown of Sweden, but to show their esteem for his 'von Gott habende vortreffliche qualitaeten'. It might be true that there was no other conceivable candidate for the position, but it was none the less an extraordinary tribute.[93]

It might seem, then, that his success in organising the League of Heilbronn had provided him with the machinery he needed for carrying out his programme. In the event it proved to be nothing of the kind. As an instrument for the safeguarding of German liberties it was from the beginning weakened by the very principles which it was designed to uphold. Its transactions revealed all too clearly that German liberties could be another name for German licence: the prosecution of private ends, dynastic rivalries, ingenuity in evading

[93] *AOSB* I.VIII.437–45, for the articles of confederation; *ibid.* 447–54, for the annexure; *ibid.* 479–87 for the treaty with the Palatinate. The standard work on the League of Heilbronn is J. Kretzschmar, *Der Heilbronner Bund* I–III (Lübeck 1922).

unwelcome sacrifices, the hostility of Lutheran and Calvinist . . .
Not even Oxenstierna's authority, nor his unremitting attention to
business, could make much head against princely particularism. And
this being so, what became of the *assecuratio* which the League had
been designed to provide? With regard to *satisfactio* the case was not
much better. For though the League might adhere to the undertaking to see to it that Sweden received proper compensation, it was
a pledge wofully lacking in weight. The League expected Oxenstierna to get his *satisfactio* from conquered Roman Catholic lands, far
from the coast; but the recompense which Sweden desired lay
outside the territories which comprised the four Circles of Upper
Germany. What they might resolve upon the matter was mere
words; what counted was the attitude of the Upper and Lower Saxon
Circles.

In one particular it did indeed seem that the League would produce
the consequences which Oxenstierna expected of it; that is, the
transference of the burden of war to German shoulders. But even
here there were problems.[94] By the articles of confederation the
members of the League had agreed to pay the large arrears,
accumulated before the League came to birth, for which the armies
were now clamouring; and those arrears provoked a serious mutiny
in the army of the Danube before the ink was dry on the instrument
which brought the League into being. Oxenstierna was forced to
meet this situation, in the first instance, by making over to the
military enterprisers, and to officers in the Swedish service, the right
to levy the contribution and taxes which were being exacted from
occupied or conc...ed lands, *jure belli*. If he could manage it, he
ensured that such ri...ts should not be surrendered without compensation: in the t...ost spectacular deals of this sort – that with
Count von Bra...nstein for the bishoprics of Magdeburg and
Halberstadt, that with Bernard for the bishoprics of Würzburg and
Bamberg – he stipulated that each should contribute 600,000 *rdr.* a
year for four years.[95] By giving or selling rights – real, questionable,
or imaginary – by ruthless and unscrupulous proceedings of one sort
or another, he seems in fact by the autumn of 1633 to have
manoeuvred the League not only into paying the army's monthly
wages but also into taking over purely Swedish debts.[96] It proved a
dear-bought success. One main object behind the formation of the

---

[94] For what follows see Nordlund, 'Krig genom ombud', *passim*.

[95] *Ibid.*, pp. 322, 334, 408, 410. In the event, Oxenstierna took von Brandenstein's money
and refused to hand over the bishoprics, and von Brandenstein died, a prisoner of war in
Saxony, almost destitute: *ibid.*, p. 417, n. 6.

[96] *Ibid.*, p. 409.

League had been to organise the payment of the armies on a regular, predetermined scale of contributions from the members, with the idea of avoiding the excesses which irregular payments inevitably produced. But this proved beyond the League's power. It lacked the self-discipline, and perhaps it lacked also the resources, to keep the machinery of contributions in smooth working order. The result, as Oxenstierna was not slow to point out, was the kind of 'exorbitances' which the League had been designed to prevent; and those exorbitances in their turn made it difficult for the members of the League to be punctual in paying their contributions. It was a vicious circle: no money, no discipline; no discipline, less money. The League was being ruined by its own soldiery. And was in consequence becoming less effective militarily, and less co-operative politically.

By the end of 1633 it seemed clear that from every point of view – *assecuratio, satisfactio,* war-finance – the League was too weak as it stood to do what Oxenstierna had expected of it. It must be afforced; and it must be afforced if possible by the adhesion of the two Saxon Circles. After the tenebrous Saxon negotiations with Wallenstein in the summer and autumn Oxenstierna can have had little hope of persuading John George to join it. The accession of George William of Brandenburg therefore became of vital importance; for the small fry of Germany would be unlikely to respond positively to an invitation which had been declined by *both* Electors. But one great obstacle stood in the way of George William's adhesion: the question of *satisfactio;* the question of Pomerania. And on that rock Oxenstierna's whole German policy foundered.

Oxenstierna took it for granted that Sweden's *satisfactio* must come mainly from the German Protestant states: it was they, after all, who were considered to owe a debt of gratitude to Sweden for their deliverance. It might, indeed, take the form of more or less masterless north German bishoprics; but at this stage the recompense which Sweden above all desired was Pomerania, and to Pomerania she advanced claims which were based partly on the alliance which Gustav Adolf had concluded with Bogislaw XIV, partly on the general ground of *jus belli.* But unfortunately it happened that George William had a long-standing and incontestable right to the succession when Bogislaw should die; and the Estates of Pomerania were wholeheartedly behind him. Sweden's pretensions to Pomerania, therefore, risked the consequence of entailing Brandenburg's enmity at precisely the moment when it was essential to retain the Elector's friendship. It had been in an effort to escape this consequence that Gustav Adolf had floated the idea of a marriage between Kristina and the Elector's heir – a proposal which the government in Stockholm took care to keep alive.[97] But whether the marriage took place or not, they were in the spring of 1633 clearly in favour of standing firm on Sweden's claim.[98]

Oxenstierna, for his part, was much less certain. Though his tactic of keeping the burdens upon Pomerania to the absolute minimum was certainly based on the supposition that the duchy would one day pass into Swedish hands, and the hope that lenity might help to reconcile it to its new masters, the imperative need to strengthen the League of Heilbronn made him revise his opinion of what could be risked. He had summoned a convention of Protestant princes to Frankfurt for April 1634: and of that convention he expected two main results: the adhesion of the states of the two Saxon Circles to the League, and the more precise definition of Sweden's *satisfactio*. In January and February he sent home serious warnings of the possible consequences of Swedish insistence upon the claim to Pomerania: it might unite the princes of the two Saxon Circles in opposition, and so defeat one of the objects of the convention: it might entail the loss of Prussia, since it might drive George William to ally with Poland.[99] Talks with George William at Stendal in February did something to relieve his anxiety; for he believed (mistakenly) that he had persuaded the Elector to join the League. In that same month a meeting of the Estates of the Lower Saxon Circle at Halberstadt, which Oxenstierna attended, took a resolution which might have had considerable significance; for they explicitly pledged themselves to join the League, and to raise their own army to act with it.[100] It is said that Oxenstierna later regretted that he had not thereupon cancelled the Frankfurt convention and rested content with his success in Halberstadt.[101] But if he indeed came to feel that it would have been better to settle for the half-loaf, it is easy to understand why he did not. The adhesion of the Lower Saxon Circle could not settle the question of Pomerania; and it in no way committed George William. Oxenstierna was playing for time; waiting for a final directive from home, hoping that when it came he might be able to induce *both* Saxon Circles to accept it, and in his own mind still uncertain as to what the best line might be. More explicitly than ever he warned his colleagues that Pomerania would prove a '*pomum eridis*', and that they would hardly obtain it without fighting for it.[102] He received the

[97] *HSH* 25. 137–9.
[98] *Ibid.*, 141–51.
[99] *AOSB* I.XI.19 (7 January 1634), *ibid.*, 178–81 (2 February 1634).
[100] *Sverges Traktater med främmande magter* (Stockholm 1909), v₂. 168–82.
[101] Oxenstierna's accounts of his meeting with George William, and of the Halberstadt conference, are in *AOSB* I.XI.286, 292, 345–52.
[102] *AOSB* I.XI.353.

directive he was waiting for about the time when the Frankfurt convention opened; and substantially it reaffirmed the Regents' previous attitude: they wanted the whole of Pomerania, if possible, and in any case a Pomeranian port; only if that should prove absolutely impossible would they settle for some unspecified bishoprics and an indemnity of six million *riksdaler*.[103]

The effects of this directive were disastrous. It wrecked the Frankfurt convention; it destroyed the League. On 12 April 1634 George William took the crucial step of insisting upon an acceptable solution of the question of *satisfactio* before committing himself to the League; on 18 June the members of both Saxon Circles associated themselves with his stipulation.[104] Sweden was now threatened with a head-on collision with Brandenburg. Oxenstierna's whole German policy was on the brink of collapse. The attempt to provide a really effective *assecuratio* was being wrecked by a quarrel over *satisfactio*. Oxenstierna fully realised the seriousness of the situation; and it was probably in an effort to retrieve it that he launched the idea of renouncing Sweden's claims to Pomerania in return for the Elector's duchy of Prussia.[105] The Regents in Stockholm, to do them justice, gave the proposal their immediate attention. They referred it to a committee of the Estates; and that committee's recommendation – though grudging and conditional – was that Prussia should be accepted in Pomerania's place.[106]

There is some reason to believe that for Oxenstierna the Prussian alternative was not merely a device to break the deadlock with George William. If one may credit his account to the Council in 1641, the Pomeranian–Prussian exchange had been his solution from the beginning, and his efforts to secure it in Gustav Adolf's lifetime had been defeated only by the opposition of Bernard of Saxe-Weimar.[107] As to Bernard's share in the business there seems to be no information, nor is it easy to conjecture what his motives may have been if Oxenstierna's assertion was true. But as far as Oxenstierna himself was concerned the idea had undeniably something to commend it. It would bring a better *assecuratio* by opening the way to George William's inclusion in a more comprehensive League. This in its turn would mean that an attack on Sweden from Germany would become less likely. Pomerania would become less necessary; and one

---

[103] *HSH* 29. 232–7.

[104] *AOSB* I.XI.596; XII.73.

[105] *AOSB* I.XI.735; cf. his rueful retrospective judgment (12 February 1635), in *AOSB* I.XIII.116.

[106] A.A. von Stiernman, *Alla riksdagars och mötens besluth* (Stockholm 1729), II. 862–4; *RRP* IV. 170–4.

[107] *RRP* VIII. 722.

might always hope that some arrangement might be made about some Pomeranian ports – as pledges, perhaps, for the payment of an unpayable indemnity. The possession of ducal Prussia would help Sweden to retain her hold upon Polish Prussia – which meant, not least, her control of the 'licenses' which were so important to her finances. Sweden's claims on Pomerania, as Oxenstierna frankly confessed, depended really upon *jus belli* – the most odious of all grounds when advanced against a Protestant state; for Gustav Adolf's Pomeranian alliance was 'so obscure, so strained in interpretation, so full of snags', that it provided a very weak base for Sweden's pretensions: indeed, in his view it probably did no more than entitle Sweden to a refund of expenses.[108]

Moved, perhaps, by considerations such as these – moved, certainly, by an increasingly anguished desire for some settlement before the Polish truce ran out – the government in Stockholm accepted his solution. But their acceptance came too late. By the time the intimation of their change of mind reached him, affairs at Frankfurt had already reached a stalemate, and the position of the League had become critical. Just how critical can be seen from two remarkable suggestions, put forward by Oxenstierna in the desperate hope of retrieving the situation. The first, in May, was an appeal to the Stockholm government to rescue the League by sending over a million *riksdaler*: so much for the principle that the German war must be paid for by the Germans.[109] The other represents the first attempt to find a substitute and a replacement for the League of Heilbronn. On 19 August Oxenstierna offered Feuquières a proposition whereby, in return for a subsidy of a million *livres* a year, Germany was to be divided into French and Swedish spheres of influence, France to take over all Sweden's holdings west and south of the Elbe, Sweden to confine her efforts to the region north and east of that river.[110] And he motivated that proposal by the admission that he could no longer control the League. In effect, he was saying that his policy had failed at all points: the League no longer provided any sort of *assecuratio*; the squabble over Pomerania had destroyed any chance that it might stand guarantor for a reasonable *satisfactio*; and its finances (and hence its ability to carry on the war) now depended upon obtaining a French subsidy, or even – intolerable thought – on support from Sweden itself. In this situation it might seem that nothing remained but to abandon central Germany to its fate, and to concentrate

---

[108] *AOSB* I.XIII.72–5 (19 January 1635, to Sten Bielke), 115–17 (12 Feb 1635, to the Regents).
[109] *AOSB* I.XI.735.
[110] Arnoldsson, *Svensk-fransk krigs- och fredspolitik*, p. 32; Falk *Sverige och Frankrike*, p. 159.

Swedish efforts in the area to which the purely Swedish troops had already been withdrawn, in the hope that such a concentration might be sufficient to obtain by arms the *satisfactio* which there now seemed little hope of obtaining by agreement. And all this *before* the catastrophe at Nördlingen, which did not occur until 27 August.

Nördlingen, nevertheless, ensured that Oxenstierna's offer would have no appeal to Richelieu; just as it also ensured that the Regents would not answer his plea for money for the League (where, indeed, could they find it?). Even before the news of the disaster reached them they had given clear signs that they were losing their nerve;[111] and after it their vacillating views on *satisfactio* – including, as the ultimate resort, seeking the friendship of the Emperor (at a moment when he was flushed with victory) and establishing a closer link with the German Protestant states (when the League was on its deathbed) – suggest that they had lost their grip upon the realities of the German situation.[112] As indeed might well be; for all their attention was now concentrated on the coming negotiations with Poland: as to Germany, they summed up their view in reiterated directives to get out of the war – amicably, if possible, but if that were impossible to get out on any terms which were reconcilable with 'reputation'. But in truth it now mattered very little what they suggested. The decisive moment, the turning-point, had been reached and passed. The League of Heilbronn could no longer do Sweden's business. And it collapsed not so much as a result of military defeat (Nördlingen was not exploited by the victors, and Oxenstierna was able to regroup his forces on the line of the Main), as of the Regents' failure to heed, in good time, Oxenstierna's warnings about the consequences of insisting on Pomerania.

The men in Stockholm might now have their eyes fixed on Poland; but Oxenstierna, left in the meantime very much to his own devices, with general instructions to get out of the war somehow, had to find some method of salving what could be salved from the wreck of his policy. It was all very well for his colleagues to exhort him, in view of the economic situation at home,[113] 'rather to follow the example of Numa than of Romulus, of Solomon rather than of David', but it was by no means obvious just what Numa and Solomon would have recommended in the circumstances in which Oxenstierna found himself.[114] One solution might lie in somehow persuading Richelieu to allow himself to be installed as the new

---

[111] *HSH* 32. 126–33.
[112] *HSH* 32. 268–71.
[113] For a dark picture of conditions in Sweden, *HSH* 32. 273, 281.
[114] *HSH* 32. 273 (5 November 1634).

target at which Sweden's enemies in Germany might 'shoot their arrows'.[115] Even before Nördlingen members of the League had been turning their thoughts to closer links with France. After Nördlingen there was no help for it; and it was with Oxenstierna's approval that the League despatched Löffler and Streiff to Paris to make the best treaty they could.[116] But the terms which they settled for were such as he could not possibly accept: they transferred French subsidies – or the hope of subsidies, for since 1633 they had been paid irregularly, or not at all – from Sweden to the League; they would have reduced Sweden to the humiliating position of being just one of a bunch of French clients; and above all they stipulated that France would declare war only if assured that John George, George William and the other Estates of the two Saxon Circles did not make peace, or enter into negotiations for it, except in conjunction with France.[117] This last provision deprived the treaty of any meaning; for already in June John George had opened peace negotiations with the Emperor, and on 14 November they issued in the Preliminaries of Pirna. In December a thinly attended meeting of the League assembled in Worms to take stock of the situation and to decide whether or not to ratify the Löffler–Streiff treaty. The result was decisive. The League, desperate for French assistance in the Palatinate, by a majority ratified the treaty; Oxenstierna refused to do so, and ostentatiously quitted the meeting. It was a clear breach. Though he continued until 1640 to style himself the League's Director, and though he attended one more meeting of a miserable rump in March 1635, from this moment the League ceased to enter into his calculations. It would no longer serve his purposes; he must seek other paths, other instruments.

By the close of 1634 Oxenstierna had become a disillusioned and embittered man, conscious that he had lost control of events, and inclined to despair of recovering it. 'Henceforward', he wrote to Johan Banér, 'I will struggle no longer, but drift where the tide may take me . . . we are hated, envied, harassed',[118] – and that hatred, he had come to see, arose from the fact that the German princes now regarded him as the main obstacle to peace. And towards peace the tide was now setting strongly. Two significant actions reveal the

---

[115] *AOSB* I.XIII.22–3.

[116] Their instructions are in *AOSB* I.XII.430 ff. Löffler was authorised to offer all Swedish holdings in Alsace in return for a French declaration of war on the Emperor and Spain: *ibid.* 437.

[117] *Sverges Traktater*, v₂. 241–52. For the Löffler–Streiff treaty, see Arnoldsson, *Svensk-fransk krigs- och fredspolitik*, pp. 56–75, 87–9; Falk, *Sverige och Frankrike*, pp. 164–7; Tingsten, pp. 182–5.

[118] *AOSB* I.XII.664 (5 November 1634).

extent of his discouragement. On 14 September 1634 he wrote to his son Johan ordering him to arrange for the removal of all his archives to Sweden.[119] And on 30 October he sent to the Elector of Mainz an extraordinary proposal. He offered, if the Elector could contrive to obtain for him a safe-conduct and pass from the Emperor, to restore to him the city of Mainz and the whole electorate; but if not, he would devastate it with fire and sword, and then hand it over to the French. The Elector had his doubts as to whether Oxenstierna's offer was seriously meant, but he did (surprisingly) succeed in inducing Ferdinand to promise the pass and the safe-conduct. But the promise contained one word which for Oxenstierna robbed it of any value: it offered him an imperial 'pardon'. This was too much for his pride to swallow; and no more was heard of this tenebrous negotiation. But he took care to make no mention of it in his letters home – not even in confidential communications with brother Gabriel.[120]

In a survey of the situation which he sent home in January 1635 Oxenstierna indicated two possible lines of action, as the only alternatives left open to him.[121] One was to take the opportunity afforded by the Preliminaries of Pirna, which had provided for the accession of Sweden and France, if they were so minded. The other was an alliance with France. Neither seemed attractive. But if he must choose, Oxenstierna clearly preferred a negotiated settlement in Germany. Somehow or other, Sweden must extricate herself from the German bog, and do it if possible without quarrelling with her alleged friends. Banér was therefore instructed not to oppose, but rather to commend, John George's efforts for peace. For if the Elector and the Emperor made peace, George William of Brandenburg would certainly adhere to it, Pomerania would follow, and so – paradoxically enough – the enemy would be shut out from the coastlands, and Sweden would gain her security on that side after all.[122] Pomerania was in any case lost, at least for the present; and Oxenstierna drifted with the tide here also. Sten Bielke was ordered not to resist a Brandenburg occupation in the event of Bogislaw's death;[123] and Oxenstierna drafted bases of negotiation which clearly recognised George William's hereditary right.[124] The best he now hoped for was that some fragments of Pomerania might be retained, as pledges for the payment of a Swedish indemnity. Nor had he any

[119] AOSB I. XII. 473.
[120] Die Politik Maximilians von Bayern und seiner Verbündeten 1618–1651, part 2 (Munich 1986), IX. 347–8, 530.
[121] AOSB I.XIII. 18–23 (6 January 1635).
[122] AOSB I.XII.666.
[123] AOSB I.XIII.74 (19 January 1635).
[124] AOSB I.XIII.117 (12 February 1635).

longer much hope of an alternative compensation in Prussia, of which he wrote that 'we hold it only by our finger-tips'.[125] There was not much comfort anywhere, at the beginning of 1635. Least of all from John George. For it soon became clear that accession to John George's peace was possible only if Sweden were willing to evacuate Germany altogether – were willing therefore, to abandon both *assecuratio* and *satisfactio*; and it entailed such a sacrifice of 'reputation' that even the Regents, desperate for peace as they now were, would hardly be willing to swallow it.

It might seem then, that nothing remained but to conclude an alliance with France. But Oxenstierna was not prepared – now, or for some years to come – to accept that conclusion. Alliance with France would involve the risk that Sweden might be used to pull Richelieu's chestnuts out of the fire, and be committed to continuing the war for as long as the alliance should last; in fact, to making the German war once again the predominant concern, at the very moment when what he wanted was a German peace. France, it appeared, was now willing to shoulder the League of Heilbronn, and Oxenstierna might well wish Richelieu joy of his bargain; but he was not minded to add himself to the list of Richelieu's puppets. His object was to use France, as once he had used the League – and even that only if his negotiations for peace in Germany failed. In that case, his hope was '*excitando aut connivendo* to give the House of Austria so much to do that they will forget about us'.[126] But since Sweden's negotiating position *vis-à-vis* John George was for the moment weak, there was much to be said for a diplomatic demonstration of Franco-Swedish solidarity. It was with this object that in March 1635 he quitted central Germany – as it proved, for ever – and made his way to a meeting with Richelieu at Compiègne. The treaty which he there concluded was in essence no more than a renewal of amity: the positive provisions were kept vague; of binding commitments there were none. But the treaty of Compiègne reflected Richelieu's growing realisation that France could not hope to effect her aims through the League alone, any more than Sweden could; and that Oxenstierna, despite the 'Gothic' manners and 'intolerable pride' which so ruffled the French diplomats, might be a disagreeable necessity, to be courted rather than kidnapped. And for Oxenstierna, on his side, the treaty served (he hoped) as a useful warning, and a demonstration that Sweden did not lack friends.[127]

[125] *AOSB* I.XIII.119.

[126] *AOSB* I.XIII.22–3 (6 January 1635).

[127] *Sverges Traktater*. v₂. 318–19, and *AOSB* I.XIII.242, 261. For an account of his visit to France, F.U. Wrangel, *Axel Oxenstiernas resa till och i Frankrike 1635* (Stockholm 1914).

But when in June 1635 he touched German soil again at Stade, the world had taken another disastrous turn for the worse. On 20 May the Emperor and John George concluded the Peace of Prague, on terms which represented a considerably tougher line on the Emperor's part as compared with the terms agreed upon at Pirna. The Palatines, William V of Hesse-Cassel, Württemberg, Baden-Durlach – the heart of the Swedish party in Germany – were now excluded from mercy; and the Emperor acquired a constitutional authority in the *Reich* such as no Emperor had enjoyed in memory of man. The princes and towns of Germany, for the moment forgetful of German liberties and anxious only for peace, flocked precipitately to accept a settlement which seemed at least to promise that: George William of Brandenburg among them. Within a few months only William V and Bernard of Saxe-Weimar were left to continue the struggle. From Stockholm Gabriel Gustafsson sent accounts of the state of the country which exceeded in gloom all his not inconsiderable achievements in that line.[128] Hard on the heels of these blows came the official news of the truce of Stuhmsdorf (2 September 1635), which – among other things – finally extinguished the possibility of retaining or regaining the friendship of George William by means of the Prussian exchange. Sweden's military resources in Germany were now reduced to Banér's small army in Pomerania and Mecklenburg. They confronted a resurgence of German patriotism under the Emperor's leadership, a universal desire for peace, a fierce hatred of the foreigner. It was a situation far more menacing than that of 1629. The overwhelming majority of the 'Swedish' forces in Germany were threatened now with proscription of themselves and their families if they resisted the Emperor's summons to return to their obedience. Where now could they look for their massive arrears of pay? In August 1635 their officers kept Oxenstierna a prisoner in their camp at Magdeburg, as a hostage whom they forced to conduct their negotiations with John George; and it was only the Elector's hectoring tone, and his unforthcomingness in the matter of money, that prevented a mass desertion from the Swedish service. Before Oxenstierna made his escape, by Banér's contrivance, he had been driven to promise them that if he did not at the peace obtain sufficient cash to pay their arrears, they might go to Sweden and collect them there in person.[129]

---

[128] *AOSB* II.III.363–4 (11 June 1635: Oxenstierna received it in the camp at Magdeburg on 7 July).

[129] The agreement between Banér and the German officers of 11 August 1635 (which Oxenstierna signed) promised that if the war went ill, and 'mancher redlicher cavallier gantz von dess reichs boden abgetrieben werden und also sein fortune anderswo suchen muste, allso haben S. Exc. *in nahmen der Konigl. Mt. und crohn* [my italics] unss versprochen, dass wir nicht

V

The mutinies at Magdeburg inaugurated a new phase – the final phase – of Oxenstierna's labours in Germany. He was now driven, almost a fugitive, to take refuge on the extreme periphery of German affairs. As he contemplated the chilly waters of the Baltic from Stralsund or Wismar, he felt the full implications of his situation: 'I sit here with empty hands, and write home, and ride around the watch like any other commander or captain.'[130] Small wonder if in such circumstances he began to feel that his usefulness in Germany was nearing its end, and that it would be better to go home. But if he went, who could step into his place to make the peace which had now become a necessity, and above all, who could make it on satisfactory terms? The Stuhmsdorf negotiations did not give him much confidence that such a person could be found in Stockholm. The humiliations of Magdeburg had not only confirmed his will to make peace, they had made very clear to him what the essential condition of such a peace must be: the contentment of the soldiery. The pledge which he had been forced to give to the mutinous officers was a pledge which Sweden simply had not the resources to honour: any peace which failed to transfer that burden to German shoulders would be disastrous.[131]

On 6 October 1635 John George formally declared war on Sweden; on 6 January 1636 George William followed his example. Protestant was now fighting Protestant: it was almost true to say that Germany was fighting the foreigners. But the peace which Oxenstierna intended was not a peace with the Electors, who were after all subjects and auxiliaries; it must be a peace between principals, a peace concluded between sovereigns, a peace with the Emperor; and it must be ratified by him.[132] This was a principle more easy to formulate than to enforce, as he had discovered already in Magdeburg. In the darkest days of the mutiny he had secretly despatched to Vienna what was almost a plea to open negotiations, and he had been crushingly snubbed: the Emperor did not even deign to send him an answer.[133] After the Peace of Prague Ferdinand II was no longer what

verlassen sondern unsere retraicte uff die crohn Schweeden nehmen und allda nach einer jedern meriten und der mügligkeit mit gelth oder güttern recompensiert werden sollen': *AOSB* I.XIII.484–5. The pledge was reaffirmed on 7 November: *ibid.* XIV.215 (to Banér's officers), and again a week later: *ibid.* XIV.233.

[130] *AOSB* I.XIV.150 (13 October 1635, to Sten Bielke).

[131] As the Estate of Nobility said very plainly: *Sveriges Rikes Ridderskaps och Adels Riksdagsprotokoll* (Stockholm 1855–   ), II.170, 193, (23 October, 2 November 1635).

[132] *AOSB* I.XIV,287 (30 November 1635): the Estates at home agreed with him: Stiernman, *Alla riksdagars och mötens besluth*, II.929–32.

[133] *AOSB* I.XIV.49 (to Ferdinand II, 17 September 1635). It was not until 10 October that

he had been before it. He was not now prepared to deal on a footing of equality with a foreign subject whose power and reputation seemed to be on the point of extinction. If Oxenstierna was still minded to treat, he must address himself to John George as the Emperor's delegate – as once the Tsars of Muscovy had condescended to treat with Kings of Sweden only through the Voyevode of Novgorod[134] – with no guarantee that any agreement reached would receive the Emperor's ratification.[135] It was all very well for Salvius to argue that this was an acceptable procedure, since the real principals had now made peace and Sweden could be considered simply as an accessory to allies who had mostly repudiated her;[136] but this was an argument so damaging to Sweden's 'reputation' that Oxenstierna could not easily accept it. Yet, in the existing circumstances, this humiliation too had to be swallowed with the others, if ever negotiations were to begin at all.

Oxenstierna saw little hope of getting an acceptable peace if he were forced to negotiate in the deplorable military situation of the autumn of 1635. The very real possibility of driving Sweden out of Germany altogether would make John George inaccessible to any proposals for a reasonable settlement.[137] The truce of Stuhmsdorf, however, did at least bring him one much-needed asset: it permitted the transference to Pomerania of 9,700 men under the command of Lennart Torstensson; and this reinforcement enabled Banér in the last months of the year to win a series of useful victories over the Saxon forces, which perhaps did something to make the Elector a little more supple. Final victory might now seem impossible; but something, perhaps, could be done by 'molesting' the Elector: in the long run, Oxenstierna believed, the Protestant princes of north Germany would prefer a settlement to the ruin of their territories.[138] But it was not sufficient simply to hang on, somehow or other, to the coastlands: if effective pressure were to be brought to bear, and above all if the armies were to be supplied, war must be waged offensively, as in the past; and Banér must be strong enough to be able to break out of the exhausted Pomeranian bastion.[139]

Oxenstierna informed his brother, in strict confidence; and he did not officially report his overture to the Regents until 30 December, when he apologised for the delay with the brazen excuse that he had been so busy at the time that he had quite forgotten to mention it: *AOSB* I.XIV.134, 374. For a differing interpretation of Oxenstierna's letter, see Goetze, *Die Politik des schwedischen Reichskanzlers Axel Oxenstierna*, p. 189.

[134] Oxenstierna himself made the comparison: *AOSB* I.XIV.23.
[135] *AOSB* I.XIV.76–7 (30 September 1635).
[136] *RRP* v. 224 (23 October 1635).
[137] *AOSB* I.XIV.376.
[138] *AOSB* I.XIV.77 146–9.
[139] *AOSB* I.XV.385 (12 April 1636).

The government at home was thinking on other lines. They lacked both Oxenstierna's nerve and his clear appreciation of what now was at stake. They had already lost any hope of territorial *satisfactio*, and some of them professed not to desire it. 'What good does it do us', cried Karl Karlsson Gyllenhielm, 'to acquire many lands, and spend money on it, and so ruin ourselves at home?'[140] The demand for a territorial *satisfactio*, said Jakob de la Gardie, had been a mistake from the beginning, for it was inconceivable that the Germans would ever agree to an arrangement which violated the Golden Bull.[141] As early as October 1635 they were ready to abandon all such claims, whether in land or money, if thereby they could keep some friends in Germany.[142] Even Gabriel Gustafsson was soon to say that it was intolerable to go on fighting a war in which they had no interest.[143] They did indeed concede that the contentment of the soldiery was the one interest that they dared not let go.[144] But it was naive to suppose (as Gabriel Gustafsson did) that they had only to say so, and peace would be tossed into their lap by a grateful and reconciled Germany.[145] Oxenstierna knew better. He was as determined on peace as they were – on the last day of 1635 he furnished them with a comprehensive and clinching list of arguments for it[146] – but he had a better appreciation of the difficulty of obtaining it, and of ensuring that it should be observed when obtained. And so, in the autumn of 1635 and the spring of 1636 he hammered home the point in letter after letter to the Regents, and in emotional appeals to his brother, that he must have reinforcements, must have supplies, must have money, if there were to be any fair chance of getting the kind of settlement which they all agreed was imperative. To Gabriel Gustafsson he wrote that given the necessary supplies they would have a short war and a quick peace; without them, a long war and a peace of ignominy.[147] No doubt the government in Stockholm did its best; but they were too inefficient, too procrastinating, to give him anything like what he was needing, and to Oxenstierna their best seemed infuriatingly inadequate.

Thus it happened that he was forced to negotiate not from strength but from weakness. Direct negotiations with John George broke

[140] *RRP* IV. 253 (4 December 1634).
[141] *RRP* V. 297 (11 November 1635).
[142] *HSH* 37. 75–90 (12 October 1635).
[143] *RRP* VI. 185. (25 April 1636).
[144] *HSH* 37. 75–90, *RRP* V. 201, 251–5, 380–1; Stiernman, *Alla riksdagars och mötens besluth*, II, 929–32.
[145] *RRP* VI. 182–3.
[146] *AOSB* I.XIV.385.
[147] *AOSB* I.XIV.406; XV.534.

down almost at once, for he demanded Sweden's immediate evacuation and adherence to the terms of the Peace of Prague, and only then was he prepared to offer a quite inadequate cash payment, with no territorial concessions.[148] Renewed negotiations, this time through the intermediary of Adolf Frederick of Mecklenburg, proved more hopeful. Substantial agreement was reached on a Swedish evacuation of Germany in stages, provided that the Emperor's ratification was forthcoming; and it was agreed also that a separate treaty covering the contentment of the soldiery and a cash *satisfactio* should be hammered out at a convention of Protestant states, designed to be held at Lüneberg early in the new year. But that was the limit of success. Oxenstierna insisted that the negotiations with the Emperor, and the Lüneberg convention, must proceed *pari passu* and take effect simultaneously: he was not going to evacuate Germany and find himself stripped of bargaining-power, in regard to the vital question of the army's arrears.[149] And on this issue the negotiations had reached a deadlock by the opening of 1636.

There were conceivable ways of breaking it: in particular, the device of another approach to France. Since Richelieu's conclusion of the Löffler–Streiff treaty with the League things had gone almost as ill for him as for Sweden. The League predictably proved more of a liability than an asset; its demise followed quickly; and the Peace of Prague left France, as it left Sweden, with no prospect of a German clientelage. In March 1635 Olivares tweaked the Cardinal's nose by kidnapping France's *protégé* the Elector of Trier, and open war with Spain followed with little delay. France could not now go it alone in Germany; and it became Richelieu's anxious concern to prevent Oxenstierna from making a separate peace, and so leaving her in that situation: at the end of the year his ambassador in Germany, St Chamont, was offering Sweden 'mountains of gold' to stay in the war.[150] Oxenstierna was thus in a position to put pressure on France by his negotiations with Adolf Frederick, and might hope that negotiations with France would soften the intransigence of John George. The diplomatic advantage was no longer in Richelieu's hands.

It was with a firm grasp of this situation that Oxenstierna opened talks with St Chamont at Wismar in February 1636. They produced two *projets* for an alliance – one Swedish, one French – to be ratified by August, and no French subsidies to be paid until then; but they also produced an agreement binding each side not to make peace in

---

[148] For the negotiations with John George, and the so-called 'Schönebeck project', see Goetze, *Die Politik des schwedischen Reichskanzlers Axel Oxenstierna*, pp. 184–7.

[149] *AOSB* I.XIV.313–14, 327, 350, 369–73.

[150] *AOSB* I.XIV.375–6, 401, 405–6.

the meantime.[151] On 1 May Louis XIII accepted the Swedish *projet*, agreed to declare war on the Emperor, and to pay Sweden a million *livres* a year in subsidy: this, after all, was the year of Corbie. But Oxenstierna on his side was in no hurry to ratify. He believed that the Emperor, confronted with the prospect of a real collaboration between France and Sweden, would choose to make peace with Sweden;[152] and he was not prepared to tie his hands in such a way as to prevent him from taking advantage of such an opportunity if it came.

Oxenstierna had been quick to grasp the implications for Sweden of the Peace of Prague: 'the Emperor', he wrote, 'has gained more by the peace than by two Nördlingens'.[153] The sovereign authority which Ferdinand II now seemed to have achieved, the collapse of any counterpoise to his power in Germany, presaged a menace to Sweden in the future. Oxenstierna had not forgotten 1629. Sweden had intervened in Germany, among other reasons, in order to save 'German liberties'; for the preservation of those liberties was Sweden's interest also. Gustav Adolf had expressed this policy in a well-remembered phrase when he said: 'As long as an Elector sits safe in his Electorate, and a duke is duke and has his liberties, then we are safe.'[154] The conclusion was inescapable: the *ultimate* objective of Swedish policy must now be the destruction of the Peace of Prague; and any settlement must have that consequence, or at the very least provide the means for it. The immediate objective, of course, remained the contentment of the soldiery. Whether in the existing circumstances the ultimate objective was attainable – that was a more dubious question. Translated into practical terms, it meant amnesty for those excluded from pardon at Prague, and the possibility of once more forming from them a nucleus of opposition to Habsburg power. The demand for an amnesty was first seriously put forward in Oxenstierna's final peace terms for Adolf Frederick, communicated around Christmas in 1635.[155] It was not that he felt any obligation to go out of his way to rescue those princes who since Nördlingen had deserted the Swedish cause: it was for Sweden's sake, and not for theirs, that the demand for amnesty was put forward. For a time he was not altogether without hope that it might

---

[151] *Sverges Traktater*, v₂. 366–72, 373–4.

[152] *AOSB* I.xv.535, 563.

[153] *AOSB* I.xiii.587.

[154] See, e.g., *RRP* vii. 423, 427; vii. 315 (22 Jan 1639, 14 Nov 1640), when this dictum was more than once quoted in the Council.

[155] *AOSB* I.xiv.354. It had however been included in the 'Schönebeck project' of 6 September 1635: Goetze, *Die Politik des schwedischen Reichskanzlers Axel Oxenstierna*, pp. 184–5.

be accepted, at least for some of them.[156] But even if it were not, and even if for the sake of an early peace it had to be postponed, the mere fact that it had been made and pressed might do something to remind the proscribed that it was Sweden that was their real friend. In a circular to the Protestant princes of Germany in June 1636 he was careful to make the point that it was just on the question of amnesty that the negotiations with Adolf Frederick had broken down.[157] It was not quite true, of course; but it was useful propaganda.

VI

Such was the situation – the treaty of Wismar still unratified, the German negotiations at a stand – when in July 1636 Oxenstierna at last took his leave of Germany, never thereafter to set foot outside his native land. For months he had been expressing a passionate longing to go home, to see his wife and friends once again, to settle down to a tranquil old age;[158] and this natural private feeling had been rein-forced by strong public considerations: the need to arouse the government from its lethargy, the need to talk to the Regents face to face of his policies and his difficulties. If only he could dash over to Stockholm for a week or two, he believed that he would be able to infuse into his colleagues some of his own steadiness of purpose, and to supply from his long experience the administrative grasp which they seemed so conspicuously to lack.[159] But in the autumn of 1635 this kind of fleeting visit was effectually barred by the protests of the officers, who feared that his departure might impede the negotiations for peace, suspected that once he got home he would probably stay there, and were not to be moved by his explanations that he was going mainly in order to expedite the despatch of the arms and supplies of which they stood so much in need.[160] This, however, was not the only consideration which weighed with him, nor perhaps even the main one. For he felt very strongly that it was his duty to stay on until his mission in Germany had been fully discharged – or at least until he was convinced that his presence there would no longer serve any useful purpose; and that was not the case before the beginning of 1636. And until he could feel sure that competent successors could be found to replace him, he scrupled to shuffle off

[156] *AOSB* I.XIV.372 (30 December 1635); *RRP* VI. 391.
[157] *AOSB* I.XV.580. To the Regents, he blamed the breakdown on Adolf Frederick's demand that he promise not to ally with France: *ibid.* XV.292.
[158] 'I am weary of myself and not less of this false world': *AOSB* I.XIII.522; cf. XV.70–1 (to Gabriel Gustafsson, 14 August 1635, 24 January 1636).
[159] *AOSB* I.XIV.99, 143; XV.70.
[160] *AOSB* I.XIV.154, 231.

his responsibilities on to shoulders less broad than his own. His letters home in these final months vividly reveal how torn he was between these conflicting obligations. Nevertheless, as winter gave way to spring, the tardiness of the government in meeting his clamorous demands for aid produced a cumulative exasperation. In his letters to his brother he took no trouble to conceal his resentments. In reply to Gabriel Gustafsson's assurance that they would welcome his return and could be relied on to give him a favourable reception, he poured out his pent-up sense of injury in a passionate tirade:

I should be glad [he wrote] to get away from this place, not only with my life, but even at the expense of it . . . The whole time I have been out here I have been a slave; I am envied and persecuted by friend and foe; and there is no afflication, no labour, no danger to life and reputation, so great that I have not had to endure it, and still have to do so. But all this is nothing to the way I have been treated since I came to these parts [*sc.* Pomerania] . . . Hitherto, I have despised it, but it has now got under my skin to such an extent that my judgement and my resourcefulness are deserting me, and – what is worse – that in order to keep things from going to pieces I must suffer everything patiently, and dare not even confide to paper the contumely with which I – and indeed my country – are treated; not because I shun, or lack the spirit, to face a quarrel, but in order that I do not damage the country's interests . . . I can't be of any use here; but if I leave, everything will collapse, and all the blame be put on me.[161]

There was worse to come. On 11 and 12 March the Regents sent him the formal leave to return for which he had been asking, with discretion to take advantage of it as he saw fit.[162] But they also suggested that leave of absence be given to Banér, who wished to come home to bury his wife. Thus, with extraordinary irresponsibility and lack of imagination, they contemplated depriving Sweden's cause in Germany simultaneously of its most experienced statesman and its best available general; and they had nothing but vague suggestions for supplying the place of either.[163] Oxenstierna allowed ten days to pass before acknowledging this remarkable communication – no doubt in order to allow time for his rage to cool before drafting his reply; but to his brother he made no attempt to temper his fury and contempt. The government, it appeared, expected that he should leave affairs in Germany in a posture which was not (in their words) 'desperate'; but they gave him no means to do so. They instructed him to take what means he needed from subsidies (what subsidies? the French were still paying none) and from local resources (though it was just

---

[161] *AOSB* I.xv.327–30 (29 March 1636).
[162] *AOSB* I.xv.407–8; *HSH* 38. 224–35.
[163] A week later they had so far come to their senses as to refuse leave to Banér: *HSH* 38. 243–5.

because local resources were near exhaustion that Oxenstierna had appealed to them for aid); and at the same time they urged him to press on with the peace negotations,

as though foreign kings and republics were so amicable and well-disposed towards us that they should, without any visible profit to themselves, lavish money upon us, or that I should simultaneously treat for peace and get money from our friends [for war] . . . Instead of an answer to my proposals and questions, I get a short extract of the annual revenue and expenditure of the kingdom – as though I were in a position to do anything to improve it, or that I should content the soldiery and supply our needs with such an extract.[164]

Three days before this letter was sent off, the Council had taken a step which must inevitably widen the cleavage between the Chancellor and the government, when they resolved to send out Salvius to make the peace which – some of them had come to suspect – was being sabotaged by Oxenstierna. Salvius was indeed to take his orders 'de modo tractandi' from the Chancellor; but 'de realibus' he was to follow instructions from home. It was a clear vote of no confidence; and Oxenstierna could hardly be blamed if he took it as a censure of his conduct. But he was too old a hand for such a move to succeed. He met it by firmly tying up Salvius in instructions which gave him only the status of a subdelegate subject to his authority, and so deprived him of any opportunity to tangle the wires.[165] Nevertheless, if he had still any lingering doubts about going home, those doubts must now have been removed: the country could not go on at this rate.

On 16 July 1636 Oxenstierna landed at Dalarö. He had missed his son's wedding; but perhaps he consoled himself with the reflection that he had at any rate ensured that Banér should miss his wife's interment. Four days later he appeared before the Council,[166] scrupulously declining to take his seat in that body until he had made his report on his mission: on the 18th he had addressed a committee of the Estates whose meeting had been postponed until his homecoming. His reception by both these bodies must have come as something of a surprise to him. His view of his colleagues had latterly been such that he may well have expected to find himself in the position of attempting to defend his record against the attacks of his political enemies. But no such attack developed. The tone was now quite altered. On 22 July the Estates passed a resolution which was in effect an unqualified vote of confidence. His policies were

---

[164] *AOSB* I.xv.411–13 (26 April 1636).
[165] *AOSB* I.xv.547 (Memorial for Salvius, 22 June 1636).
[166] *RRP* vi. 380–95.

endorsed, his services acknowledged.[167] The Regents and the Council may not have been unaffected by this emphatic manifestation of support. At all events, they associated themselves with it. In the series of protracted debates on foreign policy which occupied the attention of the Council in the last days of July and the beginning of August no one ventured the mildest criticism of his proceedings in Germany.[168] The sniping stopped; the innuendoes were heard no more. With touching unanimity they resolved that the only acceptable course of action for the moment was to fight on, as the quickest road to peace, and in the meantime to avoid giving any binding undertaking to France. Oxenstierna found himself accepted without question as the natural head of the government; and he was able at once to set about putting the administration to rights and injecting some of his own spirit into his colleagues. It was triumph of personality, an extorted tribute to the qualities which had carried him through the stormy years in Germany; and he might have been forgiven if he had received it with a sardonic smile.

We can see now that it was less surprising than it must have appeared to him. The differences between himself and his colleagues had not latterly been about policy; they had been about how that policy was carried out.[169] The Regents suspected Oxenstierna of being dilatory and half-hearted in the pursuit of peace (in which they were quite wrong); Oxenstierna's charge against them was their incompetence and tardiness in supplying him with the means through which peace could be obtained (in which he was quite right, though he ignored the mitigating circumstances). But now his rehearsal of the facts, his total command of the arguments, his formidable personal qualities, bore down their suspicions, and the long debates in the Council must have persuaded him that he could now count on having his colleagues behind him. No one was prepared to tie Sweden to France for the sake of 'a squirt of money'; everyone looked forward to a peace in Germany negotiated against a display of Swedish military strength. He and they had the same objective: the contentment of the soldiery, with some additional cash – if they could get it – by way of *satisfactio*. The only serious matter of debate was on the question of amnesty, and on that they came to the same conclusion: Sweden's negotiators must fight hard to obtain it, for the sake of William V and for the sake of Sweden's reputation; but they

---

[167] Stiernman, *Alla riksdagars och mötens besluth*, II. 946; *RRP* VI. 409–14.

[168] *RRP* VI. 502–9, 759–68.

[169] The decline of defeatism among the Regents may perhaps be connected with the marked improvement in the internal situation since 1635: in January they were describing it in unusually optimistic terms: *HSH* 38. 144.

must not let it stand in the way of peace if it appeared that peace was to be had. Only if a breach on other issues was in any case inevitable should amnesty be made the ostensible – and creditable – pretext. Which was in strict line with the instructions Oxenstierna had left behind him to guide the Swedish negotiators at the still-unsummoned Lüneberg convention.[170]Oxenstierna himself put this policy in the most uncompromising terms: if money to pay the troops could be obtained, 'I would not advise continuing the war for an hour longer'.[171] If he meant what he said – if he was not simply intent on rallying the Regents to his policy – it was an indication as strong as any of his anxiety to bring the war to an end. For it implied, and he must have realised that it implied, the postponement – if not the abandonment – of the ultimate objective: the destruction of the Peace of Prague. It was a short-term policy; and in the light of Banér's classic victory at Wittstock on 24 September 1636 it looked as though it might be the right one. In the event it proved an illusion. But that was not yet apparent in the autumn of 1636.

VII

How are we to judge Oxenstierna's achievement during the last years of his exile in Germany? On the morrow of Lützen he was confronted with alternative courses of action, each of which was liable to serious objections. He might continue Gustav Adolf's policy and fight for final victory and a dictated peace. But this, in his view as well as that of his colleagues, meant a concentration on the wrong thing: it demanded a major effort in Germany (with no assurance of real aid from France) instead of the systematic building-up of Sweden's defences against possible attacks from the neighbours, and in particular from Poland. Or he might cut short the German enterprise altogether. But that would leave Sweden with no obvious *assecuratio*, with the problem of paying the troops their arrears, and with the danger that France would seek an ally and an instrument in Denmark. He preferred a middle course which seemed to avoid these disadvantages. The idea of some sort of a permanent confederation of evangelical states had been bequeathed to him by Gustav Adolf. His solution was to take over that idea and adapt it to altered circumstances and new objectives. The League of Heilbronn was the result.

That it should have failed was by no means wholly his fault. If enormous exertions, diplomatic skill, and strength of leadership had been sufficient, the solution might have worked. But they were not

---

[170] *AOSB* I.xv.547–53, 557–62.
[171] *RRP* vi. 508.

sufficient. The fiction by which Sweden 'lent her name' to the war could not be accepted indefinitely: as soon as the German states saw the chance of a reasonable peace they would probably take it. Pirna offered that chance; and though Prague was a good deal harder to swallow, they swallowed it too, with remarkable alacrity. The device of financing the war by donations had obvious limits; and by the end of 1633 those limits had already pretty well been reached. The question of Sweden's *satisfactio* was already straining the League before the crisis came over Pomerania. Nevertheless, the League might have had a rather longer life if Oxenstierna had been content with the adhesion of the Lower Saxon Circle, as promised at the Halberstadt meeting in 1634; and it might perhaps have been saved altogether if the Prussian alternative to Pomerania had been propounded earlier, and pursued more resolutely. And for these missed opportunities Oxenstierna must undoubtedly bear a share of the blame.

After Nördlingen, and still more after the Peace of Prague, he was driven back upon a flexible defensive diplomacy, forced to make use of temporary or tactical expedients, and in the very difficult circumstances it is hard to imagine that any better result could have been obtained than that which he actually achieved, with a hand that was almost bare of trumps. He declined to be stampeded into what would have been virtually unconditional surrender, either by disasters in Germany or by pressures from home. He correctly assessed the shift in Sweden's war-aims which the new situation enforced; and he contrived to keep a free hand for realising them at whatever moment, and by whatever methods, might eventually be most appropriate. And in the end, upon his return home, he had the personal satisfaction of seeing his actions approved, and his policies endorsed, by *riksdag*, Council and Regents.

Nevertheless, it is more than questionable whether his solution was the right one. By evading for the moment the French alliance it did indeed preserve the free hand, and it did indeed put the contentment of the soldiery forward as the immediate objective; but some of the arguments upon which it was based were dubious or specious. When he told the Council that 'the Emperor is now as weak as he has ever been, and could well be resisted if one had sufficient backbone'[172] it is hard to believe that he meant what he said. And when he justified his policy of not making amnesty a *sine qua non* by the argument that if negotiations broke down on this issue and the war in consequence went on, then Sweden would be left with no option

[172] *RRP* vi. 389

but to conclude the French alliance, that was as much as to say that in order to avoid committing himself to France he was willing to leave the Peace of Prague intact, and to prefer an unsatisfactory peace to indefinite war.[173] But in the event the negotiations did break down, the war did go on, and the consequence – the immediate consequence – was not, as he had insisted, the French alliance: the consequence was that Sweden struggled on alone in pursuit of the peace that was desired. Within a year he was singing a very different tune: by May 1637 the restoration of German liberties had become the *'principalis scopus'* of the war.[174] He was to go on saying the same thing until 1641.[175] And if ever there had been a chance that this could be effected by Sweden's unaided exertions (which is more than doubtful) that prospect vanished for ever with Banér's retreat from Torgau in 1637, which was in effect a Swedish Dunkirk. In February 1638 Oxenstierna was forced to accept the inevitable, and by the treaty of Hamburg swallow the bitter pill of the French alliance.

It turned out better than he had feared. Thanks to Torstensson's brilliant campaigns, and perhaps also to France's internal difficulties, Sweden did not after all become a French puppet or client. And when peace came at last it brought with it the two essential objects of Swedish policy: German liberty restored, a comprehensive restoration and amnesty, Sweden herself an Estate of the *Reich*. It was a full *assecuratio*. So too with the contentment of the soldiery, which was firmly placed on German shoulders. These were terms which Sweden could hardly have hoped for from Oxenstierna's tactics of 1636–8. And the attainment of war-aims which were deemed essential brought with it, almost incidentally, the realisation of war-aims which since 1640 or so had been considered only as desirable.[176] It brought territorial gains which seemed to make economic and strategic sense, a large cash indemnity, and (though this had long since ceased to be a major preoccupation) the preservation of the Protestant Cause. It was a result which in July 1636 would have appeared to Oxenstierna as beyond all reasonable expectation. But it was a result which might well have been impossible without him.

[173] *RRP* VI. 505.

[174] *RRP* VII. 51–4.

[175] E.g., 'Our main concern is our security, and to prevent the Roman Empire from falling into a servitude': *RRP* VIII. 573 (16 April 1641); 'If you allow the Peace of Prague to stand, then our late king's *consilia* are annihilated, and afterwards we may be sure that we have war here at home': *RRP* VIII. 583 (4 May 1641); and cf. *RRP* VIII. 333.

[176] On 21 November 1640 Oxenstierna told the Council that the acquisition of Pomerania was 'not so important as gaining and retaining the Princes' affection and restoring them to their former state': *RRP* VIII. 333; on 16 April 1641 he told them 'Satisfactio we have insisted upon least of all. The main objectives were amnesty and the contentment of the soldiery. These points are *real*, but our *satisfactio* is not to be so considered': *RRP* VIII. 571–3.

II

Charles X and his Council: 'dualism' or co-operation?

I

In the troubled times of the fifteenth century an essential feature of the constitutional situation in Sweden had been the latent or open opposition of king and Council: until the emergence of the *riksdag* at the beginning of the following century the Council was the effective and legal check upon the crown, as well as being the natural leader of that collection of magnates of whom the Vasas were one. When in 1523 they ascended the throne in the person of Gustav Vasa this constitutional situation was soon perceived to have undergone a profound alteration. Within a decade of his accession, thanks to the need to confront external and internal dangers which were common to king and Council alike, he had effectively transformed the Council into a body of occasional *ad hoc* coadjutors; and against the possibility of their docility's proving dubious had equipped himself with an alternative ally within the constitution, in the shape of the now-emergent *riksdag*. This almost unchallenged royal dominance was eroded under his two successors. Under Erik XIV we can discern the beginning of a revival of Council-constitutionalism; under John III it becomes more conspicuous; and in the last decade of the century it culminates in the theorisings of Erik Sparre.[1] But though the Council now appears again as the advocate of limitations on the prerogative, its loyalty to the monarch, in the person of Sigismund, and its reluctance to countenance the illegal intrigues of the future Charles IX, produce that catastrophe to the constitutional cause which was consummated in the 'Blood-bath of Linköping' (1600).[2] That deed

[1] Sparre's *Pro Lege, Rege, et Grege* is printed in *Historiska Handlingar*, vol. 27, part 1 (Stockholm 1924). For a discussion of its significance see Karl Nordlund, *Den svenska reformationstidens allmänna statsrättsliga ideer* (Stockholm 1900); Fredrik Lagerroth, *Frihetstidens författning. En studie i den svenska konstitutionalismens historia* (Stockholm 1915), pp. 81–95; and Erland Hjärne, *Från Vasatiden till Frihetstiden* (Uppsala 1929).
[2] For these events, Michael Roberts, *The Early Vasas. A History of Sweden 1523–1611* (Cambridge 1968), pp. 369–93.

made a real reconciliation between the crown and the high aristocracy very difficult for so long as Charles IX lived; and it drove him to attempt to rule the country as Gustav Vasa had ruled it – i.e. as his personal domain – with assistance when he could get it from a *riksdag* still at times accessible to the inflammatory propaganda with which he had kindled revolution in the nineties. For the whole of his reign acute tension was never far below the surface; and for many his death in 1611 heralded the end of arbitrary power, and offered the opportunity to put into effect those king-yoking procedures which Erik Sparre had advocated.

Much of Sparre's programme was in fact embodied in the Charter which was imposed on Gustav Adolf in 1611.[3] But (contrary to what might have been expected) the limiting effect of the Charter turned out to be less than its tenor suggested. Thanks in no small measure to the personalities of the king and his Chancellor, Axel Oxenstierna, the reign of Gustav Adolf seemed to be a period of relative constitutional quiescence and accord. Constitutional controversies rarely obtruded themselves; the king and Council, with a few exceptions, worked together in harmony: the old problem of dualism seemed to have given place to voluntary co-operation. This better relationship provided the basis for the Form of Government of 1634.[4] The place of the crown was now taken by a regency of the five great officers of state; and it is significant of the legacy of the preceding reign that despite personal jealousies and factions within the high nobility, and though memories of Charles IX still lingered, the Council co-operated with the regents much as they had co-operated with the king in Gustav Adolf's time. But when the minority came to an end, and Christina began her personal rule, the relations of crown and Council once again grew strained, and at times stormy: her suspicion that the Council-aristocracy might be aiming at something like a Polish republic; her temporary alienation from Axel Oxenstierna, and the hostility to him of her half-brother and her uncle; and the fact that the former regents and present members of the Council were also being assailed from other quarters – all this produced, towards the end of the forties, a situation in which Christina displayed clearly absolutist tendencies, and on occasion did not hesitate to override her Council: she imposed Salvius on them against their will; she sabotaged official foreign policy at Westphalia; she forced a reluctant Council to recognise her cousin Charles, first as successor, then as hereditary prince. And in 1650 she exploited a great social and

---

[3] Printed in Emil Hildebrand, *Sveriges regeringsformer 1634–1809 samt konungaförsäkringar 1611–1800* (Stockholm 1891), pp. 195–202.

[4] *Ibid.*, pp. 1–41.

parliamentary crisis with unscrupulous skill to secure on the one hand the good-will of the Peasantry, and on the other the acceptance by the aristocracy of the fact that they could – indeed, must – for the moment look to the crown for protection against the mounting threat to their privileges. After 1651 the constellations shift a little, though Christina can still force her abdication upon her Council, though she can still declare war on Bremen without consulting them, and though she can *order* them to accept her extravagant demands for dower-lands upon her abdication.[5] In the last two years of her reign, nevertheless, she took a very active part in the Council's debates, and very rarely missed a meeting.[6]

By the time of Charles X's accession in 1654 the complexion of the central government had changed in one important respect from what it had been twenty-five years before. The Form of Government had laid it down that the Council should consist of the Regents (the High Steward, the Marshal, the Admiral, the Chancellor, and the Treasurer), together with twenty other members. It seems to have been kept to that level of twenty-five until 1643; but after Christina's accession the numbers began to rise: to twenty-nine in 1648, to thirty-three in 1649, and thenceforward dramatically: Christina called five new members to her Council in 1650, five in 1651, four in 1652, ten in 1653, and two in 1654; so that at the moment of Charles's accession the Council had no less than fifty-four members.[7] And it is at least possible that Christina's lavish additions were not merely rewards for services in the great wars, nor honours capriciously or frivolously bestowed on playboys or other unremarkable characters, but may have been intended to weaken the Council by transforming it from a serious organ of government into an honorific distinction. This, however, is to assume that its function was primarily consultative, though it is clear from the Form of Government that this was by no means the case. It was indeed expected to advise the sovereign; but it was also certainly expected to be an administration – in fact, the driving-wheel of the whole central government of the country. Each of the five *Collegia* in which the central administration was now vested was to be presided over (in theory, at all events) by one of the great officers of state; and each of them was to be assisted by other members of the Council, specifi-

---

[5] Nils Ahnlund, *Ståndsriksdagens utdaning 1592–1672* (Stockholm 1933), pp. 284–5.

[6] In 1652 the Council held thirty-two meetings, of which Christina attended twenty-four; in 1653, forty-one, and Christina attended all of them except two: figures from *Svenska Riksrådets Protokoll (RRP)*, VI (Stockholm 1923).

[7] Charles filled gaps by calling in eight new members, and added ten more on his death-bed, mostly on grounds of undoubted merit; Ulf Sjödell, 'Till frågan om Karl X Gustav och de högre ämbetena', *Karolinska Förbundets Årsbok (KFÅ)* (1971), pp. 31–3.

cally assigned to this *Collegium* or that. No less than eight were detailed to participate in the work of the Supreme Courts in Stockholm, Jönköping, Åbo, and Dorpat; three were to act as councillors to the Marshal; four to assist in the Chancery; two in the Treasury; and one was always to be Governor of Stockholm. Thus, of the twenty-five members of 1634 no less than twenty-three had important administrative functions. And this was not all. The Council might have a share in local government also, since the Form of Government laid it down that of the twenty-three provincial governors five[8] might also be members of the Council, and as long as the war should continue those whose provinces lay overseas were not to leave them. Their obligations were further increased by the establishment of new *Collegia* – College of Mines (1637), College of Commerce (1651) and the establishment of a fifth Supreme Court at Wismar (1653). Thus the expansion of the Council in Christina's time can be seen in another way also: as a necessary response to the pressure of administrative duties. Before attempting to assess Charles's view of the prerogative and his attitude towards his Council it may therefore be well first to examine the constitution and working of that body, as far as we can trace it, postponing for the moment an examination of the controversy over dualism or co-operation.

II

While there exists what appears to be a full record of the meetings of Christina's Council, minutes are lacking for the early months of the reign of her successor; and though from other sources we can see that such meetings were not infrequent, and that the king attended some – perhaps most – of them,[9] it is not until December 1654 that the series of printed minutes resumes. It is followed by another gap; and though we know of frequent meetings (sometimes in the king's presence),[10] the continuous series of printed minutes does not begin again until 9 March 1655. It is moreover unfortunately the case that publication of Council minutes at present extends no further than to December 1658, and thereafter information about such meetings is difficult to obtain. These lacunae might seem to preclude any general discussion of Charles's relations with his advisers; but it is probable

---

[8] Västergötland, Småland, Finland, Livonia, Prussia.

[9] The minutes of the Treasury record eighteen meetings between 17 June and 7 December 1654, eight of which were in the king's presence; though some of them may have been no more than consultations with individual members: *RRP* xvi. 1–2.

[10] The Treasury minutes record nine meetings with the king between 15 January and 8 March 1654; *ibid.* 37; and Bohdan Kentrschynskyj discovered another on 17 January: Bohdan Kentrschynskyj, *Karl X Gustav inför krisen i öster* (Stockholm 1956), p. 77.

that the record from 1655 to the end of 1658 may be taken as giving a fair indication of what the character of that relationship was. In the second place, the king's prolonged absences from the country, from July 1655 to March 1658, meant that his intercourse with his Council had necessarily to be conducted either by correspondence, or through emissaries from the one to the other; and it was seriously hampered by his natural preoccupation with the conduct of his campaigns. Some sort of remedy for this situation was on occasion provided by consultations with a handful of Council-members who for one reason or another were overseas, and were consequently relatively accessible; though it may be doubted whether such persons necessarily represented the views of a majority of their colleagues at home.

The thinning of the Council's effective numbers by the engage-ment of members in duties that took them away from Stockholm was in part an obvious consequence of the king's belligerent foreign policy, which committed several of them to service in the armies abroad, and involved a few in diplomatic missions. But how far that attenuation went can be clearly observed if we examine the record of attendance in the period between 4 August 1655, when the Chancel-lor, Erik Oxenstierna, made his last appearance before his departure for Prussia, and 29 March 1658, when Charles X met his first full session of the Council after his return from Denmark. During that period of two and a half years, no less than twenty-six members never attended a single ordinary meeting. Apart from soldiers such as Wrangel, Königsmarck, Douglas and Wittenberg, the Governors-General of Ingria, Livonia and Queen Christina's dower-lands in Pomerania were necessarily absent. Nine members were lords-lieutenant (*landshövdingar*), each with his own provincial responsi-bility;[11] three were diplomats[12] – or four, if we reckon Christer Bonde, who did not leave England until August 1656. The service of the law entailed the absence of some of them: Knut Posse, President of Göta Hovrätt, and bound to attend its sessions in Jönköping, had to be specially summoned when he was wanted;[13] Johan Axelsson Oxenstierna, President of the Wismar *hovrätt*, never attended at all. But even before the outbreak of war, and even on the most import-ant occasions, attendance never reached 50 per cent of the member-ship. The debate on the possibility of war either with Denmark or in

[11] Gustav Baner, E.J. Creutz, Erik von der Linde, Per Ribbing, H. Stake, Johan Ulfsparre, Göran Sparre, Johan Rosenhane, Gustaf Soop.

[12] Gustaf Larsson Sparre, C.C. von Schlippenbach, Gustav Bielke, languishing in a Moscovite prison.

[13] *RRP* XVI. 297 n.

the East attracted nineteen members on 11 December 1654, and twenty-two on 14 March.[14] Charles's proposals for a *reduktion* – a question which one would have thought was above all calculated to rally the backwoodsmen – produced a maximum of twenty-four on 6 April 1655.[15] Thereafter, when Sweden appeared to be in more or less imminent danger of attack upon her own territory, the score was no better: in November 1655 attendances ranged from fourteen to seventeen; and a similar though rather fewer number of members put in an appearance in November 1656 and February–March 1657. But on at least twenty-eight occasions the number present was six or less: on 19 November 1656 it was two.[16] In 1658 the domestic and foreign crises provoked by the second Danish war necessitated the employment of so many of them on urgent business away from Stockholm that for the fourteen meetings between 19 August and 18 December the average attendance was four.[17] In such circumstances the consultative function of the Council plainly fell into abeyance. Under the strain of war it had disintegrated, and had become transformed into a corps of *ad hoc* executive officers. It was not that the Council had proved too large: it was rather that it was proving not large enough, if this was how its members were to be employed.

Before 1658, however, this process was not carried intolerably far: in spite of hastily organised defensive measures, in spite of temporary dispersals to cajole provincial meetings or bring recalcitrant peasants to a better mind, it did, until August 1658, remain a serious consultative body; striving earnestly to carry out the king's instructions – or what it guessed them to be, if precise instructions were lacking. Who, then, really did the work of government during the period of the king's absence? Attendance, in itself, is no sure indication of a member's usefulness or importance: it might be that for some attendance was possible precisely because the state's business could be carried on (by more efficient members) without their quitting Stockholm. Nevertheless, a count of attendances, and a comparison of recorded contributions to the debate of those who did attend, does perhaps give some indication of who were at the heart of the government. It suggests that the effective conduct of affairs lay

---

[14] *RRP* XVI. 11, 65.

[15] *RRP* XVI. 131.

[16] *RRP* XVI. 688. In Gustav Adolf's absence the Council had suffered equally acutely: though his Instruction of 1630 had ordered that there were always to be at least ten in Stockholm, on 1 July 1631 there were only four – not, in Gabriel Gustafsson Oxenstierna's opinion, because their duties took the others elsewhere, but mainly because they were lazy and slack: *Axel Oxenstiernas skrifter och brevvexling, (AOSB)* II.III.232.

[17] *RRP* XVIII. 89–131.

mainly in the hands of those members whose record is listed below.[18] The dominant figure was certainly the High Steward, Per Brahe, and this not only or mainly in view of his official precedence. It seems clear that his colleagues looked to him for leadership: when he was ill, meetings were held in his room.[19] In times of crisis he took the lead in organising defence; he was personally responsible for initiating the holding of provincial meetings in 1656; he himself took charge of military operations in Västergötland; and he was prepared to risk royal displeasure in an emergency without waiting for the king's orders or approval. Long experience in various capacities equipped him to deal with all kinds of business. But equally indispensable were those who had to provide the men and resources without which the defence of the country could not be ensured, nor the king's exigences satisfied. The Treasurer, Magnus Gabriel de la Gardie, was mostly engaged in waging ineffective war in Livonia, and though he appeared in Council a score of times in 1656 he could not be said to be discharging (or to be capable of discharging) the duties of his office.[20] Those duties devolved upon two highly competent and overworked members: Herman Fleming and Gustav Bonde. But Fleming, besides being in fact in charge of the 'ordinary' finances, was also President of the College of the *reduktion*, and as such was directly responsible for contriving resources which might be diverted to current expenditure; while Bonde was a partner in the great consortium with Mårten Augustinsson Leijonsköld which was engaged in raising vast loans against the security of the Great Customs and the crown's *régale* on copper.[21] A third, closely associated with them, was Christer Bonde, who on his return from his embassy to England succeeded, on the death of Erik Oxenstierna, to his office of President of the College of Commerce; and a fourth was Herman Fleming's brother Erik, President of the College of Mines. And finally, the crucially important questions of naval equipment and deployment were dealt with, not by the somewhat ineffective Admiral, Gabriel Bengtsson Oxenstierna (until Karl Gustav Wrangel

[18] The record for attendances easily went to Seved Bååt (299), followed by the financial expert Gustav Bonde (213). Then a group with around 180 attendances: Thure Sparre, Erik and Johan Gyllenstierna, Arvid Forbus; then Schering Rosenhane (153); Per Brahe, who though twice disabled by illness, appeared on 169 occasions and led the discussion on every one of them; and the two economic experts Erik and Herman Fleming (142 and 131, respectively).

[19] *RRP* xvi. 259–74, 481–8, 410–55.

[20] Christina had arbitrarily dismissed him from the office of Treasurer in December 1653, and Fleming took his place as President of the Treasury College. Charles reinstated de la Gardie in 1655, but Fleming continued to do the work.

[21] For the organisation of extraordinary war-finance see Hans Landberg, 'Krig på kredit', in *Carl X Gustaf inför polska kriget. (Carl X Gustaf-studier, 4,* ed. Arne Stade) (1969) and

succeeded to that position in 1657), but by an experienced naval officer, the indefatigable Claes Bielkenstierna.

It fell to these dozen members, then, with support as it might happen from less regular attenders, to carry out the king's orders, ensure that the domestic situation gave him no unnecessary cause for anxiety, and apply such remedial measures as the case might seem to admit of. They had no easy time of it. A disastrous fall of rock at Falun dealt Swedish copper-production a blow from which it never wholly recovered.[22] Twice they were driven from the capital by outbreaks of plague. The crisis of 1650 was too fresh in their memory for them ever to be unmindful of the possibility of its recurrence. They were troubled, as Axel Oxenstierna in his day had been troubled, by the influx into Stockholm of hordes of beggars.[23] Though Charles had forbidden them to exercise the revisionary jurisdiction which inhered in the king's prerogative, he had also ordered them to clear off the heavy arrears of cases which had piled up in Christina's time,[24] and the task proved no light one: they were forced to spend more time than they could afford in settling the quarrels of a litigious landowning aristocracy. This presented special difficulties, for the amount of legal expertise available to them was small: on 7 June 1656 the court had to be afforced by four members of the *reduktion* College, two assessors from *Svea hovrätt*, and five Chancery councillors. Once, and once only, they ventured to ask the king to excuse them from acting 'since they are too few'.[25] The instructions with which they were provided, though they were sufficiently explicit on what the Council might *not* do, could not in the nature of the case cover all the problems that might unexpectedly arise. From time to time they would send off a budget of questions to the king – much as the Council had done to Oxenstierna between 1632 and 1636 – and if they were lucky they might receive answers which were still relevant at the time of their arrival: Charles, though no mean letter-writer, could not emulate Oxenstierna's full, precise, and (on the whole) prompt replies. The king on his side was not sparing of enquiries, demanding a full report of their doings, and supplementing it by private information: of this the Council was not

idem, 'Kungamaktens emancipation. Statsreglering och militärorganisation under Karl X Gustav och Karl XI' *Scandia* (1969).

[22] *RRP* XVI. 251–2, 254 ff., 262, 267 ff., 269, 281–2 etc.

[23] *RRP* XVI. 256. cf. Oxenstierna's complaint (3 November 1651) 'begging has now so much got the upper hand that a little boy will soon have nothing to do but beg – as though it were a trade': *Svenka ridderskaps och adels riksdagsprotokoll (SRARP)* IV₂. 559; and cf. Herman Fleming's remarks on the same topic: *ibid.* 561.

[24] Stellan Dahlgren, 'Charles X and the Constitution', in *Sweden's Age of Greatness, 1632–1718*, ed. M. Roberts (1973), p. 198; *RRP* XVI. 349.

[25] *RRP* XVI. 474; XVIII. 99.

ignorant, and it did not make their task the easier.[26] Some of the questions that he sent to them were difficult enough to answer; others were virtually impossible.[27] On occasion he did ask them questions to which they might feel themselves reasonably competent to reply: for instance, as to whether he should offer, as the price of an English alliance, trade concessions in the Baltic, or the pawning of Bremen in return for a subsidy.[28] But as a rule they tended to give him the answers which they imagined he desired; and on occasion they could endorse 'with applause' quite preposterous proposals.[29] Only once during the period of Charles's absence did they risk a *decision* involving foreign policy, and that was when they failed to promulgate the king's stringent Ordinance on Religion, on the ground that it would have impeded Christer Bonde's negotiations for an English alliance, since it was directed against Calvinists.[30] But on receiving Charles's emphatic order to do as they were told, they promulgated it without further ado.[31]

The Council was hamstrung in two respects: one general, one particular. In general, they usually did not venture to take any important action without the king's permission; and, in particular, they were expressly debarred from meddling (as a body) in the business of the *Collegia* – which meant, above all, in the affairs of the Treasury and the *reduktion*. The great loan-operations were wholly outside their province; and 'ordinary' finance was the affair of Herman Fleming, in charge of the Treasury. The operations of the *reduktion* were his sole responsibility also, though the question of how far he might on his own authority extend it, and on what terms the 'quarter-part rent' was to be managed, was never resolved very clearly; for Charles, however much he relied on Fleming, was never prepared to let the general control slip out of his own hands.[32] The result of this situation was that the Council might take measures, or order them as might seem most expedient; but they must rely on the Treasury to find the necessary money for them. Sometimes – indeed, frequently – this simply could not be done. Wages were being drastically cut at

---

[26] Dahlgren, 'Charles X and the Constitution', p. 197.

[27] E.g. his letter of 31 January 1656, informing them that he had a choice of alliances between France, England and Transylvania (a highly dubious statement) and asking them which to choose. They replied that 'since they have no information as to H.M. intentions' they contented themselves with listing Sweden's enemies, in order of priority; and not surprisingly got it wrong.

[28] *RRP* XVII. 278; XVIII. 24–5, 39.

[29] *RRP* XVIII. 57, 67; below pp. 92, 140.

[30] *RRP* XVI. 278 (22 September 1655).

[31] *RRP* XVI. 456 (1 May 1656).

[32] Stellan Dahlgren, *Karl X Gustav och reduktionen* (Uppsala 1964), pp. 131–5, 140, 169–72, 333–4.

all levels, and often not paid at all; and the Council had repeatedly to come cap in hand to Fleming for assistance. Could he not contrive to squeeze a modest sum from somewhere for an urgent need? Might they, or might they not, anticipate next year's revenue? In October 1656 they did secure Fleming's approval for it, mainly so that they could repair the fleet and pay the crews; but he soon thought better of it: revenues, by the king's instructions, were tied to the special uses for which he had designed them. The king's recruiting-agents committed excesses which the Council could not control, and discontent at this state of affairs took the ominous turn of complaints that 'in the king's absence there was no one to give them justice'.[33] They felt themselves in acute difficulties also on the question of whether to send help to Riga, then besieged by the Russians, and apparently in imminent danger of falling.[34] They had had no reply from Germany as to who was to be considered in command of the defences of Finland, now obviously threatened with a Muscovite invasion: was it Gustav Edvartsson Horn or Gustav Leijonhufvud? Or was it perhaps Magnus Gabriel de la Gardie?[35] Per Brahe lamented that they could do nothing to avert the loss of Narva, having no instructions about it.[36] At a moment when the Swedish blockade of Danzig had provided one of the main reasons for Dutch intervention in the Baltic the Council had to ask the king what the state of affairs was in regard to the levying of toll there, since 'they really do not know what has happened there in the preceding year'.[37] No information about Danzig; no information about Finland; Riga apparently in extremities, and a royal order that no troops were to be sent there from Sweden![38] Per Brahe, contending that *facies rerum* had altered in the meanwhile, was characteristically in favour of taking some action.[39] But if anything were to be done, where were the resources to come from that should pay for it? Dared they pawn crown lands? Fleming told them No: not without the king's orders.[40] It was not until 25 September 1656 that they received the news that Charles was intending to send help to Riga from Poland, and that he had ordered ten ships to be despatched to the town's assistance.[41] In the event, Riga was saved not by his action or theirs, but by the sorties of the

[33] *RRP* xvi. 298.
[34] *RRP* xvi. 628–9.
[35] *RRP* xvi. 436.
[36] *RRP* xvi. 469.
[37] *RRP* xvi. 571.
[38] *RRP* xvi. 534, 628.
[39] *RRP* xvi. 630
[40] *RRP* xvi. 633.
[41] *RRP* xvi. 636, 638, 642.

defenders, and the epidemics and shortages that decimated the enormous Russian forces that were besieging it. But though this anxiety might be relieved, the problem of the fleet remained; and throughout the whole period up to the conclusion of the treaty of Elbing they struggled to solve it: mutiny of shipwrights; crews unpaid; workmen on the fortifications at Vaxholm (designed to bar any Dutch attack on Stockholm) forced to work barefoot since there was no money to provide them with shoes;[42] doubts whether even if the fleet could be got ready for sea they could risk sending it out, or whether (as Charles seemed to think) a fleet in being was not after all better than a fleet at the bottom.[43] Not until the arrival of Charles's letter of 19–20 June 1657 was the Council's anxiety relieved by an order to the Admiralty that it might take 'the most available means' (whatever those might be supposed to be) to equip the fleet for action.[44]

In the summer of 1656 the threat from the Dutch and the Danes, the imperative need to take measures for self-defence, and the deplorable state of the finances, moved the Council under Per Brahe's leadership to a step whose boldness reflected their desperation. They offered Charles unsolicited advice. They were careful to call it a *consilium*, and to disclaim any notion of its being a 'Resolution' (*rådslag*); but even so it was a *consilium non rogatum*, and thus of dubious constitutional propriety.[45] Of this they were very conscious. But with a courage born of despair they put their programme into effect before any answer reached them. The calculated risk came off: Charles's approval, though it came too late, justified their action. This was hardly surprising; for the essence of their *consilium* was a plan to raise more men, and the money to pay for them. This they proposed to do by summoning – not a *riksdag*, which Charles would never have tolerated in his absence,[46] any more than Gustav Adolf would have done – but a number of provincial meetings, who might, perhaps, be more susceptible to persuasions than would be the case with a general meeting of the Estates,[47]

When the war began, Swedish finances were in the last year of a

---

[42] *RRP* xvi. 411, 593.

[43] *RRP* xvii. 148 (6 June 1657).

[44] *RRP* xvii. 210.

[45] *RRP* xvi. 360, 440. It was not until 1680 that *consilium non rogatum* was definitely declared to be unconstitutional.

[46] E.g. his letter of 12 February 1657: *RRP* xvii. 19.

[47] The list of signatories gives some idea of those whose advice might be expected to carry weight; it ran: Per Brahe, Gustav Horn (Marshal), Gabriel Gabrielsson Oxenstierna (a member of the Council since 1643), Erik Gyllenstierna, Seved Bååt (whose membership also dated from 1643), Herman Fleming, Gustav Bonde, Arvid Forbus and Johan Paijkull (reputable generals), Claes Bielkenstierna, and Erik Fleming: *RRP* xvi. 725–9.

triennial arrangement which had been determined on by the *riksdag* of 1652.[48] In that year the Estates had agreed to a militia-levy for the years 1653, 1654, and 1655 at the very heavy rate of every eighth man on the lists of those eligible for service (in the case of crown-peasants and tax-peasants) and every sixteenth man (in the case of peasants of the Nobility, with no exceptions save for the noble's personal servants and the cottars who did day-work on his manor); though for 1655 they were to be lightened to every tenth man, or every twentieth, and exemption was to be granted to peasants of the Nobility living in the immediate environment of their manors. In similar fashion, taxation was fixed in 1652, on a quite heavy basis, for 1653, with only limited exemption for peasants of the Nobility, and with the provision that for 1653 and 1654 the Nobility should pay four silver *daler* for every peasant homestead on their estates, manors only excepted. It is astonishing that at a moment when Sweden was really in no danger of attack, and only two years after the alarming social crisis of 1650, the *riksdag* should have been induced to commit itself for three years to grants on a scale appropriate only to time of war; and almost more so that the Nobility should have acquiesced in the serious erosion of their privileges for the first two of them. However that may be, the precedent proved useful when the Diet met again in 1655. Once again a triennial arrangement was agreed upon:[49] for 1656 militia-levies at the rate of one in ten for crown- and tax-peasants, and one in twenty for peasants of the Nobility, with noble exemptions straitly limited, as before; taxation substantially unaltered at its previous level.[50] But by the summer of 1656 Per Brahe and his colleagues could no longer feel that these were sacrifices adequate to the emergency. Hence their *consilium* proposed that meetings be held in the provinces, each under the chairmanship of its *landshövding*, with additional supervision from Stockholm to give support to the efforts of the local authorities.[51] Such support might well be needed; for what was asked of these assemblies was the advancing to 1656 of the militia-levy granted for 1657, at a flat rate of one in ten, nobles as well as others; the doubling of the Nobility's knight-service and of the contribution in grain granted by the Clergy for 1657, every parson moreover being to furnish one cavalryman,

---

[48] A.A. von Stiernman, *Alla riksdagars och mötens besluth* (Stockholm 1729), II. 1186–92.

[49] This really foreshadows the decision of 1660 that meetings of the *riksdag* henceforward should be at least triennial.

[50] Stiernman, *Alla riksdagars och mötens besluth,* II. 1,253–8.

[51] Gustav Horn took on four provinces, Per Brahe two, the College of War three, the Admiralty one. There had been a clear anticipation of this procedure in 1639: C.T. Odhner, *Sveriges inre historia under Drottning Christinas förmyndare* (Stockholm 1865), p. 90.

every canon one foot-soldier; and the Burghers to advance the contribution which they would have been due to pay next year.[52]

These were drastic measures, and the Council's representatives had enough to do to secure their acceptance. In Kronoborg *län* the demand for the extra levy was met with 'riot and tumult'; in Värmland the *landshövding* recommended that no levy be attempted, since only one man had a musket, and the yield of levy would be insignificant. The local authorities in Österbotten considered it unwise to put arms into the hands of the peasantry, since they might use them against their masters. There were vexatious delays because most of the Nobility were said to be abroad, and their bailiffs or stewards did not venture to agree to anything without obtaining their consent. But the most determined resistance came in Östergötland, where the clergy, led by Bishop Enander of Linköping, contended that the Council had no right to call such meetings in the king's absence, and buttressed their arguments by ominous (if inaccurately dated) precedents from the revolutionary years of the 1590s.[53]

Nevertheless, the Council on the whole carried its point. The *landshövdingar* mostly co-operated well; the stubbornness of the Östergötland clergy was conveniently blamed on the mismanagement of Johan Rosenhane;[54] and in due course a letter from the king gave *ex post facto* approval to Per Brahe's initiative. Not only that; for it evidently occurred to Charles that what the Council had contrived to do in 1656 might well be possible – and would certainly be necessary – in 1657. On 30 January 1657, therefore, he sent an order authorising 'the leading members' of the Council to negotiate with the Peasantry on a provincial basis, and promised to send them written full-powers to do so: the ground was to be cut from under Enander's feet this time.[55] The meetings of 1656 had been an improvisation; those of 1657 were carefully planned in detail by Charles himself. He sent home a lengthy Proposition, of the type normally laid before a full *riksdag*, in which the international situation as he saw it – or at least, as he wished them to see it – was elaborately displayed, with a wealth of propaganda to exemplify it.[56] Each of these meetings was in fact treated as a miniature *riksdag*, all four Estates being present, and each being provided with a Speaker. Procedural arrangements were carefully laid down; and each was even to have something corresponding to a Secret Committee. The Council was

[52] *RRP* XVI. 505–30.
[53] *RRP* XVI. 548, 584, 599, 601, 604.
[54] *RRP* XVI. 603.
[55] *RRP* XVII. 31, 34.
[56] *SRARP* VI. 132–54.

given firm guide-lines for action. There were to be six provincial meetings for Sweden, three for Finland, and they were to take place at the end of April. What was to be demanded of them bore a dire resemblance to what had been asked of the meetings of 1656: the levying of militia already granted for 1658 was to be brought forward to 1657; the number of recruits for the navy was to be doubled; taxation was to be still heavier, particularly for the Nobility and the Clergy.

This time the Council had a much tougher job than on the previous occasion. In the first place, the fact that there were to be nine meetings meant that it was difficult to reach agreement between them on the replies to the demands upon them: lengthy correspondence took place between one meeting and another. Secondly, the Council was uneasily conscious that what they were asking violated promises they had given in 1656. At the meetings in that year the Peasantry had been assured that there would be no militia-levy in 1657; and the Nobility had likewise been promised that the flat rate for all Estates, to which they had then reluctantly agreed, should be for one year only.[57] Thirdly, and much the most important, Nobility and Peasantry alike were outraged by the demand that this time the levy was to be on a *per capita* basis (*på mantal*). But since 1643 it had always been based on the number of homesteads (*på gårdatal*). And though, as Charles rightly explained, the change represented no more than a return to the practice in Gustav Adolf's time, he was conscious that it might provoke resistance, and was prepared with alternatives.[58] In almost all the meetings the Peasants offered obstinate opposition to *mantal*: Knut Posse lamented that he had been dealing with them for years, but had 'never found them as bad as now'.[59] Christer Bonde drew up a memorandum for his colleagues on the Council, suggesting that the demand be abandoned in return for other concessions.[60] After much persuasion the Council's representatives succeeded in inducing the meetings to swallow this bitter pill, but only when the Stockholm meeting, where resistance was strongest, learnt that their colleagues at Jönköping (under the firm supervision of Per Brahe and Seved Bååt) had yielded on this point.[61] Just how bitter the pill was appeared from Gustav Bonde's calculation that its acceptance would mean that at a stroke the king tripled his manpower-income.[62] In the end the Council could come

[57] *SRARP* VI. 199–202.
[58] *SRARP* VI. 200.
[59] *SRARP* VI. 90.
[60] *SRARP* VI. 165–6.
[61] *SRARP* VI. 168.
[62] *SRARP* VI. 75; cf. *RRP* XVII. 80, 96, 112.

home with a general agreement: for the three years 1657, 1659, and 1660, there was to be a levy at a flat rate of one in ten *på mantal*, though for the Nobility only of one in twenty for the years 1659 and 1660. But the Nobility were further constrained to accept a new levy of 100 *rdr.* for every horse due from them in knight-service (not excepting widows and orphans), and other extraordinary burdens also. The Burghers agreed to a doubled levy for the navy and a doubling of the excise for 1657–60. The once-recalcitrant clergy of Östergötland were lucky to escape with a contribution of eight *tunnor* of grain for every sixty-four homesteads; their brethren of Västergötland (more exposed to the danger of Danish invasion) with a promise of one artillery-horse per parish.[63]

In return for these far-reaching concessions the Council gave an undertaking that there should be no militia-levy in 1658; but having taken the initiative once without incurring royal displeasure, they were tempted to repeat the performance. Between December 1657 and February 1658 they twice considered breaking their promise, and were dissuaded only by Gustav Bonde and by Herman Fleming, who made the cogent point that if they raised more troops there was no means of feeding them.[64] And they pleaded (in vain) with Dalarna to agree to a special levy, despite the fact that by a compact dating from Gustav Adolf's time the Dalesmen were specifically exempt in return for providing a fixed contingent always to be kept up to strength (which, given the heavy mortality in Poland, was sacrifice enough).[65] Nevertheless, when Charles came home at last in 1658 Per Brahe and his colleagues were entitled to feel that they had deserved well of their sovereign.

A main reason for their success in 1657 lay in the fact that the number, and the wide dispersal, of the provincial meetings of that year made it very difficult to organize any common front in opposition to the government's proposals: a calculation which doubtless lay behind Charles's refusal to allow any full meeting of the *riksdag* in his absence. But even after he returned, ennimbused in the glory of his triumph over Denmark, he took good care to summon to Göteborg a meeting which was far from being a full *riksdag*. The Resolution of that meeting was signed by forty-seven members of the Nobility (including members of the Council), twenty of the Clergy, and eight

---

[63] Stiernman, *Alla riksdagars och mötens besluth*, II. 1282, 1285.

[64] *RRP* XVII. 300; XVIII. 7.

[65] This arrangement, known as *ständigt knektehåll*, had been violated already in 1630: *RRP* II. 79. It applied in some other provinces also, notably Jämtland and Västerbotten: Birger Steckzén, *Krigskollegii historia I 1630–1697* (Stockholm 1930), p. 215. Charles XI was greatly to extend it.

of the Burghers:[66] in reality, it was much the same as a meeting of the Secret Committee. This type of meeting had been not uncommon in Gustav Adolf's time, and had come to be termed a 'Committee-riksdag'. Not until the last month of Charles's life, in January 1660, was there a full riksdag once again – after an interval of four and a half years. Does the gap imply a growing disposition to rule without a parliament? If so, are we to see Charles's reign as some sort of constitutional watershed? Are his policies and tactics a foreshadowing of the absolutism which was to be established by his son after 1680? And, supposing that were true, what light would it shed upon his relations with his Council?

III

It is only comparatively recently that the relations of Charles and his Council have become a matter of debate among Swedish historians. The general assumption was that in this matter, as in so much else, Charles shaped his actions in accordance with what had been the practice under Gustav Adolf. For Emil Hildebrand, for instance, the position of the Council under Christina and Charles X could be dismissed in a single brief paragraph: in his view there was apparently nothing of significance to record; sovereign and Council worked together as they had done in Gustav Adolf's time.[67] So too Nils Ahnlund, who, observing that 'it was generally noted' that Charles endeavoured to imitate his great predecessor, specifically cited the continuing co-operation between king and Council as an example of this.[68] A.B. Carlsson, though he considered that it was no part of Charles's purpose to collect a standing Council round him, saw this only as another example of his wish to rule as Gustav Adolf had ruled.[69] And Sven Ingemar Olofsson wrote that on Charles's accession the Council 'once again took its constitutional place by his side'.[70]

The first challenge to this long-held assumption came with the publication of an article by Stellan Dahlgren in 1960.[71] That article suggested that the Accession Charter to which the king subscribed in 1654 was less stringently binding than had been the case with the similar Charters given by Christina and Gustav Adolf; that it

[66] SRARP VI. 350–2.
[67] Emil Hildebrand, Den svenska statsförfattningens historiska utveckling (Stockholm 1896), p. 271.
[68] Ahnlund, Ståndsriksdagens utdaning pp. 291–3.
[69] A.B. Carlsson, Den svenska centralförvaltningen 1592–1809 (Stockholm 1913), pp. 56–7.
[70] Sven Ingemar Olofsson, Carl X Gustaf. Hertigen-Tronföljaren (Stockholm 1961), p. 8.
[71] Stellan Dahlgren, 'Kansler och kungamakt vid tronskiftet 1654', Scandia (1960).

deliberately left the king with freer hands, under the specious argument that any further guarantees against his abuse of power were adequately provided for by the Coronation Oath; and finally that this modification of the arrangements was the work of Axel Oxenstierna, who hoped (vainly, as it turned out) to obtain in return a new Chancery Ordinance, which would in effect have made him sole *ephor* – and probably hoped too that it might deter the king from prosecuting that *reduktion* which could already be perceived to be imminent. Four years later there followed Dahlgren's great dissertation on Charles X and the *reduktion*,[72] which for the first time sifted that complex matter to the bottom, and in the course of doing so shed a great deal of light on Charles's constitutional attitudes. And in 1973 he summed up his views in an article conveniently available in English.[73] He contended that Charles at the time of his accession deliberately attempted to lay a basis for an extension of the prerogative, and in particular that the constitutional instruments which were then agreed upon enabled him to pursue a foreign policy unrestrained by any checks either from *riksdag* or Council. In pursuing it, he resorted to 'mobilisation-measures which strained the constitutional framework almost to breaking-point'.[74] The *reduktion* was not only a measure designed to provide a sound financial basis for governments in peacetime no less than in wartime, as distinct from the expedients to which he had recourse in order to carry on a belligerent foreign policy; it was also designed to have the consequence of undermining parliamentary control of taxation by obviating the need to come to the *riksdag* for grants of taxes, new or old. And the position of the *riksdag* was further eroded by the holding of provincial meetings, and by the long hiatus between one *riksdag* and the next. The king's resort to small meetings of members of the Council who happened to be abroad, and his use, even after his return home, of 'secret' meetings with a mere handful of members, constituted an attack upon the special status and authority of the Council:[75] an attack which was not less real by reason of his especial care to treat Council members with consideration (as compared with the rest of the community) in the matter of payment of their salaries, and by his comparatively gentle handling of them in regard to the *reduktion*.

In 1965, however, five years after Dahlgren's *Scandia* article, and one year after the appearance of his dissertation, there came a chal-

---

[72] Dahlgren, *Karl X Gustav och reduktionen*.
[73] Dahlgren, 'Charles X and the Constitution'.
[74] *Ibid.*, p. 189.
[75] *Ibid.*, pp. 190–1.

lenge to some of his conclusions in an article by Ulf Sjödell on the problem of ' "dualism" or co-operation as a theme in Swedish constitutional history'.[76] Sjödell considered that from the time of Fryxell and Geijer onwards the prevailing trend had been to see that history in dualistic terms: either as a struggle between king and aristocracy; or as a conflict between 'static' and 'dynamic' views of the constitution;[77] or – with the late middle ages in mind – as a question of *regimen politicum* or *regimen regale*. Dahlgren, he thought, was not really a dualist, and Oxenstierna's manoeuvres in 1654, however inspired by personal considerations, made it clear that he believed that it was possible, and perhaps necessary, to come to terms with the prerogative – an attitude which had, indeed, already been apparent during the regency for Christina.[78] Sjödell's own views were developed in his dissertation,[79] in which he examined the relations between crown and aristocracy, mainly under Charles XI, but also under Charles X. In Charles X's time the situation was not to be seen in dualistic terms: king and Council were two centres of power which kept each other in balance; and the Council played a mediating role between king and *riksdag*;[80] though in the king's absence it necessarily became more active. Throughout the whole period 1600–60 no attempt was made to define the relationship between them, and there was no real conflict:[81] Ahnlund was therefore correct in seeing Charles's reign as a continuation of the accord which had existed under Gustav Adolf. There is nothing to suggest that Charles at the time of his death was contemplating the introduction of an absolutism.[82] And he sums up: 'Characteristic for all of them [Gustav Adolf, Christina, Charles X] is a personal stamp on government, and the fact that they do not deal with it [the Council] unfairly at the expense of other institutions; that they are willing to hear the Council's views before deciding important questions, especially of foreign policy; and that the chance of Council member's attaining an influential

[76] Ulf Sjödell, 'Kungamakt och aristokrati i svensk 1900-tals debatt', *Historisk tidskrift* (1965).

[77] This distinction originates with Erland Hjärne, in his study *Från Vasatiden till Frihetstiden* (Uppsala 1929), who used it to distinguish between political systems which emphasize rights, and those which emphasize duties.

[78] Sjödell, 'Kungamakt och aristokrati', p. 57; Nils Runeby, *Monarchia mixta. Makfördelningsdebatt i Sverige under den tidigare stormaktstiden* (Uppsala 1962), p. 251.

[79] Ulf Sjödell, *Kungamakt och högaristokrati. En studie i Sveriges inre historia under Karl XI* (Lund 1966).

[80] Which hardly squares with his dictum that 'the Council, as an independently operating, distinct factor in the life of the state . . . has never existed in modern times under a king of full age': Sjödell, 'Kungamakt och aristokrati', p. 320.

[81] Sjödell, *Kungamakt och högaristokrati*, p. 22.

[82] *Ibid.*, p. 18.

position depends not on constitutional claims or mere membership, but on ability.'

Two further contributions to the debate came from Hans Landberg and Göran Rystad. Landberg was concerned mainly with the devices by which Charles financed his campaigns; but his examination of these problems led him to conclusions about the constitutional situation. Unlike Sjödell, he saw a latent if not quite explicit conflict between the crown and the Council; and he summarised the outcome of that conflict in the title of one of his articles, which ran: 'The Emancipation of the Monarchy. Budgeting and military organisation in the reigns of Charles X and Charles XI'.[83] He agreed with Dahlgren in thinking that Charles's financial measures 'seriously disturbed the financial and constitutional balance in the operations of the state';[84] but he differed from him in his interpretation of the obligations laid upon the king by the Charter of 1654: to him it seemed that that document, even when linked to the Coronation Oath, did not relieve Charles from the obligation to obtain the assent of Council and *riksdag* to a war of aggression. What happened in December 1654 was that the Council felt that the extent of Charles's recruitment of mercenaries, and the heavy financial burdens which it implied, left them with no real option but to agree that there was nothing for it but to employ the regiments that had been recruited; but as to where to use them, against what enemy, and when – all these things were explicitly left to the king's discretion, though subject to the consent of the *riksdag*. And when the *riksdag* met, the argument of financial necessity which the Council had found irresistible proved irresistible to the *riksdag* also, however reluctantly they might come to that conclusion.[85]

Göran Rystad was concerned to identify the location of power within the state; and in his view the decisive criterion was the power of appointment to offices. As he put it in his most recent article on this theme: 'The gatekeeper who controls the entrance to offices and positions within the administration, he is in charge. Find him – or them – and you will be able to determine the distribution of power in the country at any given time'; for in seventeenth-century Sweden 'the bureaucracy is the key element'.[86] The programme of the high

[83] Hans Landberg, 'Kungamaktens emancipation' and cf. his two contributions to the collective volume *Carl X Gustaf-studier*, 4 (1969): 'Krig på kredit. Svensk rustningsfinansiering våren 1655', and 'Statsfinans och kungamakt. Karl X Gustav inför polska kriget'.

[84] Hans Landberg, 'Statsfinans och kungamakt', pp. 151–2.

[85] Hans Landberg, 'Decemberrådslagen 1654. Karl X Gustav, rådet och rustningsfrågan', *KFÅ* (1968), pp. 57, 59, 65.

[86] Göran Rystad, 'The King, the Nobility and the Growth of Bureaucracy in 17th Century Sweden', in *Europe and Scandinavia. Aspects of the Process of Integration in the 17th Century*, ed.

aristocracy in the 1590s, as set out in Erik Sparre's *Postulata nobilium*, had demanded that all appointments be made 'with the Council's counsel'; but though Gustav Adolf's Charter of 1611 did indeed secure to the nobility a monopoly of major offices, it had stopped short of insisting on the Council's counsel. Thereafter, this item in Erik Sparre's programme became increasingly unrealisable, with the establishment in Gustav Adolf's time of a regular civil service, and with the growing jealousy with which much of the lesser nobility viewed the pretensions of the great Council families. By the time of Charles X it had ceased to be practical politics; and 'In matters of appointment Charles X felt himself to be under no obligation to seek the advice of his Council.' The keeper of the gate was now the king, and the Council had no say in the matter.[87] Thus Rystad, like Dahlgren, and to a limited extent like Hans Landberg, saw the reign of Charles X as a period, not of collaboration as in Gustav Adolf's time, but as one in which the crown established an ascendancy over its potential rival.

IV

The accession of Charles X was followed by – and in one case entailed – formal constitutional changes. The first of these consisted in his refusal (as Christina had also refused) to confirm the Form of Government of 1634. This, as Axel Oxenstierna himself observed,[88] was no more than logical, for much of that document applied only to the circumstances of a royal minority; and one point in it, in particular, must have been unacceptable to Charles. That was the provision for a regency whenever the sovereign should be a minor, or incapacitated, or *absent*; and there is good reason to suppose that at the moment of his accession the possibility of his being absent on campaign must have been in his (and perhaps in Oxenstierna's) mind. At all events, the Form of Government was tacitly ignored, despite the feeling that it in some sort constituted a fundamental law. That feeling would emerge strongly in 1660, once Charles was dead.

More immediately controversial was the replacement of Gustav

Göran Rystad (Lund 1983), pp. 65, 70. For a fuller treatment of this theme by the same author, see 'Med råds råde eller efter konungens godtycke? Makten över ämbetstillsättningarna som politisk stridsfråga under 1600-talet', *Scandia* (1963).

[87] This involved, of course, the right *not* to appoint; and Charles exercised this right to refrain from appointing a successor as Chancellor, on Erik Oxenstierna's death in 1656, or a successor as Marshal, on Gustav Horn's death in 1657: on the possible constitutional significance of this, see Runeby, *Monarchia mixta*, pp. 446 ff. Ulf Sjödell considered that Runeby made too much of this.

[88] Runeby, *Monarchia mixta*, p. 454.

Adolf's Charter of 1611 (which the Estates in 1654 had wished to retain) by the Charter of 1654. The Charter of 1611 had limited the prerogative in three essential points:[89] it had bound the king:

(i) not to make war, peace, truce or alliance without the knowledge and consent of the Council and Estates;

(ii) not to change the law without the consent of the Council and the lower Estates (*meniga ständerna* – as against Duke Johan and the Queen Mother) and

(iii) not to impose aids, tolls, or other imposts, nor militia-levies, without the Council's knowledge and the consent of 'those concerned'.

Charles's Charter of 1654[90] had significantly different wording. He promised:

(a) to maintain all men in their lawfully-acquired (*välfångna*) rights, privileges, and property;

(b) to safeguard the peace of the country 'to the best of our ability', so that 'no war is begun or undertaken' (clause 6); and

(c) [in the same clause] that 'if anything is necessary to be altered for the welfare, *safety*, advancement and requirements of the country, all such things' be done with the Council's counsel and the knowledge and consent of the Estates.

It was Dahlgren who first raised the question as to whether (b) and (c) were intended to be separate provisions: whether 'all such things' referred to both, or only to (c), and whether the final provision in (c) for assent by Council and Estates could properly be interpreted to apply also to (b). Dahlgren thought it could not; and Sjödell agreed with him,[91] seeing in (c) the hand of Oxenstierna erecting a barrier against a *reduktion* by mere prerogative (though he apparently did not consider whether 'lawfully acquired', in (a), did not in fact restrict the limits of the guarantee). The barrier was however reinforced by the terms of Charles's Coronation Oath; for that oath conformed to the wording of Gustav Adolf's Coronation Oath of 1617, which (in its second version) had pledged the king to maintain *all* noble privileges, and not (as he had originally intended) all *ancient* privileges.[92] The subsequent course of events showed both kings diminishing those privileges almost to vanishing-point; but in both cases they did so 'with the consent of those concerned' – i.e. the Estate of Nobility.

---

[89] Hildebrand, *Sveriges regeringsformer . . . samt konungaförsäkringar*, pp. 195–202.

[90] *Ibid.*, pp. 206–13.

[91] Dahlgren, 'Kansler och kungamakt', p. 137; Sjödell, *Kungamakt och högaristokrati*, p. 46.

[92] Dahlgren, 'Kansler och kungamakt', p. 129 n. 90 and *Karl X Gustav och reduktionen* p. 9.

Moreover, some doubt about the constitutional position arose from the wording of the mediaeval Land Law (*c.* 1350), which was still considered to be a fundamental law; for that law bound the king not to 'diminish the realm' by alienating the lands of the crown, and authorised him if necessary to retake them 'by force'.[93] It is possible that this was intended to apply only to alienations to foreign powers; but it is clear from the terms of Gustav Vasa's Testament (which also enjoyed great constitutional authority in the seventeenth century) that *he* considered it to apply also to alienations to Swedish subjects – in his case, to the duchies conferred upon his sons.[94] And in 1650 the Estate of Burghers (and Archbishop Lenaeus) insisted that a *reduktion* was conformable to the Land Law and to Gustav Vasa's Testament.[95]

The change of wording, as between 1611 and 1654, may indeed have been motivated by Axel Oxenstierna's hope of a tacit bargain which would strengthen the position of the Chancery and the authority of the Chancellor; and it is true that he caused a draft Chancery Ordinance to be prepared which would have had that consequence. But it is reasonable to suppose that he was anxious to protect himself and his office against, for example, the jealousy of the Treasury, and against the habit of conducting the Chancery's relations with the crown through minor officials and secretaries, of which he had had embittering experience in Christina's reign.[96] Dahlgren's suggestion that Oxenstierna, by omitting any explicit mention of the *riksdag*, deliberately framed the Charter of 1654 to open the way to provincial meetings in place of the *riksdag* seems mere conjecture: he had indeed resorted to this device (as Gustav Adolf had done before him) for a short time after his return from Germany in 1636; but from 1638 onwards he seems to have regarded full meetings of the Estates as a safer, and therefore preferable, means of proceeding. And as Dahlgren himself pointed out, in 1654 he indicated that the tax-granting machinery prescribed by the Land Law 'was now operated by the *riksdag*'; and he informed Whitelocke that the *riksdag* was the normal channel for such business.[97]

The question with which we are concerned, however, is not what Oxenstierna intended, but how king and Council perceived and followed the arrangements of 1654. In regard to foreign policy the

[93] *Utdrag ur Magnus Erikssons Landslag*, ed. Emil Olsson (Lund 1927), clause 5.

[94] Roberts, *The Early Vasas*, pp. 194–5.

[95] Birger Lövgren, *Ståndstridens uppkomst. Elt bidrag till Sveriges inre historia under Drottning Kristina*. (Uppsala 1915), p. 108.

[96] Nils Forssell, *Kansliet från Gustav II Adolf till år 1660. Kungl. Maj:ts kanslis historia* (Uppsala 1935), I. 51, 55–7, 69; Runeby, *Monarchia mixta*, p. 435.

[97] Dahlgren, 'Kansler och kungamakt', p. 131; Bulstrode Whitelocke, *A Journal of the Swedish Embassy in the years 1653 and 1654*, ed. Charles Morton (1885), II. 280–1.

Charter of 1654 was notably less restrictive than that of 1611. Gustav Adolf had been debarred from making truce, peace, or alliance without the knowledge and consent of Council and Estates: no such limitation was imposed on Charles X. This is no great matter for surprise, since Gustav Adolf had for the most part ignored this obligation: the Peace of Stolbova, the truce of Altmark, the Pomeranian and Hessian treaties, and the treaty of Bärwalde were made without seeking the advice of his Council or the consent of the *riksdag*. When Charles X made his treaties with Brandenburg or the Dutch, or concluded the peace of Roskilde, he was under no obligation to consult anybody. The situations were analogous: wartime, and a king abroad; and Axel Oxenstierna was of all men best qualified to realise from experience what the common-sense answer was. Whether this liberty was also to apply to a war of aggression was another question, and the answer to it might depend upon whether (b) and (c), above, were or were not to be considered distinct provisions. Despite Dahlgren and Sjödell, the record suggests that they probably were not: (c), after all, had referred to the *safety* of the country, which might well depend upon the hiring of mercenaries, with war as the necessary consequence of the need to employ them. In the Council debates of December 1654 Erik Oxenstierna (now Chancellor, in succession to his father) emphasised over and over again that a decision for an attack (whether on Denmark, or Poland, or Russia) was not within their competence: all they could do was advise on the expediency of arming. War required the assent of the *riksdag*;[98] and the king himself took no little pains to obtain it when it met in 1655. The common acknowledgement by Council and king of the need for the assent of the Estates suggests, surely, that the division of (c) from (b) is arbitrary and unlikely. And, as we shall see, even in regard to the second war with Denmark the king resorted to implausible arguments designed to show that it had been authorised in advance by the Committee-*riksdag* which met at Göteborg in May, and had been backed unanimously by six members of the Council at the Wismar meeting of 28 July 1658. His patent anxiety to put himself right with the law suggests that, though the prerogative might have been significantly enlarged in 1654, neither he nor the Council felt that his hands were wholly free.

In fact, though the wording of clause 6 of the Charter may conceivably have been designed to enlarge the limits of the prerogative, Charles X never behaved as though it did. The issue of peace or war could not be decided simply by his will. The burden of war – and

[98] See below, pp. 115 ff.

especially of the preparations for war – was so heavy that the moral support of the Council, and the consent of the Estates, were indispensable. And the argument which the king adduced, the justification of the sacrifices he demanded, was his constitutional duty to preserve the country's *safety*, and to seek the aid of Council and Estates in discharging that duty. In 1655 he sought to enlist the support of the *riksdag* by depicting the situation as one in which Sweden was menaced, not only by Poland, but by Muscovy, by the Emperor, by Denmark, by the Dutch: the recruitment of mercenaries, they were told, had 'a *general* application'. So too in 1658, when the Committee-*riksdag* gave him a free hand 'to provide for his *security*'. In short, if it is insisted that clause 6 of the Charter is divisible into two halves with differing constitutional implications, in the existing circumstances (b) turned out to be irrelevant: what mattered was (c).

Dahlgren also suggests that the Charter of 1654 weakened – and perhaps was intended to weaken – the position and competence of the *riksdag* in that the *riksdag* as such was nowhere mentioned in it:[99] the nearest it came to doing so was in the obligation, under (c), to obtain the consent of the 'Estates' (*ständerna*), without any more precise indication whether by this was intended a full *riksdag*, or not. But it is also true that the Charter of 1611 does not mention the *riksdag* either: it refers to 'the lower Estates', or to 'the consent of those concerned'; and in the Coronation Oath of 1617 the word is 'the commonalty' (*allmogen*). Gustav Adolf had certainly not considered himself bound to deal with a full *riksdag*: for him, as for Axel Oxenstierna later, it was purely a matter of expediency and tactics at any particular time, rather than a constitutional issue. In 1620 the Stock and Land Tax was granted by a Committee-*riksdag*, supplemented later by the consent of the 'commonalty' after negotiations with the peasantry in various parts of the country, and it was reimposed in 1626 without the consent of anybody, though this was one of the first taxes seriously to infringe the privileges of the Nobility. In 1628 the Three Marks Aid (a poll tax affecting every subject) was never granted by the Estates: once again the king relied on local negotiations. The Mill Toll of 1625 was granted by a Committee-*riksdag*; but in 1631 the king drastically increased its burden by a simple order demanding that henceforth it be paid in silver: this was taxation by mere prerogative, and Axel Oxenstierna could offer no explanation.[100] The use of the device of the consent of 'those concerned' was exemplified in the Trade Meeting (*handelsdag*) of

99 Dahlgren, 'Kansler och kungamakt', p. 129 and 'Charles X and the Constitution', p. 184.
100 *AOSB* I. vi. 322.

1613. Provincial meetings for Finland were held in 1614 and 1616. The institution of the Secret Committee in 1627 in effect withdrew all important matters of state (except finance, with which the Committee always declined to concern itself) from the cognizance of the *riksdag* as a whole. Thus when in 1656 the Council called provincial meetings and imposed increased taxation and militia-levies they had ample store of precedents to rely on; and when Charles adopted and systematized their initiative in 1657 the only possible constitutional question that arose was provoked by his desire to levy the militia on a *per capita* basis, and even here he was prepared to compromise.

V

When Dahlgren wrote that Charles's consultations with small meetings of advisers 'constituted in practice an attack upon the special status and authority to which the Council, as the recognized advisory body to the sovereign, was entitled by the constitution',[101] he overstated his case. In the first place, we should have expected that if the charge were well founded there would have been some reaction from the Council's side – if not in Charles's lifetime, then at least after his death. Just as in 1660 the Estates (not the Council) took care to insert into the *Additament* to the Form of Government a clause forbidding provincial meetings, as subversive of the authority of the *riksdag*, so one might have expected the Council to secure the prohibition of the type of meeting which had been held at Frauenburg, Vordingborg, Flensborg, and Wismar in the years 1656 to 1658. But this was a point which does not seem to have occurred to anyone. Next, there is the general point that nothing in the constitution debarred a king from seeking counsel wherever he might think proper: nowhere was the Council described as the king's *sole* adviser. To consult with commanders in the field, to discuss problems with secretaries and other administrators near his person, was not an unreasonable action for a king waging war at a great distance from his own country. Even when he was at home there was nothing improper or unconstitutional in the so-called 'secret' meetings of May 1658. Their purpose was to discuss what attitude Sweden should adopt if – as seemed possible – an aristocratic Fronde should erupt in Denmark.[102] Though there were six members of the Council present on the first occasion, and a rather differently constituted six on the second, the proceedings on the two days, if the minutes are a fair record, were virtually a triangular debate between the king, Per Brahe, and Chris-

---

[101] Dahlgren, 'Charles X and the Constitution', p. 191.
[102] *RRP* XVIII. 150–7.

ter Bonde: Brahe being on the whole for aiding the Danish nobility, Christer Bonde for non-intervention. And Charles himself? It has been suggested that his remarks indicate a disposition to approve of Frederick III's supposed plans to make himself absolute, as providing a useful example for imitation on the other side of the Sound.[103] But it seems rather that his main concern was how best to ensure the fulfilment of the terms of the peace of Roskilde: this becomes especially clear at the close of the second meeting. It is difficult, then, to draw from these meetings the constitutional inferences which Dahlgren drew from them.

Equally innocuous were the discussions of 2–18 January 1658, and those at Vordingborg on 11 February. The January meetings were concerned with diplomacy and foreign policy; and Dahlgren took particular exception to them since they included the secretaries P.J. Coyet and Anders Gyldenklou, who were not members of the Council at all. But they also included two diplomats who were, as well as three other Council members. The meetings were essentially consultative: no decision was taken.[104] At Vordingborg Charles discussed the terms to be imposed on Denmark (a matter wholly within his discretion in terms of the Charter) with a general, a diplomat, and a Danish traitor.[105] Just so had Gustav Adolf proceeded: no Resolution of the Council, no *riksdag* debates, had preceded the peace of Stolbova or the truce of Altmark.

The meetings at Frauenburg in September–October 1656, and the succession of meetings which ended in the second Danish war, require perhaps more particular attention. As to the Frauenburg meetings,[106] what stands out is the king's urgent need to get his own mind clear about the alternatives which were open to him. When he told those he had summoned '*Ergo subjicior omnium judicio, ergo quaere consilia vestra, nam ob solam famam malevolii spargunt infelicia*'[107] he meant exactly what he said – as Gustav Adolf had done when on 3 November 1629 he told the Council 'And as I hope that this measure shall conduce to the welfare *patriae*, so I hope too, that if it prove not so, no man will impute it to me for a fault.'[108] Like Gustav Adolf, and like Axel Oxenstierna when he sought the approval of Council and *riksdag* in 1643 for the attack on Denmark on which he had already determined, he was seeking absolution in advance. With Erik

---

[103] E.g. Jerker Rosén, *Det karolinska skedet* (Lund 1963), p. 75; Lennart Thanner, '1680 års statsrättsförklaring', *Historiska arkiv* (Stockholm 1969), XI. 61.
[104] *RRP* XVIII. 131–41.
[105] *RRP* XVIII. 141–3.
[106] *RRP* XVI. 730–5.
[107] *RRP* XVI. 733.
[108] *RRP* I. 228.

Oxenstierna he had no doubt debated the issues already – and most of the time of the meetings was taken up by debating them with him all over again – but his mind seems to have been so distracted between one possibility and another that it is not surprising that he should have wished to canvass a wider range of opinion. Consultation with the Council in Stockholm would be slow, and some early decision seemed imperative. He had therefore to advise with such persons as were readily available. The group he collected seemed (on paper) a reasonably representative body: the Chancellor (Erik Oxenstierna), the President of the Supreme Court in Wismar (Johan Axelsson Oxenstierna), the Master of the Buckhounds[109] (Gabriel Gabrielsson Oxenstierna), the Governor of Stockholm (Schering Rosenhane), that old soldier and future Admiral, Karl Gustav Wrangel, with seven other members of the Council: a total of twelve – which was distinctly above the average attendance in Stockholm. It is true that only Schering Rosenhane could be counted as one of the effective government at home; but still, the meeting could as fairly be considered an authentic Council meeting as those rumps over which Per Brahe had presided: it did not necessarily imply any infringement of the Council's 'special status and authority'. For the decision reached seems to have been intended to be embodied, as at other Council meetings, in a formal Resolution (*rådslag*), and may even have been so: the minutes leave two lines vacant for its insertion; and the minutes of the meetings of 2 and 5 October are in fact headed '*in Senatu*'.[110] No doubt there existed an *obiter dictum* of Gustav Adolf to the effect that Council meetings might not legally be held outside the country;[111] but this appears to have been conveniently forgotten.

Very different was the case in regard to the meetings which preceded the second war with Denmark. Four members of the Council attended the meetings at Flensborg on 24 and 26 June, when the military prospects of a possible attack on Denmark were discussed; on 28 June the same four, with one addition, came to a provisional decision to launch it; on 23 July six unanimously reaffirmed that decision at a meeting in Wismar.[112] The precedent of 1655, if it went for anything, suggested that the waging war ought properly to be notified in advance to the Council, and obtain the approval of the *riksdag*. None of these preliminaries was observed on this occasion. Charles might seem to be interpreting the Charter as giving him

---

[109] This is perhaps the closest approximation to the Swedish 'Riksjägmästare'.
[110] *RRP* XVI. 739, 744, 749.
[111] C.G. Styffe, ed., *Konung Gustaf II Adolfs skrifter* (Stockholm 1861), p. 83.
[112] *RRP* XVIII. 81–8, 163–6.

unlimited freedom in foreign policy: (b), it appeared, was not covered by (c) – which is what Dahlgren had contended.[113] This is a very different situation from that at Frauenburg in 1656. Yet even now Charles was apparently anxious to appear to be behaving within the limits of the Charter; and he contended that in effect the Committee-*riksdag* at Göteborg in the spring of 1658 had given him authority to attack any enemy which might seem to be endangering the country: once again, it was to be considered as a question of security. The question on foreign policy which he had then put to the Estates, and the Council debates which preceded the Resolution, had been essentially concerned with the dangers from Austria on the one hand and Brandenburg on the other; and the Resolution of the Committee-*riksdag* had been unanimous in authorising him to solve the problem of quartering and paying his armies by transferring them to Brandenburg territory, and to attack the Elector if he should be so unreasonable as to resist that necessary measure. Nothing had then been said about Denmark, except expressions of concern that the peace of Roskilde should be loyally observed. But it was not without significance that Charles had taken care to provide the meeting with a schedule of instances in which Denmark had failed to observe them: the pretext for war had already been laid before the Estates.[114] And the course of the negotiations in Copenhagen suggests strongly that the king privately exhorted P.J. Coyet (one of his negotiators) to sabotage the conciliatory efforts of the other (Sten Bielke).[115] The Resolution of the Committee-*riksdag*, at all events, was drawn in terms so vague that those dangers to which it adverted could be construed to refer to Denmark, no less than to Austria or Brandenburg. The Estates declared that they hoped

that Almighty God may have a regard to, and may assist, H.M.'s righteous cause, and may chastise those who have been unwilling to acquiesce in honest solutions, *or to provide for H.M.'s security*; which the Committee in all humility submit, in general, to H.M.'s most gracious and sapient dijudication.[116]

Whatever we may think of this mandate, it did at least prove one thing: that Charles had a constitutional conscience, and that for the moment it was giving him trouble. It was a view of the Charter which hardly squares with Dahlgren's. Yet the attack on Denmark seems to have been received by the Council with shock and consternation: how, they asked themselves, can we break it to the Swedish people? How justify Charles's consequent demand that the

[113] Dahlgren, 'Charles X and the Constitution', pp. 191–3.
[114] *RRP* XVIII. 345–9.
[115] C. Adlersparre, ed. *Historiska samlingar* (Stockholm 1822), v. 23–175.
[116] Stiernman *Alla riksdagars och mötens besluth*, I. 1,300.

militia-levy for 1659 be brought forward to 1658?[117] The argument that military necessity – i.e. the maintenance of the army – left no alternative but to transfer the troops to Danish soil was an argument which they must have found hard to swallow, since the Resolution of the Committee-*riksdag*, and the Council debates that had preceded it, had plainly indicated that there *was* an alternative: namely, to park them in Brandenburg. These reactions were perhaps a trifle naive – unless they, too, believed that in foreign affairs the king's hands were not (or, at least, ought not to be) wholly free.

Nevertheless, the ordinary Council meetings after Charles came home – that is, between March and June 1658 – look remarkably like a reminiscence of the supposed harmony of Gustav Adolf's time: there are free discussions in the king's presence, the king himself intervening; though now there is no visible pressure from his side to push the Council to a desired conclusion. Not least because he found it difficult to decide what it was that he desired. The debates show him wavering unpredictably between irreconcilable expedients, prepared to give favourable consideration to quite surprising proposals.[118] At these meetings the Council does its best to sort out his ideas, on occasion by a *pro-* and-*contra* debate, every member individually declaring his opinion,[119] and the decision tends to be unanimous. And the conclusion that seems to emerge from all these meetings – including those held overseas – is, first, that king and Council do, in principle, agree that in foreign policy the king is bound by the Charter to seek and obtain the sanction of his constitutional advisers, and of the *riksdag* – or at least of a Committee-*riksdag*; and secondly, that the king's opinion always prevails. The paradoxical situation was this: Charles accepted that his freedom of action was limited; but in fact his foreign policy was entirely his own.

VI

In the reign of Charles X, as in that of Gustav Adolf, the country was burdened by increasingly onerous militia-levies. In 1627 Karl Karlsson Gyllenhielm had asserted that this was entirely a matter within the king's prerogative.[120] A year later, when the question was raised in the Council, Gustav Adolf, in a temperamental outburst, had said:

Nec quaeritur, an ego jus habeam imponendi sine consiliis, et quid nostra privilegia

---

[117] *RRP* XVIII. 89, 91, 94, 97.
[118] E.g. *RRP* XVIII. 27, 29; cf. below pp. 138–40.
[119] *RRP* XVIII. 301.
[120] *AOSB* II. III. 110–11; *RRP* I. 58, 62.

admittebant, sed observanda natura vulgi et necessitas temporis, nec tantum quid debeant, sed quid possint subditi, et lex velit, ut quod faciunt, voluntarie faciant.[121]

And Axel Oxenstierna in 1636 had also ruled that the consent of the *riksdag* was not necessary for such levies.[122] Neither king nor Council would have made such an assertion in Charles's time. In 1656 the initiative in increasing the burden had come from the Council; the consent of the provincial meetings had somehow been obtained; and their example had been followed by the king in 1657. This aspect of Charles's mobilisation-measures, at all events, can hardly be said, in Dahlgren's phrase, to have 'strained the constitutional framework almost to breaking-point'.[123]

How was it, then, in regard to the mobilisation of financial resources? When the reign began, taxation had been fixed, as we have seen, by the triennial arrangement agreed to at the *riksdag* of 1652, which was succeeded by another triennial arrangement determined on at the *riksdag* of 1655; and thereafter by the concessions extorted from the provincial meetings of 1656 and 1657: so far, all was constitutionally regular, however disagreeable. As to the large mercenary forces required to fight Charles's wars, in themselves they had no necessary constitutional implications at all: nothing debarred the king from hiring foreign troops, provided he could pay for them. But unfortunately this was far from being the case in 1654–5: times had changed. This time there were no subsidies to be hoped for; the old maxim that war must sustain war, which had been applied more or less successfully in Germany, could not be made to work in Poland; and the hope of extracting from Danzig or Pillau anything equivalent to the *licenter* on which Gustav Adolf had thriven proved a delusion. The resources had to be found at home, and this at a moment when the budget for 1654 could be made to appear to balance only by massive reductions in debt-repayments.[124] The money needed to begin the war was raised, partly by large loans from private individuals such as H.C. von Königsmarck or Beata de la Gardie; but above all as the result of a contract concluded in April 1655, whereby the crown pawned one of its basic revenues – the Great Toll on exports – to a consortium of Mårten Augustinsson Leijonsköld and Gustav Bonde, and at the same time concluded

---

[121] Nils Ahnlund, 'Öfverläggningar i riksrådet om tyska kriget 1628–1629', *Historisk tidskrift* (1914), p. 115.

[122] *AOSB* II. III. 210–11; cf. *AOSB* I. VI. 320.

[123] Dahlgren, 'Charles X and the Constitution', p. 189. Or again: 'It is clear that the influence of the *riksdag* upon taxation, and upon the raising of troops, was in many ways nullified in Charles's reign': *ibid.*, p. 197.

[124] Hans Landberg, 'Kungamaktens emancipation', p. 100; cf. Dahlgren, *Karl X Gustav och reduktionen*, p. 59.

another agreement which assigned to Leijonsköld the *régale* and the export-duties on copper.[125] The effect of these arrangements was that the main financial responsibility for the raising and fitting-out of the armed forces rested almost entirely in their hands.[126] Again, there was in this nothing that was plainly unconstitutional: it was within the king's prerogative to raise loans against the crown's assets and standing revenues and to apply the money as he might think best, as it also was to alter the rates of duty as he saw fit. But it was a different matter when large sums were diverted to war-expenses from the yield of taxes granted by the *riksdag* – the Little Toll, for instance, or the Stock Tax – and in 1655 nearly a million was taken from such sources to meet the needs of the armies.[127] It is true that the contract with Leijonsköld and Bonde stipulated that they should pay a million *rdr.* annually to cover the deficit on the 'ordinary' budget,[128] but in fact a mere 60,000 *rdr.* seems to have been applied to civilian purposes: all the rest went to the army. The resulting deficiency in the 'ordinary' budget meant that in 1655 the crown defaulted on the wages due to its servants to the extent of 650,000 *rdr.*[129] This *was* a constitutional issue. Members of the Council felt strongly that 'ordinary' expenses ought to be met out of 'ordinary' revenue, and that 'extraordinary' expenses – by which they meant military expenses – ought not to be supplied by measures which it was not in their power to oversee. Such measures included a *reduktion*. Erik Oxenstierna was prepared to swallow a *reduktion* if it helped to balance the 'ordinary' budget; but Magnus Gabriel de la Gardie (for instance) was not prepared to see a *reduktion* designed to cover expenses which were 'extraordinary'.[130] What they wanted was some sort of constitutional check. They did not get it.

Nevertheless, Charles's contrivances to cope with his financial problems did not establish a new constitutional norm, nor were they in fact innovations. Gustav Adolf had pawned or sold the crown's estates or revenues; in 1629 he had diverted 120,000 *dlr.* of the proceeds of the Stock Tax to supply the needs of his armies;[131] his contracts with Louis de Geer, or Erik Larsson, to manage the crown's revenues from copper, provided some sort of precedent for Leijonsköld. What was new in Charles's time was the *scale* of all these operations. Nevertheless Hans Landberg's perception of the signifi-

---

125 Hans Landberg, 'Krig på kredit', pp. 43–8.
126 *Ibid.*, pp. 48, 50.
127 *Ibid.*, pp. 111–13.
128 Dahlgren, *Karl X Gustav och reduktionen*, p. 64.
129 *Ibid.*, p. 113.
130 Hans Landberg, 'Kungamaktens emancipation', pp. 106–8.
131 Roberts, *Gustavus Adolphus*, II, 80.

cance of Charles's policies as amounting to 'the Emancipation of the Monarchy'[132] seems at least premature. Once the wars were over the customary controls of the finances would again become operative; the 'ordinary' revenue would be applied to 'ordinary' expenditure; the debt would be to a considerable extent paid off; and Gustav Bonde – so lately Leijonsköld's partner – would balance the budget – until the second war with Bremen upset it again.

VII

Perhaps no issue sheds more light on the relationship of king and Council than the question of the *reduktion*. For Charles, the *reduktion* was essential to the economic recovery of the country from the financial chaos in which Christina had left it, and therefore to the maintenance of its status as a great power. For the Council, a *reduktion* threatened a catastrophic subversion of the privileges and immunities of that aristocracy of which they were the leading representatives. The demand for the recovery of lands alienated by the crown had been raised by the three lower Estates as early as 1611; and from that time forward it had never been wholly silenced. In the great social and constitutional crisis of 1650 it had reached a climax out of which a civil war had seemed for a time to be a conceivable outcome. Meanwhile, from the time of Gustav Adolf onwards, the Nobility had on repeated occasions been persuaded to agree to curtailments of their privileges; and to many of them it seemed that the process had gone so far that any further concession could not reasonably be expected of them. They were safeguarded, they might think, by that clause in the Charter which required the assent of Council and *riksdag* to any measure which might be necessary for the 'welfare . . . and needs' of the country. But not a few of them must have viewed with misgiving any proposal which might necessarily entail investigation of the circumstances surrounding the donations which the crown had bestowed upon them: were they 'lawfully acquired' in terms of the Charter? Probably most of them were; but in the case of many the carelessness of the crown (Christina might on occasion give the same land to two different persons) and the state of confusion which was the consequence of administrative slackness (and, in some cases, corruption) had produced a situation in which some donations, though they might not strictly be 'unlawful', could hardly fail to be branded as irregular. If the demand for a *reduktion* were now to be pressed by the king, it seemed not impossible that it

---

[132] Hans Landberg, 'Kungamaktens emancipation'.

might entail a major constitutional crisis in which king and Council would confront each other from irreconcilable positions, and in which the king might be tempted, by enlisting the support of the lower Estates, to renew, more explicitly than Christina in 1650, that 'strife of Estates', which had been in the background of politics for decades. In the event, confrontation was avoided; the constitutional crisis did not occur; the strife of Estates did not break out. And though the respite turned out to be temporary, it was one of Charles's major achievements to have contrived it.

Even before his accession Charles had made up his mind that there must be a *reduktion* of some sort. His first draft of such a plan dates from March 1654, and already at that time he was discussing tactics with Herman Fleming, who was destined later to be the *reduktion*'s leading champion and instrument.[133] Talks seem to have been held in the early months of Charles's reign with other members of the Council also; and in October 1654 he was demanding to be supplied with accurate information as to what crown lands had been alienated, and which could be considered 'indispensable' to the ordinary operations of government.[134] Draft after draft in his own hand, minute calculations of fiscal possibilities, record the development of his ideas of what was requisite. And though on 23 December 1654 (perhaps as a tactful *quid pro quo* for the Council's virtual endorsement of his foreign policy) he confirmed the privileges of the Nobility which Gustav Adolf had granted (in its second version) in 1617, he deliberately refrained from confirming the extension of them which Christina had granted in 1644; and he took care to delay the formal confirmation of the privileges he did grant until after the *riksdag* of 1655 – that is, until *after* the question of the *reduktion* had for the moment been settled:[135] he began operations, therefore, with a small trump in his hand. Meanwhile, he continued with his drafting and his calculations. Two drafts, which Dahlgren considers were written shortly before the Estates assembled, were first discussed by the Council on 13 March 1655.[136] They were ominously far-reaching. They suggested the *reduktion* of all allodial grants made since 1632, and the immediate restoration to the crown of lands considered 'indispensable'.[137] For six weeks the king left the Council to ponder

---

[133] Dahlgren, *Karl X Gustav och reduktionen*, p. 12.

[134] *Ibid.*, p. 43.

[135] *Ibid.*, p. 53: cf. Charles's nonchalant answer, when they enquired about it: *RRP* XVI. 193.

[136] *RRP* XVI. 45; Dahlgren, *Karl X Gustav och reduktionen*, pp. 49, 51 and 'Charles X and the Constitution', p. 189. Christer Bonde had already presented a memorial to the Council on the previous day: R. Swedlund, 'Krister Bonde och reduktionsbeslutet 1655', *KFÅ* (1937).

[137] Dahlgren, *Karl X Gustav och reduktionen*, pp. 57–8 and 'Charles X and the Constitution', p. 197.

these proposals in his absence: he did not, as Gustav Adolf might have done, attempt to convert them by appeals to their patriotism or ominous signs of his displeasure; he simply allowed time for the gravity of the situation to sink in. The members of the Council were left to make up their own minds: from 23 March to 18 June the king never set foot in the Council chamber – a length of absence unparalleled since his accession. The tactic proved effective. The grim facts could not be shrugged off; patriotism – which the high aristocracy, with all its many faults, rarely failed to show in a crisis – nerved them to self-sacrifice once again. Almost at once the Council, led by Erik Oxenstierna, accepted the idea of a *reduktion* in principle – though they found it less easy to agree on how best it was to be effected. And they found too that it was to them that was allotted the embarrassing task of persuading their brethren of the Nobility to come to the same conclusion: the king, it appeared, was not disposed to lend them a helping hand. The labyrinthine debates with committees of the first Estate, the innumerable special cases which pleaded for consideration, the tangled webs of landholding which required to be unravelled, the thorny question of 'merited' as against 'unmerited' donations, the alternative of a contribution instead of a *reduktion*[138] – all these he silently left them to struggle with. But though he thus remained in the background he took care to provide himself with a weapon, to be used at need, which neither Council nor Nobility would be able to resist. This was nothing less than the draft of a formal Proposition to the *riksdag* as a whole, which would have depicted the country's critical economic condition and invited all four Estates to consider how best the crown was to be relieved. It was the tactic which Gustaf Vasa had used in 1527 to carry the Reformation. If the king resorted to it, the Council and the Nobility would find themselves confronted with a 'strife of Estates'. And though no Proposition in this form was ever made, either the knowledge that it had been drafted, or the possibility that it might be, was decisive.[139] When on 26 April he sent to the Council the explicit proposal that either one-quarter of all estates alienated since 1632 be at once restored to the crown, or alternatively that pending their restoration they should be charged with a contribution of 200,000

[138] For the dilemma see Sven A. Nilsson, 'Reduktion eller kontribution? Alternativ inom 1600-talets finanspolitik', *Scandia* (1958), pp. 90–3. The Council would have preferred contribution, but the Nobility opted for *reduktion*, hoping that thereby their other privileges in regard to fiscal immunities might be left intact; and they accepted *reduktion* in principle on 22 May: SRARP v₂. 320 ff.

[139] Dahlgren, *Karl X Gustav och reduktionen*, pp. 62–3; Ahnlund, *Ståndsriksdagens utdaning*, p. 298.

rdr. a year,[140], the battle was as good as over as far as the Council was concerned, though for another six weeks the endless meetings with a committee of the Nobility would continue in an effort to decide which alternative to choose, and to define in detail the procedures to be followed, with such safeguards against abuse as might be contrived. By early May the Nobility had resignedly opted for the restitution of a quarter of the alienated lands rather than pay a contribution, and a *reduktion* Ordinance had been formulated.[141] It might, no doubt, have been promulgated simply as a royal Ordinance, since in practice its effects would be virtually limited to a single Estate; but it was felt desirable that it should be included in the final Resolution with which the *riksdag* was to close its proceedings. But it was not until 24 April that the Council for the first time gave to committees from the Clergy and the Burghers an inkling of what was impending,[142] and when the Ordinance came before the three lower Estates it met with vehement opposition. For the Ordinance declared itself to be an 'eternal and unbreakable' arrangement, and the three non-noble Estates refused to regard it either as the one or the other. The Nobility might feel constrained to accept a settlement which on the face of it was final; the other Estates did not.[143] Nor Charles either. The opposition of the lower Estates played into his hands; and when the Peasants proposed that the whole *reduktion*-settlement should be deferred until the next *riksdag*, but that in the meantime contributions from the lands affected should be paid (the so-called 'quarter-part rent'), pending a thorough investigation of their legal status, the suggestion was welcomed by (significantly) Herman Fleming.[144] And on 18 June Charles at last attended a meeting of the Council. Pent-up exasperation at the difficulties which had been started by some of the Nobility found expression in an outburst in the authentic Vasa tradition:

Jura majestatis are now so disputed . . . that H.M. must assert his own rights, just as other Estates seek their own security . . . H.M. sees very well what they are aiming

---

[140] Dahlgren, *Karl X Gustav och reduktionen*, p. 80, where however he maintains that the king overtrumped the Council by putting this direct to the Nobility. A committee of the Nobility did indeed meet the Council on 26 April, and the king's proposal was put to them by Erik Oxenstierna, but Charles's presence at the meeting is not recorded either in the Council's or the Nobility's minutes: *RRP* XVI. 158, 174; *SRARP* v₂. 58–9. A committee of the first Estate had met the king earlier on that day, but only to report on how they had settled a quarrel between Per Brahe and Ernst Creutz: *ibid.* 57. And it is clear that the king communicated his proposals regarding 'indispensable' revenues 'through the Council': *ibid.* 47, 285–9.

[141] Dahlgren, *Karl X Gustav och reduktionen*, pp. 101, 110; *SRARP* v₂ 61, 64, 82; *RRP* XVI. 176.

[142] *RRP* XVI. 143, 146.

[143] *RRP* XVI. 220.

[144] *RRP* XVI. 235.

at. If they are minded to continue along these lines, H.M. for his part must look to how the rights of himself and the realm are to be safeguarded: in his view a king should have as great a share of rights as a nobleman. They have begun to lay the foundations of what H.M. will not tolerate, and he must take his measures to thwart their design.[145]

But this salvo was followed by the proposal (echoing the views of the Peasants) that pending detailed scrutiny of the terms on which lands had been alienated (i.e. until the next *riksdag*) the revenue of the lands scheduled to be reduced be paid to the crown. On this the Council – exceptionally – took a vote.[146] They endorsed the suggestion. And they voted too that Charles be asked to intervene personally, and use his authority to obtain the acceptance of this solution by *all* the Estates. But the king had no intention of doing any such thing: 'to use *authoritate regia simpliciter* and without any proper basis was not for H.M., nor could he favour one Estate more than another'.[147] And so it was left to Erik Oxenstierna to confess with embarrassment to the Nobility that the 'eternal' Ordinance could in fact be amended, and that a stringent investigation of the legal position was essential.[148]

The decision, as embodied in the Resolution of the *riksdag*,[149] was not, for Charles, the optimal solution: what he really was after was an assured income, in commodities and services, from land, and a further lessening of the privileges of the Nobility, which would combine to secure to the crown a steady fixed revenue, and relieve it from the need to solicit grants from the *riksdag* – an objective which commanded the cordial support of the tax-paying community, which either did not perceive, or was indifferent to, the constitutional implications. But this for the moment could wait: the principle of a *reduktion* had been accepted; and before the next *riksdag* the perquisitions of the new College of the *reduktion*, with Fleming at its head, might well open the way to its extension beyond the limits contemplated in 1655. Meanwhile, he had handled the situation with notable tactical skill. He had avoided an immediate 'strife of Estates' by first tackling those who were destined to be the most conspicuous victims of any *reduktion*: that is, the Council; and thereafter leaving it to them to argue it out with the Nobility as a whole. And the three non-noble Estates, confronted with major concessions by Council and Nobility, had obligingly handed him the opportunity for his

---

[145] *RRP* XVI. 228–9.

[146] *RRP* XVI. 228, 230.

[147] *RRP* XVI. 233.

[148] He told them that 'the whole *secretum* lies in the fact that it is not possible at this time to make such an Ordinance that no alterations in it can occur': *SRARP* v₂. 183.

[149] Stiernman, *Alla riksdagars och mötens besluth*, II. 1, 231–58.

legists to pick holes in titles, dispute the terms of donations, convict beneficiaries of deceiving or swindling the crown, and so lay the basis for that great 'retribution' (*räfst*) which would in the 1680s reduce many a family to comparative (if temporary) ruin.[150]

From the point of view of Charles's relations with his Council two things suggest themselves. First, the events of 1655 demonstrated that in this matter – as in the case of foreign policy – whatever the interpretation of the Charter of 1654 it did not in fact restrict the king's liberty of action: the assent of Council and *riksdag* was indeed sought and obtained; but the king's will prevailed. The technique employed was the same as in the Council debates on foreign policy in December 1654: the king to all appearances distances himself from the discussion, which proceeds without him; but he influences it by providing indisputable facts, or tendentious questions, or (in the case of the *reduktion*) by tacit menace. Secondly, though it might appear that in consequence the Council had suffered a serious defeat, that did not impair their good relations with the sovereign; for he took care by his propitiatory attitude thereafter that good relations should continue. It is true that members of the Council were among the heaviest losers by the *reduktion*, but the king and Fleming between them did their best to let them down lightly, to offset their losses by maintaining their salaries at a time when all other salaries were cut, and by exceptional favouritism in cases of exceptional merit – for instance, towards distinguished soldiers among them.[151] For Charles needed the good-will of his Council, and he strove to keep it: in his situation he could not do without it.[152] He never had cause to complain of their insubordination, nor – at least until after August 1658 – of any serious difference of opinion on the essential question of foreign policy. Gustav Adolf's Council, on the other hand, could on occasion offer real resistance to the king's will: there were stormy passages which have no parallel in Charles's reign. In 1627, for instance, after 'long and sharp' deliberations with the king upon a general militia-levy and the Stock Tax, they put forward an alternative which the king rejected. Gustaf Adolf then took the autocratic step of drafting the Council's Resolution himself, and demanding that they sign it. Their reply was to leave it unsigned for a fortnight,

---

[150] It may perhaps be true, as Sven A. Nilsson suggested, that if the process of stripping the Nobility of their fiscal exemptions – already pushed very far – had been continued, there might have been no need of a *reduktion* at all: that is, from a purely financial point of view: Nilsson, 'Reduktion eller kontribution?', p. 97.

[151] Dahlgren, *Karl X Gustav och reduktionen*, pp. 165 ff., 176, 218, 237, 330.

[152] Already in 1654 the Danish envoy, Peder Juel, had commented that Charles was disposed to 'caress' the Council: A. Fryxell, *Historiska bref rörande Sveriges historia utur utländska arkiver* (Stockholm 1830), p. 108.

'*usque ad indignationem regis*'. The conciliatory Gabriel Gustafsson Oxenstierna succeeded in persuading them to give way; but when the king included his draft in his Proposition to the *riksdag*, the Estates too delayed their answer, secretly invited the Council members to discuss the situation with them, and then proposed the same alternative as the Council had put forward. And they asked (as the Council had also done) that the king should give a guarantee that if they yielded to his demand, it should be without prejudice, saying that they acquiesced in it 'from their affection and good inclination'. To which the king replied in anger that he had no need of their affection: it was a simple matter of duty. And therewith proceeded to draw the Resolution of the *riksdag* himself, as he had drawn that of the Council.[153] The situation was equally tense in 1631, though now the king's fulminations were at long range. He was angry because the yield in men and money of the measures which had been taken fell below his expectations; the Council on their side complained that the commonalty were saying that the burdens imposed upon them were the Council's 'inventions'. Gustav Adolf's reaction was to send home Dr Bothvidi to teach them their business, with a swingeing rebuke for their impertinence.[154]

Not until 7 November 1658 can we see anything like flat opposition by Charles's Council to the king's policy. It was provoked by his astonishing suggestion of ceding Prussia to Austria, and by the incredible argument he advanced in support of the idea: '*De potestate maritima. Futuram negavit esse copiam Austriacis ob defectu portuum.*' Had he forgotten Wallenstein? This was too much for the Council. Magnus Gabriel de la Gardie asked for time to think; but Christer Bonde had his thoughts ready, and needed no delay: '*prolixius rem deduxit*', urging the dangers and the difficulties, and the whole Council rallied to his support. The only answer Charles could make was '*Acheronta movendo, si non licet flectare caeteros*'.[155] And though he briefly recurred to the idea three weeks later,[156] he did not succeed in persuading anybody. But by this time his foreign policy was already in ruins, as the Council must have realised: all that remained were expedients – any expedients – to free himself from the entanglements in which his second Danish war had involved him.[157]

---

[153] *AOSB* II. III.110–1; *RRP* I. 59, 62.
[154] *AOSB* II. III.210–1: cf. Axel Oxenstierna's caution to the Council, in reply to their lamentations, that '*Regum aures sua natura sunt tenerae*': *ibid*, I. VI. 320.
[155] *RRP* XVIII. 176–8.
[156] *RRP* XVIII. 180.
[157] A revealing survey of the expedients to which he resorted is provided by Torsten Gihl, *Sverige och västmakterna under Karl X Gustafs andra krig med Danmark* (Uppsala 1913).

VIII

We are now perhaps in a position to weigh the arguments in the controversy between Dahlgren and Sjödell. In general, it seems clear that as between Gustav Adolf and Charles X there was a real difference in king-Council relations. In 1636 Per Brahe had remarked that Gustav Adolf had been inclined to enlarge his powers by diminishing the privileges of others.[158] But little as Brahe relished the *reduktion* of 1655, he never seems, either at that time or after 1660, to have levelled the same criticism at Charles X. In part the difference between the two reigns was a question of personalities. Gustav Adolf was imperious, as Charles never was except in isolated instances when he lost his temper; Charles's Council was a much better team than Gustav Adolf's, once Axel Oxenstierna had departed for Prussia. Gabriel Gustafsson Oxenstierna, though generally respected, was too easily disheartened to be such a leader as Per Brahe was; and the Treasury in Gustav Adolf's absence could show no official as trusted or as capable as Herman Fleming, at least until the management of the finances was put into the hands of Johan Casimir of the Palatinate. Sjödell was right to see the reign as a period of co-operation. The accord of king and Council is indeed obvious: few kings can have had better collaboration or more loyal support from their Council; few Councils can have worked harder to implement the king's policies. The accord was based (as had also been the case under Gustav Adolf) on a common attitude to the general principles of foreign policy; and that made it easier for the Council to swallow the *reduktion*, since without it that policy could hardly be carried on. It was therefore possible for the Council to reconcile itself to another basic fact of the situation: the dominance of the crown. There was accord, certainly; but it was not an accord of equal parties. It represented loyal service to a master.[159] It is impossible to see the Council as *balancing* the crown, as Sjödell did, if only because no issue arose on which balance seemed to be called for. Though we can and do see the Council acting as an intermediary (not a mediator!) between crown and *riksdag* in 1655, it never, as far as we know, advanced a claim to discharge a constitutional function as mediator while Charles was alive; and still less to be an ephorate. Yet it was, on the whole, strong: strong with the strength that comes from solidarity. Unlike the Council from 1630 to 1648, or from 1660 to

[158] Georg Wittrock, *Regering och allmoge under Kristinas förmyndare* (Uppsala 1948), p. 130. Jakob de la Gardie had made a similar remark about the same time: Lövgren, *Ståndsstridens uppkomst*, p. 11.

[159] This was how Axel Oxenstierna had conceived the relationship also: *AOSB* I. VI. 321 (to Gabriel Gustafsson Oxenstierna, 17 May 1631).

1680, it was not weakened by factions: the Oxenstierna–Skytte quarrel, the clash between Magnus Gabriel de la Gardie and his enemies, had no parallel in 1654–60. Though Per Brahe and Herman Fleming represent opposing extremes in their attitude to the *reduktion*, that did not prevent them from co-operating closely as colleagues, or lead them to betray state secrets to the emissaries of foreign powers.

If then the Council (or at least the central core of ten or a dozen members) was emphatically a working body, Charles X was no less emphatically a working king, as manifested in a flood of letters and memoranda. A skilful tactician at home no less than in the field; an excellent administrator, a diplomat of wide experience; he was a cultured man of his time, fluent in Latin and modern languages: Anders Schönberg, writing a century later, judged that he was probably the most learned of Swedish sovereigns.[160] Like many of his predecessors on the throne, he was a competent theologian, capable of putting a bishop right on the vexed question of marriage with a deceased wife's sister;[161] and like many of them also he had the gift of effortless oratory.[162] He was indeed a very different character from the buccaneer of traditional Polish historiography, or the Protestant Hero of Cromwell's wishful thinking. Though with Axel Oxenstierna's help he secured a Charter, which (as it turned out) freed his hands in regard both to foreign policy and to the *reduktion*, he does not seem to have attempted to exploit his advantage in such a way as to alienate his Council. His authority remained within the limits that had been prescribed to him. He neither sought nor needed any acknowledgement of it (though any rash author who presumed to make a distinction between 'mediate' and 'immediate' subjects might find his book hurled against the wall),[163] and no voice was raised in the Council to question it – for the moment. For from 1611 onwards the cause of Council-constitutionalism had one danger to fear above all others: the danger of an alliance of crown and commonalty against

[160] Anders Schönberg, *Historiska bref* (Stockholm 1850), II. 178.

[161] *RRP* XVIII. 79.

[162] As was evidenced by his performance on 8 April 1658, when he opened the Göteborg Committee-*riksdag* with a lengthy survey of foreign policy. To this succeeded *A Short Relation*, drafted and read by Secretary Edvard Ehrensteen: it covers thirty-five closely printed pages, and is a chronological survey of the events since the provincial meetings of 1657. This, one might suppose, would have been enough for one day; but the king, 'drawing his chair rather further forward' delivered another speech, covering the same ground all over again, which (the exhausted minute-taker recorded) 'lasted two whole hours'; and had in other respects something of a Cromwellian flavour: *SRARP* VI. 287–9, 292–6; and (for the *Short Relation*), ibid. 307–42.

[163] The author was Michael Wexionius Gyldenstolpe. The anecdote dates from 1680: Runeby, *Monarchia mixta*, p. 400.

the aristocracy. In Charles IX's time that alliance had been nefarious; in Christina's, fortuitous and sentimental. But under Charles X it never became explicit, nor would he have desired that it should be; for in 1655 – as in 1650 – political wisdom dictated the maintenance of good relations with the aristocracy at a particularly delicate moment; and to secure that he needed the Council's help. In the absence of that danger, Council-constitutionalism had no obvious bogy to alarm it, no spur to make it scrutinise the prerogative with jealousy, no political or constitutional issue on which to fight. For Charles, the possibility of such an alliance was useful *in terrorem*: no more; for it would have done nothing to win the war, of which the three lower Estates quite clearly disapproved. And from the point of view of the Council, 1655 must have appeared a singularly inappropriate moment for advancing constitutional claims, with a war on their hands, ever more mercenary armies needing to be paid, and the dilapidation of the finances unquestionably demanding radical measures. In 1660 men would draw a distinction: 'it is one thing to rule with the Council's counsel, but another thing to rule with its consent'; but in Charles's lifetime they were not ready for such hairsplitting: they were content with the old rule of 1602, which had laid it down that 'it is for the Council to advise, and not to govern'. If Charles's constitutionalism was tactical, tactical considerations were not lacking on the Council's side either.

This leaves open the question whether Charles may not have intended to extend the prerogative beyond the limits of 1654 in the direction of absolutism, when once the restraints imposed by a war situation had been removed by victory. Despite his good relations with Axel Oxenstierna at the close of Christina's reign, he can hardly have failed to assimilate some of the political ideas of the anti-Oxenstierna group of the 1640s, of which his father and his uncle had been at times the leaders. That group had leaned towards a strong monarchy; and in 1649 Carl Christopher von Schlippenbach, who was close to it, and was one of Charles's closer associates in 1654 and after, had put out a pamphlet of strongly monarchical complexion.[164] Sven A. Nilsson has suggested that from Gustav Adolf to Charles XI there is a clear trend towards some kind of military monarchy.[165] It first becomes apparent, in his view, in Gustav Adolf's War Ordinance of 1620, with its careful provision for numbering the

---

[164] Runeby, *Monarchia mixta*, pp. 339–41.
[165] Sven A. Nilsson. 'Reduktion eller kontribution?, pp. 91–5 and 'Krig och folkbokföring under svenskt 1600-tal', *Scandia* (1982) and *Den karolinska militärstaten . . . Tre Karlar: Karl X Gustav, Karl XI, Karl XII* (Stockholm 1984).

people in the interest of the state's control;[166] and it appears in the Mill Toll of 1625, which was expressly declared to be designed to provide a standing army. It surfaces again in Charles X's plans in 1658 for the extension of *ständigt knektehåll* from a few provinces to the whole country, which would have freed the crown from the need to seek the consent of the *riksdag* to militia-levies.[167] One main purpose of the *reduktion* was to use the lands so recovered as a financial base for the army, and thus (among other things) diminish the crown's need to hire expensive cavalry from abroad.[168] The steady process whereby, from Gustav Adolf's time onwards, 'extra-ordinary' grants were tacitly transmuted into ordinary revenues requiring no further parliamentary sanction, looks like another element in the same development. An anecdote, dating from some time after 1660, reported that Charles thought of altering the Council's title from 'Council of the Realm' to 'King's Council', as Charles XI was to do in 1682.[169] In the 1650s, it appears, the dons at Uppsala were ceasing to inculcate a political theory based on contractualism enforced by ephors, and were veering towards the idea of a mixed monarchy in which the crown should predominate; and Charles himself is said to have read Bodin, and perhaps had not failed to take note of Bodin's *dictum* that 'nothing is so just as that which is necessary'.[170] A strengthening of the power of the crown was an obvious consequence of Charles's uncontested intention of weakening the power of the aristocracy. It seems unlikely that he would have been willing to accept indefinitely the quasi-regal pretensions of the great counts such as Per Brahe, who was accustomed to speak of his 'subjects' in his county of Visingsö, and who provided for a regency against the contingency of his premature demise; and on this issue it had already appeared from the debates on the *reduktion* that Charles would be able to rely on the backing of the lower nobility. The terms of Charles's Testament of 1660, with its evident intention of entrenching the dynasty by allotting seats in the Regency to the queen mother, to Charles's unpopular brother Adolf Johan, and to his brother-in-law Magnus Gabriel de la Gardie (perhaps he remembered how his own father had been thrust aside after 1634), and its arbitrary attempt to treat the realm as though it could be disposed of by private testamen-

---

[166] Styffe, *Gustav II Adolfs skrifter*, p. 18. For the suggestion that education and church-discipline were dominated by the same determination to supervise and control the subjects of the state, see Bengt Sandin, *Hemmet, gatan, fabriken eller skolan* (Lund 1986).

[167] Hans Landberg. 'Kungamaktens emancipation', pp. 114–16, 118, 120.

[168] Dahlgren, *Karl X Gustav och reduktionen*, pp. 117, 176, 207, 218.

[169] Göran Rystad, 'Claes Rålambs memorial 1665', *KFÅ* (1963).

[170] Runeby, *Monarchia mixta*, pp. 363–5, 396–400, 402.

tary disposition,[171] led the Estates to annul it: an act which Charles XI never forgot or forgave. And at least one shrewd and percipient foreign observer came to the conclusion that if Charles had lived he might have followed the example of Frederick III.[172]

There is no doubt that Charles was a soldier at heart, who would for choice have followed the profession of arms, and who was not sorry to be able to follow it after his accession. He had been present at the final triumph of the Thirty Years War, when the Swedes at last entered Prague; and he may well have had always with him the memories of those glorious days: in 1649–50 he, more than any other statesman, decided the settlement of Germany. And soldiering for him meant not only command; it meant personal engagement in the mêlée, as it had for Gustav Adolf; and he would have counted death in battle an appropriate end to his career. A military monarchy, nevertheless, is not quite the same as an absolutism. It could exist within the framework of the constitution – and especially within the terms of the Charter of 1654. It remains to be demonstrated that Charles desired more than that. His domestic policies were essentially conditioned and made necessary by his foreign policy: by his determination to equip Sweden, militarily and economically, for the role of a great power – a role which he never renounced, even in adversity. And to play that part the Council, as before, was an indispensable instrument, just as the good-will of the Estates was necessary if his attention were not to be distracted from the foreign dangers with which he believed Sweden to be menaced, or from the fleeting opportunities for expansion which seemed to present themselves. Co-operation was therefore necessary; dualism might entail possibly fatal handicaps. Only when the Peace of Roskilde had been imposed, and when the logic of expansion might seem to have reached its reasonable limits – both from a domestic and an international point of view – had the time arrived for his collaborators to call a halt and break the partnership. How far they would have risked it if Charles had not succumbed to pneumonia may be questionable; but once he was dead, military monarchy was no longer relevant – until the time, fifteen years later, when it re-emerged as (among other things) the saviour from a disaster which the Regency had striven in vain to avoid, and which it had proved incapable of confronting.

If Magalotti's conjecture was correct, however, it would help to explain what happened in 1660. It is as though long-stifled aspira-

---

[171] Georg Wittrock, *Carl X Gustafs testament. Den politiska striden i Sverige 1660* (Uppsala 1908).

[172] Lorenzo Magalotti, *Sverige under år 1674*, trans. C.M. Stenbock (Stockholm 1912), p. 74.

tions and frustrations come boiling to the surface. The basic social crisis emerges once again: men talk, as they had talked in the 1640s, of the danger of civil war.[173] Constitutionally and socially it seems that the clock has been turned back a quarter of a century. The foreign adventure is over; the *reduktion* has slowed down almost to nothing; the consensus on foreign and domestic policy which had marked the years of 1654–60 exists no longer. For the Council, it is a moment of triumph. If Charles's reign had, in Landberg's phrase, seen the emancipation of the monarchy, 1660 witnessed the emancipation of the Council. Per Brahe asserts the Council's inherent right to be 'mediators'; its members once again begin to talk of themselves as ephors.[174] The Council now controls appointments: it has supplanted the king as keeper of the gate.[175] Effectively it controls the Regents also; for one single dissentient voice among them entails reference of the point at issue to the Council for decision.[176] But simultaneously the *riksdag* (and especially the Estate of Nobility) emerges as the Council's chief rival and critic. It is the *riksdag*, under Noble leadership, that annuls Charles's Testament; it firmly establishes its right to the parliamentary initiative and its monopoly of legislation (no more provincial meetings or Committee-*riksdagar*); it insists on triennial meetings for the future. The *Additament* to the Form of Government, recurring to a clause in the Charter of 1611 which had been conspicuously omitted in 1654, lays it down that no official be dismissed without condemnation by due process of law.[177] All this reads like a general condemnation of practices which had obtained in the preceding reign. It is true that the implied censures on Charles are nowhere made explicit: this is not a replay of 1611. The point about arbitrary dismissals did not touch Charles, but may well have been prompted by what Christina had done to Magnus Gabriel de la Gardie in 1653; and to some extent the censures are irrelevant, since the *Additament* applied only to the period of Charles XI's minority, and it was the Regents who were thus to be subject to constitutional restraints.

By the time that minority ended, in 1672, we can already detect the signs of a change of climate. The Charter which was prescribed for Charles XI in that year reiterated *verbatim* that clause in the Charter of 1654 which so engaged the attention of Dahlgren and Sjödell: Charles XI was to be free to interpret his constitutional obligations as Charles X had interpreted them. It was a clear victory

---

[173] Wittrock, *Carl X Gustafs testament*, pp. 127–8. Magnus Gabriel de la Gardie (not ordinarily stupid) was disposed to blame the social crisis on the Jesuits.

[174] Sjödell, *Kungamakt och högaristokrati*, pp. 275, 302.

[175] Rystad, 'The King, the Nobility and Growth of Bureaucracy', pp. 67–8.

[176] Hildebrand, *Sveriges regeringformer*, p. 56: *Additament*, clause 15.

[177] *Ibid.*, clause 8.

for the non-noble Estates over the aristocracy and the Council.[178] As the constitutional pendulum swings back and forth, the Charter of 1654 appears for the moment as a balance-point. But the balance would soon be disturbed; a common front between crown and lower Estates would become an ominous possibility; in 1675 and 1678 it would draw nearer; and after 1680 a new form of co-operation would triumph (for a time) over dualism. What emerges from the turmoil after 1660 is neither consensus nor dualism, but trialism: a protracted struggle, with shifting alliances, between Regents, Council, and *riksdag*.

When Dahlgren wrote that a conflict between crown and Council must have 'underlain' the whole of Charles's reign he was probably right; but what mattered was that in that reign the conflict did not emerge into the open. On the other hand it is equally clear that Sjödell's picture of constant co-operation during the whole period 1600–60 is a distortion. Conflict had in fact underlain co-operation all the time. Erik Sparre's doctrines were not annihilated by his death at Linköping: as Åke Hermansson has demonstrated,[179] they were not without influence even on the agents and collaborators of Charles IX. During the two minorities the challenge to the virtual *pro tempore* sovereign – Axel Oxenstierna in the one case, the Council in the other – is transferred to other shoulders: to the *riksdag*, in particular. *Regimen politicum* could find at need other champions than the Council, as the events of 1719–20 would demonstrate. In short, some form of dualism was normal throughout the period: even under Charles XI it was not wholly silenced. But collaboration and co-operation were also normal, if only because war, or the fear of war, tended to be normal too, and was powerful enough to rally men to government. It remains true that before Charles XI dualism was never quite as silent and subdued as in 1654–60; but the conflicting views of Dahlgren and Sjödell on a brief period of six years must not tempt us to apply either the one or the other to impose a pattern upon a complex century.

[178] Sjödell, *Kungamakt och högaristokrati*, pp. 67–8, 77, 222. Even in 1660 the lower Estates, though they welcomed the *Additament*, had been less than eager to annul Charles's Testament; a strong monarchy, they thought, might have its uses.

[179] Åke Hermansson, *Karl IX och ständerna. Tronfrågan och författningsutvecklingen i Sverige 1598–1611* (Uppsala 1962).

III

Charles X and the great parenthesis: a reconsideration

I

On 6 June 1655 a Swedish army of 18,000 men under the command of Arvid Wittenberg, having traversed Brandenburg territory with the Elector's leave, crossed the frontier into Polish Prussia, and so initiated a catena of wars which was to be protracted without intermission until the peace settlements of 1660–1. On the 25th the Resolution of the *riksdag* declared its acceptance of the necessity for war with Poland.[1]

Though in terms of Charles X's Accession Charter the assent of the Estates was probably required for the undertaking of an offensive war,[2] and though the Council of State in its debates in the previous December had certainly assumed that it was, they seem on the whole to have supposed that assent would be forthcoming; and in the end the event proved them right. But in reality the decision had been made almost inevitable before the *riksdag* met. It was the sequel to a series of Council meetings in December 1654 and January 1655. Early in December the king had instructed his Chancellor, Erik Oxenstierna, to elicit the Council's opinion on three points which he submitted to them. First, as to whether the international situation made it necessary for Sweden to arm; secondly, whether in such a case the military measures to be taken should be adequate only for defence, or whether they should be calculated with a view to the possibility of offensive action; and thirdly, against which of the dangers which seemed to threaten the country the armaments ought to be directed.[3] This last point referred, on the one hand, to the risk of a Danish attempt to reverse the verdict of the peace of Brömsebro; and, on the other, to the threat to Sweden's actual or potential interests in the Baltic which might arise from the prevailing turmoil

[1] A.A. von Stiernman, ed. *Alla riksdagars och mötens besluth* (Stockholm 1728), II, 1233–4.
[2] See above, pp. 75–7.
[3] *Svenska Rikstrådets Protokoll* (*RRP*) XVI. 11–12.

in eastern Europe, and in particular from Tsar Alexis's invasion of Poland in the spring of 1654. After four days of debate, in the course of which the Danish option at first had strong support, the Council decided to advise the king that Sweden should arm; that the arming should be offensive; and that it should be directed to the danger from the east.[4]

II

The decade which followed the Westphalian settlement brought no peace to Europe. Though exhaustion imposed comparative calm upon Germany, the dragging Franco-Spanish duel continued, in Flanders and in Italy; the Portuguese struggle for independence likewise; and new crises came to reinforce the old: the Ukrainian revolt; the first Anglo-Dutch war; Cromwell's assault upon the Indies, and the war which was its consequence; clashes between Dutch and Portuguese in Brazil which for a moment seemed likely to involve both France and England. In this stormy weather Swedish policy after 1650 was marked, as a rule, by caution and restraint.[5] The ending of French subsidies suggested that this was by no means a time for expensive initiatives, and there was a correspondingly diminished concern for the affairs of Germany. Sweden's interest in the federative movements was cool; and the leadership of German Protestantism seemed for the moment likely to pass into the hands of Brunswick or Brandenburg.[6] Queen Christina, even while her religious principles were still unquestioned, looked a less convincing champion of the Protestant Cause than her father, and for valid political and personal reasons she cultivated the good-will of the Habsburgs, both in Vienna and in Madrid. In the face of the Anglo-Dutch war, Swedish statesmen were resolute in rejecting invitations to ally with one belligerent or the other, and devoted themselves to serious efforts to establish, with Denmark, a common front of neutrality, each country being anxious to keep the naval operations well away from the Sound.[7] The view eastward from Stockholm induced – though less consistently – much the same disposition to be

[4] *RRP* XVI. 35–6.
[5] Sven Ingemar Olofsson, *Efter Westfaliska freden. Sveriges yttre politik 1650–1654* (Kungl. Vitterhets Historie och Antikvitets Akademiens Handlingar. Historiska serien 4) (Stockholm 1957) is the fullest and best account of Swedish foreign policy in this period.
[6] Hjalmar Crohns, *Sveriges politik i förhallånde till de federativa rörelserna i Tyskland, 1650–1658* (Helsingfors 1901), I *passim*; Olofsson, *Efter Westfaliska Freden*, pp. 83–6, 91, 150 ff., 361–79, 409–44.
[7] *RRP* XV. 477–8 for Oxenstierna's decisive interview with van Beuningen, 24 September 1653; Åke Lindqvist, *Politiska förbindelser mellan Sverige och Danmark 1648–55* (Lund 1944), pp. 102–5, 136–8; Olofsson, *Efter Westfaliska freden*. pp. 271–90, 479–94, and chapter X; Birgit

quiet. As Swedish statesmen contemplated the crisis in Poland which followed Chmelnicki's revolt, though they watched it with attention, kept themselves well informed, and engaged in occasional intrigues which led nowhere,[8] it was only occasionally that they seriously contemplated fishing in these troubled waters.[9] They had, indeed, important controversies with Poland, and sooner or later they must settle them: the claim of the Polish Vasas to the Swedish throne, or at least to the Swedish royal title; the claim of the Polish Republic to Livonia, conquered by Sweden after 1626; and on the other hand the desire of the Swedes for the recovery of 'royal' Prussia and the 'licences' levied at its ports:[10] assets of great financial importance which had in 1635 been temporarily lost in terms of the truce of Stuhmsdorf. That truce was due to expire in 1661, and it was the earnest wish of Axel Oxenstierna and his colleagues to conclude a firm peace with Poland before it did so. But conferences at Lübeck in 1651 and 1652–3 had ended in deadlock; John Casimir of Poland would not abate one jot of his pretensions; the Swedes would neither hand back Livonia nor abandon the hope of regaining what they had lost. At the *riksdag* of 1652 there were prolonged debates on the desirability of forestalling their enemies by an attack on either Denmark or Poland.[11] Queen Christina, for the moment donning the helmet of Bellona, urged that this would be a good moment to attack Poland and recover what had been lost 'and perhaps even more'; though Oxenstierna soberly observed that 'to flounder into a war would be a grave matter'.[12] At all events, Christina and the Council in 1652 gave consideration to a plan of attack on Poland which foreshadowed the strategy employed by Charles X in 1655; and they were keenly conscious that the native army was much in need of reinforcement.[13] But these impulses were not pursued, and were indeed nullified beforehand by the prevailing financial stringency.[14] As to the Ukrainian upheaval, Oxenstierna's view was that Cossacks, in general, were a nuisance that ought to be abated; and he

---

Grabe, 'Den nordiska allianstanken under holländsk-engelska kriget', *Historisk tidskrift* (1938), pp. 270–87.

[8] Bohdan Kentrschynskyj, 'Ukrainska revolutionen och Rysslands angrepp mot Sverige 1656', *Karolinska Förbundets Årsbok [KFÅ]* (1966), pp. 25–33.

[9] Bohdan Kentrschynskyj, 'Till den karolinska Ukraina-politikens förhistoria', *KFÅ* (1959).

[10] For their importance see Einar Wendt, *Det svenska licentväsendet i Preussen 1627–1635* (Uppsala 1933).

[11] *Svenska ridderskaps och adels riksdagsprotokoll* (SRARP) v₁. 114ff.

[12] *Ibid.* 123, 115–16.

[13] *Ibid.* 103, 116 ff.

[14] Yet Georg Landberg wrote 'Time and again [in 1652–3] there are signs of the idea of using the disturbed situation to attack Denmark or Poland': Georg Landberg, *Den svenska utrikespolitikens historia*, section I, part 3, *1648–1697* (Stockholm 1952).

took upon himself to advise Tsar Alexis to have no truck with them.[15] Alexis, however, had other ideas. The treaty of Pereyaslavl in March 1654 incorporated the Cossack community into the Russian state;[16] and it was followed almost immediately by a Muscovite invasion of Poland, seconded by a renewed Cossack onslaught.

As long as Christina reigned and Axel Oxenstierna lived this new twist to the confused situation in south-east Europe had little visible effect in Stockholm. Since the 1630s Sweden had regarded Muscovy as a friend to be relied on, in virtue of a common enmity to Poland; and it was the constant hope of Swedish statesmen to induce the Tsar to agree to the channelling of Russian trade to the West through Swedish-controlled ports in the Baltic.[17] This confidence was reflected in the Proposition to the *riksdag* on 11 May 1654, when the Estates were assured that Alexis's invasion of Poland implied no threat to Swedish interests;[18] and it was in reliance on Swedish good-will (and perhaps as a test of it) that the Tsar turned to Oxenstierna with a request to buy 20,000 muskets for his army.[19] Nevertheless, though men in Stockholm might be slow to admit it, the advance of Russian troops into Poland did radically change the situation: even Oxenstierna found it prudent to respond to the Tsar's request for muskets by cutting down to 4,000 the number he was prepared to provide. For though the thrust of the Russian invasion might be towards White Russia, the debility of the Polish republic might conceivably tempt the Tsar to enterprises which would put him in possession of areas long considered to be of vital interest to Sweden: in the first place, Livonia, which it seemed that the Russians might encircle, or even overrun. Equally alarming was the possibility of a Muscovite advance into royal Prussia, culminating – in the very worst case – in the taking of Danzig, and the consequent control of all the trade that flowed down the Vistula. The Peace of Stolbova, as Gustav Adolf had triumphantly proclaimed, had shut off Muscovy from access to the Baltic;[20] but it was unlikely that the Tsars would for ever accept that situation. A determination to open a window to the sea, once attained in the time of Ivan IV, was in fact the master-element in the foreign policy advocated by the Tsar's minister,

[15] *RRP* xv. 4 (17 January 1651); Kentrschynskyj, 'Till den karolinska Ukraina-politikens förhistoria', p. 177.

[16] A. Choulguine, 'Le traité de Péreyaslav', *Révue historique* (1959).

[17] See *Ekonomiska förbindelser mellan Sverige och Ryssland under 1600-talet. Dokument ur svenska arkiv*, ed. A. Attman, A.L. Narotjnitskij et al. (Stockholm 1978).

[18] *SRARP* v₂. 283.

[19] Olofsson, *Efter Westfaliska freden*, pp. 528–9.

[20] *Tal och skrifter av Konung Gustav II Adolf*, ed. Carl Hallenberg (Stockholm 1915), pp. 134–5.

Ordyn-Nashchokin, in the full consciousness that this must entail a war with Sweden; and though for the present Alexis inclined rather to the policy of Nikon and Matveev, who preferred advances in a more south-westerly direction, it could not be assumed that their influence would continue to prevail.[21] Russian mercantile and commercial ambitions did not go unremarked in the College of Commerce. By the late summer of 1654 it was no longer possible to accept Axel Oxenstierna's tradition of friendship with Moscow without reservations, or to swallow the anodyne declaration that nothing was to be apprehended from Russian actions in Poland. It had become patent that Swedish foreign policy must be reassessed in the light of what was happening on the other side of the water. It seems very probable that Charles appreciated that fact; though the 'impenetrability' upon which more than one historian has remarked[22] makes any precise statement on the point hazardous. When in December he submitted his questions to the Council he took care not to be present at their debates: it suited him better to make sure that whatever the outcome the responsibility should be theirs as well as his, with no ground for recriminations later.

III

Such was the situation, such the problems, which confronted Charles on his accession. How did he react to them? When and why was the decision to attack Poland taken? Does it represent an enforced capitulation to circumstances, or was it the implementation of a deliberate policy?

The answer to these questions must, to a considerable degree, be conjectural, for surviving evidence does not enable us to see very far into the king's mind, particularly in 1654. But until 1956 there was among Swedish historians a fairly general disposition to agree that the answer to the last of them must be in the affirmative: Poland, they thought, really was his objective; though they might differ as to the moment when it certainly became so.[23] In 1956, however, there appeared in *Karolinska Förbundets Årsbok* a weighty article by Bohdan Kentrschynskyj which advanced a quite different interpretation.[24] Kentrschynskyj had the advantage of a command of all the

[21] Bohdan Kentrschynskyj, 'Karl X Gustav inför krisen i öster 1654–1655, *KFÅ* (1956), p. 9.

[22] Among others, Nils Edén, 'Grunderna för Karl X Gustafs anfall på Polen', *Historisk tidskrift* (1906), pp. 17–18.

[23] So Pufendorf, Anders Fryxell, F.F. Carlson, Ellen Fries, Nils Edén, Gustaf Jacobson, Sten Bonnesen, Georg Landberg.

[24] Kentrschynskyj, 'Karl X Gustav'.

Slavonic languages (not to mention others such as Magyar and Rumanian); he was himself of Ukrainian origin; a warm Ukrainian patriot, writing in the era of the Cold War. No previous historian had based his argument upon such an overwhelming abundance of material, spanning the whole of northern and eastern Europe. He followed this article with others which shed important new light on Chmelnicki's revolt and its consequences both for Europe in general and for Sweden in particular. Thus armed with sources inaccessible to most previous Swedish historians, he propounded an explanation of the events of 1654–5 whose main theses may be summarised as follows: from the outset of the reign – and indeed probably already before Charles's accession – the king had realised, more clearly than any of his countrymen, that the most serious threat to Sweden's safety, now and in the predictable future, lay in the expansive might of Russia and the Tsar's designs upon the Baltic ports. It followed that Sweden had no alternative but to meet the onward march of what the Swedes were in the habit of referring to as 'Russian barbarism', and to meet it at once before it became too formidable. Charles was thus the forerunner and political ancestor of Charles XII. In the face of this threat there was one logical ally: Poland. His policy, therefore, until the late spring of 1655, was not a war with Poland, but a Polish alliance; and he attacked Poland when that hope proved to be vain. It was not mainly, as Carlson and Edén had maintained, a question of 'better to forestall than be forestalled',[25] nor was it true that Russia was no more than one factor in what for them was the main question – i.e. 'the coastlands' (sjökanten). The whole Polish adventure was therefore to be regarded as what he termed 'a parenthesis', the inconvenient postponement of a consistent design which would be resumed after the parenthesis had been dealt with.

Fourteen years later, in 1970, Kentrschynskyj's article was challenged by Birger Åsard.[26] From an examination of the military preparations which were made in the spring of 1654 and the months that followed, Åsard came to the conclusion that the objective must have been not Russia but Poland, and in particular royal Prussia. Not all historians have been prepared to accept his argument.[27] It therefore seemed that it might be useful to look again at the evidence

---

[25] Kentrschynskyj, 'Karl X Gustav', pp. 132–3 – a dictum which does not square too well with his earlier remark: 'Even if the Russians were to be content to leave the Swedish provinces unmolested and direct their attention exclusively to the Polish coastlands, they must be forestalled and prevented from attaining their objective': ibid., p. 46.

[26] Birger Åsard, 'Upptakten till Karl X Gustavs anfall mot Polen 1655. Till frågan om krigets mål och medel', KFÅ (1970).

[27] Lars Tersmeden, Carl X Gustafs Armé (Carl X Gustaf-studier, 8) (1979), pp. 124, 227 n. 64. Kentrschynskyj was by this time dead.

which Kentrschynskyj adduced, and to re-examine, more fully than
Åsard did, the inferences which he drew from it.

IV

First, then, what do we know about the king's attitudes before
December 1654? At the moment of his accession Axel Oxenstierna's
traditional policy of friendship with Russia still held the field, as the
Proposition to the *riksdag* on 11 May plainly testified. Indeed, it had
seemed possible that relations might be drawn still closer, for in
January the Tsar had offered an alliance, and Oxenstierna was
reported by the Danish envoy Peder Juel to be hesitating whether to
consider the proposal or not.[28] And when the Polish emissary
Canasilles – apparently with the object of repairing the damage done
by his earlier refusal to acknowledge Charles as Christina's legitimate
successor – proposed a defensive alliance against Russia, he was
coldly informed that Sweden had no need of such an alliance, her
relations with the Tsar being entirely satisfactory.[29] Whether they
would continue to be so satisfactory was another matter. It was
ominous that after the treaty of Pereyaslavl the Tsar assumed new
titles, some of them expressive of Muscovy's historic pretensions:
henceforth, it was to be understood, Ingria, Karelia, and Kexholms
län were to be accounted part of the Tsar's *votchina*. The Swedish
government took no action apart from declining to accept the Tsar's
new relationship with the Ukraine;[30] but they can hardly have failed
to feel uneasy. A more immediate Russian ambition was probably
Kurland, for Duke Jacob had created a small but efficient navy; and if
that fleet should pass under Russian control the Tsar might eventually be in a position to challenge that *dominium maris* which all
Swedish governments had been asserting for the last thirty years.
Charles had been anxious on this score already before his accession.[31]
Yet for the first few months of the reign it is hard to discern any
clearly defined policy towards Russia. It was not until July that the
progress of the Tsar's armies in Poland provoked an overt reaction.
On 22 July orders were sent to Gustav Horn, the General-Governor
of Livonia, to look to the defences of the province: a very necessary
step, for on Charles's accession the garrisons in Balticum numbered

[28] F.F. Carlson, *Sveriges historia under konungarne af pfalziska huset* (Stockholm 1855), I. 166
n. 2.

[29] Ellen Fries, *Erik Oxenstierna, Biografisk studie* (Stockholm 1889), p. 210. The dramatic
narrative of the Canasilles-affair in Pufendorf is reduced to its proper proportions in Edén,
'Grunderna för Karl X Gustafs anfall på Polen', pp. 20–2.

[30] Kentrschynskyj, 'Ukrainska revolutionen', p. 34.

[31] Sven Ingemar Olofsson, *Karl X. Gustav. Hertigen – Tronföljaren* (Stockholm 1961), p. 245.

only 6,125 men.[32] Further orders to Horn in August showed mounting anxiety, as the situation in Poland became more alarming: they culminated in an order of 9 September giving Horn full authority to take any steps he might think necessary without now being constrained by any concern lest the Russians should take offence at the movement of troops to the frontiers.[33] There can be little doubt that this last order was written under the influence of the news, which arrived in Stockholm on that same 9 September, of the annihilation of Janusz Radziwiłł's army at the battle of Szepelewicze.[34] But the sense of crisis which obtained on 9 September seems to have died down, for the moment; no doubt because Horn's report of 17 September was to the effect that the Tsar's objective in the immediate future was not Livonia but Smoleńsk; that his strategy was to secure his communications with Chmelnicki by occupying the country between Smoleńsk and Kiev; and that in any case it would be unwise to give him 'any unseasonable ground for taking umbrage'.[35] In short, Charles was exhorted not to panic.

As to Russia, then, it seems a reasonable assumption that at this time he was more concerned with providing adequate defensive measures against a possible emergency than with any plan of attack; and there seems only Kentrschynskyj's bare assertion to support the idea that he had such a plan in mind from the earliest days of his reign. Outwardly, relations with the Tsar are still friendly: the king lets him have 8,000 muskets;[36] care is taken to avoid provocative military movements which might be misconstrued; Horn is instructed not to get involved in Poland. As things stood, Sweden had as yet no quarrel with Russia; but indubitably had one with Poland. What was Charles's attitude to that quarrel? Did he already regard Poland as the logical ally?

In the early fifties Charles had on more than one occasion expressed anxiety lest John Casimir might be meditating war; and in January 1653 he was thinking in terms of a preemptive strike against Poland.[37] That, of course, is no indication of what he may have been thinking in the rather different circumstances of 1654. Nevertheless, the idea, if he still had it, does not seem to have been peculiar to himself, if we may believe the Danish diplomat Peder Juel, who

---

[32] Tersmeden, in *Carl X Gustafs armé*, pp. 235, Appendix 1.

[33] Kentrschynskyj, 'Karl X Gustav', pp. 35 n. 1, 36 n. 8, 37 nn. 9–12; Edén, 'Grunderna för Karl X Gustavs anfall på Polen', pp. 23–4.

[34] Kentrschynskyj, 'Karl X Gustav', p. 36 n. 8, citing John Thurloe, *A Collection of State Papers* (1742), II. 593, for the date.

[35] Kentrschynkyj, 'Karl X Gustav', p. 37 n. 12.

[36] Olofsson, *Efter Westfaliska freden*, p. 529.

[37] Carlson, *Sveriges historia*, I. 149 nn., 158 n. 4; Fries, *Erik Oxenstierna*, p. 350 n. 2.

reported to his government soon after the receipt in Stockholm of the news of the treaty of Pereyaslavl 'they entertain some hope here of possessing themselves of Prussia, no matter by what means'.[38] Yet when (rather late: not until August) Johan Kock was sent to Warsaw to announce Charles's accession, his instructions contained no hint of menace.[39] His reception was correct, if hardly cordial, and John Casimir gave Charles his title without any other reservation than a reminder of their 'fraternal relationship'. But Kock's mission had other purposes of a less formal nature. By this time the king was clearly very anxious for information about what was really happening in Poland and what the Poles were thinking about it. Kock was therefore to reconnoitre, and to ascertain ('discreetly') what the prospects were of Poland's making peace with the Tsar; or whether perhaps the Republic might be willing to look for aid to Sweden, and on that basis he prepared to renew the negotiations which had been broken off in 1653. But before Kock's report could arrive, Charles's impatience had led him, on 30 September, to send Johan Meyer af Lilienthal to conduct a more thorough investigation. He was given a comprehensive assignment. He was to find out whether the Poles would seek help from the Emperor; whether parts of the country were likely to put themselves under the protection of the Habsburgs, or of George II Rákóczy of Transylvania, or of the Elector of Brandenburg (possibilities which were almost equally disagreeable); whether the Tsar would be content if he regained what had been lost at the peace of Polyanovo (1634), or if, perhaps, he intended to subject the whole of Poland; what the attitude of the Estates of Prussia would be in the event of a Russian conquest; and whether after making peace Poland and Russia were likely to combine against Sweden.[40] The answer to some of these enquiries must necessarily be speculative; and equally speculative are any conjectures as to the precise considerations that inspired them. But if it should turn out later that one of the motives which was to determine Charles's actions was 'better forestall than be forestalled', it is tempting to think that behind this questionnaire may have lain some idea of this kind. However that may be, Lilienthal's report, which arrived in Stockholm on 23 November, had solid information of the most disturbing kind: it was a devastating description of the chaos, dissensions, and military weakness of the country. In Nils Edén's view it

---

[38] Carlson, *Sveriges historia*, I. 166 n. 2.
[39] Kentrschynskyj, 'Karl X Gustav', p. 38; Edén, 'Grunderna för Karl X Gustavs anfall på Polen', p. 134; Gustaf Jacobson, *Karl X Gustav* (*Sveriges historia till våra dagar*, VII) (Stockholm 1926), p. 272. But contrast Fries, *Erik Oxenstierna*, p. 210 and Åsard, 'Upptakten', p. 16.
[40] Kentrschynskyj, 'Karl X Gustav', p. 41.

was decisive in determining the king to put his questions to the Council in December.[41]

Kentrschynskyj did not think so. The situation in Poland, he contended, was no worse at the time of Lilienthal's mission than it had been before it: Lilienthal's report can therefore have had no great influence.[42] But even conceding that it may have been a matter of some delicacy to assess the precise degree of Polish demoralisation, Kentrschynskyj's judgment ignored two major catastrophes: the first, the battle of Szepelewicze; the second, the Russians' success in taking Smoleńsk. The news of the fall of Smoleńsk reached Stockholm on 16 November. [43] The arrival of Lilienthal's report, a week later, must surely have led Charles and his advisers to feel that Polish affairs had reached a crisis. And that feeling must have been strengthened by the tidings that came from the Hague. Since the end of March the Swedish agent Harald Appelboom had been reporting to Stockholm on the progress of the negotiations which Nicolas de Bye, John Casimir's private agent, was conducting with the Dutch. They resulted in a draft treaty which would have provided John Casimir with a fleet of his own, a large Dutch subsidy to pay for it, and the promise of Dutch naval support to the extent of twenty ships in case of war.[44] This was a flagrant violation of the truce of Stuhmsdorf, which had laid it down (Article XXI) that Poland should neither keep a fleet of war in the Baltic, nor assist any other power to do so.[45] Even before Lilienthal's report reached Stockholm this was known to the king, and its influence can be seen in his letter to Appelboom of 18 November, in which he commented on vague Dutch proposals for an anti-Habsburg league by indicating that he considered them as designed to amuse him 'until they can attack us, with Poland and perhaps with Denmark'.[46] He might well feel that Sweden was menaced with a threat to her *dominium maris* more immediate (and more formidable) than any contingent threat from Kurland; and the way would have been barred to any settlement with Poland which restored royal Prussia to Sweden, with all the economic advantages which its recovery would bring with it.

There is one circumstance which might suggest that even before Charles's accession he could have been thinking in terms of a

---

[41] Edén. 'Grunderna för Karl X Gustavs anfall på Polen', p. 27.

[42] Kentrschynskyj, 'Karl X Gustav', p. 33.

[43] Arne Munthe, *Studier i drottning Kristinas och reduktionens historia* (Studier utg. av Svenska Riksarkivet, 2) (Stockholm 1971), p. 47 n. 39, citing Christer Bonde's journal.

[44] Åke Lindqvist, 'Svenskarna och de Byes beskickningar 1654–1655', *KFÅ* (1941), pp. 10, 16–17.

[45] *Sverges traktater med främmande magter*, v₂. 34.

[46] Carlson, *Sveriges historia*, I, 170 n. 1.

reconquest of this territory. Among the bitterly contested issues raised by the abdication of Queen Christina had been the provision of dower-lands upon whose revenues she could live in a style appropriate to her dignity. In the prevailing financial stringency this could be contrived only by a fairly sweeping *reduktion* of donations now in the hands of the nobility, and in particular of the 'ducal domains' in Pomerania which had been alienated to great magnates and leading army commanders. These interested parties naturally fought hard to keep their lands; and their resistance was overcome only when Charles, whose accession was only a few days ahead, placated them with a promise that those who were to be sacrificed should obtain compensation.[47] But where, at a time when plans for a *reduktion* were already under discussion between Christina, Herman Fleming, and Charles himself, was such compensation to be found, without compromising the economic reform which was their objective? To alienate crown estates in the Swedish dominions would make nonsense of their policy. Charles's promise provided the answer to this difficulty; and it was an answer which was apparently convincing, for it proved acceptable. Is it not at least possible that he undertook that they should have their 'compensation' in Poland? At all events, on 8 July 1655 – at a moment when he was still at Dalarö waiting to sail for Pomerania – Beata de la Gardie, who was one of the victims of the Pomeranian *reduktion*, appealed to the king for compensation *in Poland*.[48] Was she claiming a promise? Or was she only exceptionally quick off the mark?

This is mere conjecture, but it is in a measure supported by the affair of Schlippenbach's mission. Schlippenbach had been sent in July to the courts of Germany to give formal notice of Charles's accession. Upon his arrival in Berlin he had taken upon himself to propose to the Elector of Brandenburg an alliance on the basis of joint action in Poland; and had declared that Charles for his part desired the acquisition of royal Prussia, with some harbours (perhaps Pillau and Memel) in ducal Prussia also. This produced an immediate protest from the Elector, and Schlippenbach was eventually disavowed by his government. But the Brandenburg envoy in Stockholm, Dobrczensky, was nevertheless of the opinion that Schlippenbach had in fact blurted out the king's real intentions; and when at the end of the year Bartholomeus Wolfsberg was sent to

---

[47] For the difficulty about compensation see Sven Ingemar Olofsson, *Drottning Christinas tronavsägelse och trosförändring* (Uppsala 1953), pp. 189–90, 197–203; Munthe, *Studier*, p. 38 n. 19.

[48] G.H. von Essen, *Alienationer och reduktioner i f.d. svenska Pommern* (Stockholm 1900), p. 47 and n.

Brandenburg with the formal disavowal, that disavowal did indeed disclaim any designs upon the Elector's ports; but it renewed the suggestion of a common policy towards Poland, and it was significantly silent about royal Prussia.[49] On the whole, it seems not improbable that Dobrczensky was correct in his conjecture. Nils Edén summarily dismissed the episode as giving no sure evidence of Charles's intentions.[50] But though Schlippenbach may have been a blundering diplomat,[51] he had been the confidential intermediary between Christina and her successor in the weeks preceding her abdication,[52] and he is perhaps as likely as any other to have been aware of Charles's real views – even though (as Edén objected) there survives no written evidence of any communication to him on the question. A private conversation may have been enough to prompt Schlippenbach to an indiscretion. And what, after all, was the Swedish share in any 'common policy' likely to be?

These are speculations; but one thing at least is certain: that from the outset of the reign – and indeed even before it – Sweden was vigorously rearming; and of this Kentrschynskyj (like all his predecessors) was unaware. It was upon this fact that Åsard mainly rested his argument. In March Charles had a meeting with Axel Oxenstierna at Eskilstuna, and it seems to have been then decided that there should be a very large-scale mobilisation of the native army. The desirability – and the difficulties – of an increase in the size of the militia had been pointed out already in 1652; but little had been done.[53] But now it was a very different story. By December 1654, 158 companies of native foot had been mobilised in Sweden, and a further 78 in Finland; and of these, 58 Swedish companies had been sent to Pomerania, and a further 24 were scheduled to go there; while 52 of the Finland companies had been transferred to the Baltic provinces.[54] The distribution of the new levies, and especially the size of the reinforcements sent to Pomerania, might well suggest that they were destined for action against Poland: whatever the case as regards Livonia, Pomerania did not in March 1654 appear to be in immediate danger. Åsard contended that what we are seeing is the revival of the plan which had been mooted in 1652, for a pincer-movement against royal Prussia from Pomerania and Livonia simultaneously.[55] The

[49] Fries, *Erik Oxenstierna*, pp. 215–16.
[50] Edén, 'Grunderna för Karl X Gustavs anfall på Polen', p. 19.
[51] If so, that did not prevent Charles from continuing to employ him on diplomatic missions, and consulting him on critical occasions: see below, p. 138 n. 192.
[52] See, e.g., Olofsson, *Drottning Christinas tronavsägelse*, pp. 186–9, 204.
[53] *RRP* xv. 116–25.
[54] Åsard, 'Upptakten till Karl X Gustavs anfall', p. 34.
[55] *Ibid.*, pp. 12–13; cf. Edén, 'Grunderna för Karl X Gustavs anfall på Polen', p. 17.

timing of the decision to mobilise is certainly suggestive. The meeting at Eskilstuna occurred at the beginning of March. The news of the treaty of Pereyaslavl seems to have reached Stockholm by 24 March. The Proposition to the *riksdag*, declaring that Sweden had nothing to fear from Russia, is of 11 May. Already before Christina's abdication troops were being fitted out to move, not, as might perhaps have been expected, to Bremen but to Pomerania.[56] It seems unlikely, then, that the mobilisation was directed(at all events, in the first instance) against Russia.

Equally significant are the measures taken for the raising of mercenaries. Hans Landberg believed that this did not begin until the conclusion of the war with Bremen – that is, until after the signing of the convention of Stade on 28 November 1654.[57] But in fact it began some months earlier. In July, contracts to raise mercenary regiments were concluded with Königsmarck, G.O. Stenbock, and other Swedish enterprisers.[58] Alexander Leslie, earl of Leven, who arrived in Stockholm on 7 July,[59] thought the moment opportune to offer to raise a regiment of 2,000 Scots for the Swedish service, but was informed that a commission to do so had already been issued to Robert Douglas, until recently Christina's Master of the Horse.[60] The initiatives thus taken in the spring and summer were greatly expanded from October onwards, and were now on a scale appropriate to a major war.[61] The convention of Stade left the regiments who had been fighting in Bremen unemployed. It was impossible financially – or at least, highly inconvenient – to disband them; but they might, no doubt, have been quartered on Bremen–Verden. Instead, they were transferred to the already overburdened Pomerania.

Taking all these circumstances together, it is difficult to see them as evidence for a settled design to confront the Russians. The indications are rather that the reinforcements for Livonia are intended to be precautionary and defensive; care is to be taken to avoid provoking the Tsar; and after the arrival of Horn's reassuring letter of 17

[56] Munthe, *Studier*, pp. 36–7.

[57] Hans Landberg, *Krig på kredit. Svensk rustningsfinansiering våren 1655.* (Carl X Gustavs-studier, 4) (Stockholm 1969), p. 10.

[58] Tersmeden, *Carl X Gustafs armé*, p. 119.

[59] Wilbur C. Abbott, ed., *The Writings and Speeches of Oliver Cromwell* (Cambridge, Mass., 1907–47), III. 268.

[60] Peter Julius Coyet to Charles X, 27 April 1655, reporting a conversation with Leven: printed in summary in M. Roberts, ed., *Swedish Diplomats at Cromwell's Court* (London 1988), p. 60. There is no mention of this in Archibald Douglas, *Robert Douglas, En krigaregestalt från storhetstiden* (Stockholm 1957): he did not raise a regiment (of dragoons) until October 1655: *ibid.*, p. 182.

[61] Tersmeden, *Carl X Gustafs armé*, p. 120, who gratuitously adds: 'a war with Russia'.

September the anxiety about Livonia seems to diminish. But it is replaced by anxiety about Poland: internal chaos, as reported by Lilienthal; Dutch interference, as foreshadowed by Appelboom. If, as the disposition of the newly embodied troops might suggest, the object was to have them conveniently available for a campaign in royal Prussia, they might be robbed of that opportunity either by a Polish collapse and a Russian advance to Danzig, or by a Dutch rescue-operation which would at least make Danzig a prime objective, and so deprive Sweden of the most valuable prize which a campaign in Prussia had to offer. It looks likely, then, that by the end of November Charles's main fear in regard to Prussia may have been that the Tsar (or the Dutch) might forestall him. Whether this is a justified inference or not, the record of the months from the accession to the Council meetings of December enforces one conclusion: though it may be uncertain at this stage against what enemy he was preparing – it might be Poland, it might be Russia; that would depend, perhaps, on how the military situation developed, and a little, maybe, upon the efficacy of diplomacy – there can be no doubt that he was contemplating a major war, and had probably been doing so since March. The raising of more and more mercenary regiments, the impossibility of any domestic financial measures which would yield returns speedy and abundant enough to enable him to make cash settlements with all the enterprisers with whom he was contracting, left their employment in active operations the only option open to him.

The purpose of the Council meetings in December, therefore, was not to advise him on the issue of war and peace, but rather to endorse increased recruiting, and to canvass opinion as to the most eligible enemy. But the ultimate decision for war – timing, method, objective – was to be left in the hands of the king, who must take his chance at a *riksdag* in the hope that the assembled Estates would be as unable to withstand a *fait accompli* as the Council had been.[62] In all this there was nothing new: in 1652 Council, Secret Committee, and *riksdag* had been asked much the same questions, had made not very dissimilar answers, and had happily thrown the decision into the hands of the queen.[63] In that year the domestic situation was such that Christina had been in no position to make use of the discretion that was given to her. In 1654 her successor had firmer ground to stand on, a more pressing need for action, and perhaps a more clearly formulated purpose.

[62] This is the argument of Hans Landberg, 'Decemberrådslagen 1654, Karl X Gustav, rådet och rustningsfrågan', *KFÅ* (1968).
[63] *SRARP* v₁. 113, 117, 118, 121.

V

From the time of F.F. Carlson to the present the four meetings of the
Council on 7, 8, 11, and 12 December have attracted the attention of
those historians who deal with the origins of the Polish war;[64] the
most recent contribution to the debate being that of Hans Landberg.
No record of the meeting on the 7th appears to have survived, and
the minute of that on the 8th begins in the middle of a discussion; but
for the meetings on the 11th and 12th the minutes appear to be
reasonably full. That does not mean that they are easy to follow:
Edén (not alone) found them 'somewhat confused'.[65] Decisions,
apparently firm, may be taken at one meeting and the same issues
discussed as it were *de novo* at the next; speakers may take discrepant
attitudes at successive meetings; the position of the Chancellor, Erik
Oxenstierna, as the king's presumed spokesman, seems at times to
be usurped by his colleague the High Steward, Per Brahe. The two
best and fullest accounts are those of Edén and Kentrschynskyj:
Kentrschynskyj, in particular, clears up the matter of the missing
minutes, offers a convincing explanation of the three days' delay
between the second and third meetings, and displays the structure of
the discussions more clearly than any of his predecessors. But in
order to get the debate into perspective, to trace the fluctuation of
opinion, and to mark the critical points which facilitated (or constrained) its resolution into something not far from unanimity, it is
desirable, and indeed necessary, to adhere strictly to chronology; for
it is all too easy, and may well be misleading, to confuse the speeches
of one day with those delivered on another. Both Edén and Kentrschynskyj fall into this trap on occasion.[66] Both, moreover, slur over,
or miss, what appear to be significant points. Each interprets the
record differently; each arrives at a conclusion which could not be
accepted by the other. There is nothing for it, then, but to conduct
our own examination of the text for the three days for which a record
is available.

The truncated report of the meeting on the 8th begins in the
middle of what is probably a speech by Erik Oxenstierna, from
which it appears that at least some of them are willing to contemplate
a war, if it is '*cum honestate coniunctum*': indeed, there follows a
somewhat discursive and unorganised discussion which Oxenstierna
summarises as being '*generale* on *honestate et utilitate belli*'.[67] It is
difficult to believe that this was no more than an abstract philosophi-

---

[64] A remarkable (and, it seems, unique) exception is Sten Bonnesen.
[65] Edén, 'Grunderna för Karl X Gustavs anfall på Polen', p. 29.
[66] E.g. *ibid.*, pp. 30–1; Kentrschynskyj, 'Karl X Gustav', pp. 62–5.
[67] *RRP* xvi. 3, 6.

cal debate about international ethics. However that may have been, throughout the next three meetings Oxenstierna is seen repeatedly intervening to point out that they are *not* talking of going to war, for that is a matter for the *riksdag* to settle with the king. But as the discussions proceed these reminders become ever more clearly formal and irrelevant: they are tributes to constitutional propriety; they offer a useful escape-clause from responsibility. Members slip easily enough from talking about mobilisation to talking about war: even Oxenstierna himself, in incautious moments, is no exception. The reason for this is sufficiently obvious. On 7 December, as the debate on the 8th makes clear, they had already accepted that arming was necessary: the king's question on this point had answered itself already; and what he was really asking them was their approval of arming on a larger scale. But in view of the fact that Sweden was in no financial condition to provide the cash outlay that would be required, 'the contentment of the soldiery' (to borrow the ominous phrase which had dominated the closing years of the Thirty Years War) almost inevitably meant their employment: as Per Brahe said, even at this early stage, 'to put ourselves in such a state of readiness as to be able to sit still, without 6 or 7 German regiments (for less would be scarcely adequate) is to make war on ourselves'.[68] His colleagues can scarcely have been unaware of the point. As Kentrschynskyj rightly remarked, 'from the start their ideas seem to go beyond purely defensive preparations'.[69]

More difficult was the second question: against whom should their arming be designed? – against dangers threatening from the west, or against those impending in the east?, against Denmark, or against the possibilities inherent in the Russian–Polish conflict? This was no new dilemma: it had perplexed men already in 1652, when it was much debated in the Secret Committee, though the alternatives then – more precisely than in 1654 – were Denmark or Poland?[70] The Chancellor at this stage came down decidedly in favour of arming against Denmark, on the ground that it was necessary to secure the entrance to the Sound before venturing on any other undertaking.[71] Karl Gustav Wrangel supported him; and Christer Bonde, among other points, alleged the possibility of Danish involvement in the plans which de Bye was known to be hatching in Holland.[72] On the other hand, Per Brahe gave a vivid and alarming picture of the

[68] *Ibid.* 5.
[69] Kentrschynskyj, 'Karl X Gustav', p. 56. Contrast Hans Landberg, 'Decemberrådslagen 1654', pp. 52–4.
[70] *SRARP* v₁. 114.
[71] *RRP* XVI. 3–4.
[72] *RRP* XVI. 6–7.

growing might and 'insolence' of the Tsar.[73] But though his arguments for arming against the east were strong, and though he was
afraid that the Tsar might be contemplating large territorial gains in
Poland, he did not at this stage appear to be advocating war. Still less
was this the case with some of the others. Gustav Adolf Leijonhufvud feared that if Sweden were involved in a war with Russia
'others might start something against us';[74] Carl Soop was decidedly
against 'letting rip against the Russians'.[75] Bengt Skytte thought the
danger from Russia exaggerated, and Magnus Gabriel de la Gardie
inclined to the same opinion.[76] The Council, it is plain, was far from
unanimous. But the Chancellor, on whom Per Brahe's eloquence
had already made an impression, pointed out that the king was
expecting a Polish emissary any day, that their advice was required
before his arrival, and that there was no time for protracted discussion; and he put it to the meeting that most members were in favour
of arming against the east: to which somewhat precipitate conclusion
'all members assented'.[77]

Having reached this point they began to consider the implications
of their decision. What, for instance, was to be their attitude to
Poland? Once again Per Brahe intervened with a speech which was
ultimately to be decisive. He contended that Sweden was now
presented with a great – perhaps a unique – opportunity: an opportunity not merely to settle the old controversies about the royal title
and about Livonia, but also to secure important advantages – territorial, and therefore economic also – at Poland's expense. After
dilating on Poland's weakness and inability to stand up to threats, he
suggested that in return for 'certain concessions' Sweden might
render to Poland 'chivalrous assistance'. The Poles might be offered
an alliance against their Russian enemies – not without a grim
reminder that 'we are quite as ready to take a slice from them as the
Russians are'. And the eminently satisfactory result of such an
arrangement would be that 'we could either help'em or skelp'em to
our advantage'.[78]

None of Brahe's colleagues showed much interest in any
'chivalrous assistance'. Erik Oxenstierna, his anxieties about
Denmark apparently forgotten in the face of the prospect of recovering royal Prussia, came in with enthusiasm to Per Brahe's idea: he
resurrected all the old grievances, alluded to the new provocation of

[73] *RRP* XVI. 5.
[74] *RRP* XVI. 8.
[75] *RRP* XVI. 8.
[76] *RRP* XVI. 4, 5.
[77] *RRP* XVI. 8.
[78] *RRP* XVI. 9.

de Bye's intrigues, dwelt on the faithlessness of Polish negotiators and the probability that Morsztyn (the expected Polish emissary) would prove not to be furnished with full powers,[79] and drew the conclusion that all this suggested the expediency of using the chance to present the Poles with a virtual ultimatum.[80] Per Brahe observed that if Swedish troops were moved from Bremen to Pomerania, Sweden would be in a position to 'negotiate in the winter and fight in the spring'. There must, of course, be negotiation first; but the aim should be to secure 'a piece of land which they could cede, which would be of no great consequence to them, but of great advantage to us'.[81] The Chancellor considered the financial equation: say that action against Poland cost six or seven barrels of gold, or a million *rdr.*, how was this to be compared with what they would gain in Poland? – and presumably answered the question to his own satisfaction.[82] Only Bengt Skytte reminded them that the terms of the truce provided that even if differences proved irreconcilable, the suspension of arms was to be maintained.[83]

So ended the meeting; thin in numbers, apparently rather rushed by the Chancellor, its conclusion by no means following from the debate as recorded in the minutes. But among much that is unclear it seems apparent that so far from there being a general feeling for offensive action against Russia, only Per Brahe was prepared to consider it. No one else suggests anything more than a defensive posture. Nor can we see, as yet, any serious disposition towards an alliance with Poland: in so far as the possibility is aired, it is an acknowledgement of the propriety of at least giving negotiation a trial. Per Brahe, no doubt, contemplates the possibility of an alliance with Poland to attack Russia – but only as part of a blackmail bargain, and even he is thinking of war with Poland if his 'certain conditions' are rejected: indeed, he professes himself to be ready to take on Poland and Russia simultaneously. Once the majority has acceded to the view that preference should be given to the danger from the east, what happens is that Erik Oxenstierna and Per Brahe combine to use the remainder of the time available to press for the seizure of the opportunity to gather rich pickings from the chaos of Poland while the going is still good.

Kentrschynskyj was probably correct in thinking that members found the meeting on the 8th unsatisfactory, partly because the

---

[79] Kentrschynskyj, 'Karl X Gustav', p. 60, mistook his meaning: cf. *RRP* xvi. 10.
[80] *RRP* xvi. 9–10.
[81] *RRP* xvi. 10.
[82] *RRP* xvi. 10.
[83] *RRP* xvi. 10.

attendance was small, partly because some of them, feeling they had been stampeded into a decision, desired an interval for reflection.[84] At all events, despite the king's demand for their advice as soon as possible – that is, before the expected arrival of the Polish envoy Morsztyn – they did not meet again until three days later.

When they resumed their deliberations on the 11th they were a much more representative body: no less than nineteen members spoke in the ensuing debate. The proceedings began with a recapitulation by the Chancellor of the questions before them for decision, no doubt for the benefit of those members who had not been present on the former occasion. But he added two new questions, both of them significant. Was Morsztyn, when he arrived, to be answered 'without beating about the bush'; to be told that the Poles must now 'conform'; and that if they do not do so with good will 'they must expect other measures'? And finally, the loaded question: 'Or shall we let this chance slip, and allow this man [Morsztyn], like the previous envoys, to put us off with compliments and fair words?'[85] The last two questions spring directly from Per Brahe's speech on the 8th: they are a clear continuation of the anti-Polish, imperialist line which Erik Oxenstierna had so warmly embraced on that occasion. It is true that he now took care to repeat that they were not discussing war, but only arming: if they had been debating whether to make war on Poland or Russia that would have been another question.[86] But the best comment on this reminder was immediately provided by the formal debate which followed; for it assumed, in fact, the shape of an argument between peace and war. Bengt Skytte was put up to argue the case for peace; Christer Bonde the case for arming. Skytte's contribution contained one passage which was in the light of after-events prophetic: 'If everything should go as we would like it to go, and we could have the good fortune to overcome first one obstacle and then another . . . all our neighbours – indeed, all nations – would league together against us rather than allow such a thing'[87] – a prediction which came near to fulfilment in 1658. Bonde's more lengthy exposition went far beyond his brief. It was from the beginning an undisguised argument for war. He contended that Sweden, as in the past, should use the opportunities that presented themselves; that to remain at peace would be to entail heavy expense in maintaining a large army which might just as well be used in war; that war is good for trade; that (as

[84] Kentrschynskyj, 'Karl X Gustav', p. 60.
[85] *RRP* xvi. 12.
[86] *RRP* xvi. 13.
[87] *RRP* xvi. 15.

he had already argued on the 8th) since a rupture with Poland must come when the truce expired in 1661, they might as well provoke it now. He had a good deal to say about Muscovite commercial ambitions, the Tsar's desire for a foothold on the Baltic, and the menace implied in his recent assumption of new titles; but this did not lead him, as might have been expected, to suggest war with Russia: the plundering of Poland presumably appeared an easier prospect. He had not altogether forgotten his original preference for the Danish option; but (as with Oxenstierna) his ideas had since undergone considerable modification: it would not be difficult, he now considered, to dispose of the Danes if they tried to make trouble.[88]

Before the vote of members was taken Per Brahe and the Chancellor each contributed significant, if somewhat cryptic, observations. Brahe for his part disclaimed any idea of rushing to attack anybody; but he pointed out that one of two things might happen: either Poland and Russia might be reconciled and combine to attack Sweden; or Poland might succumb altogether. Sweden had legitimate grievances against all three of her neighbours – Poland, Russia, Denmark; but Poland (unlike Russia) 'may well come to terms'. In the circumstances, it would be best to keep talking with Morsztyn until 'we see how things develop'.[89] Oxenstierna, for his part, commented that in view of the troops Sweden already had in Livonia and Germany. 'which can also be used for this design', and in view also of 'the recruited troops we have, and how much can still be furnished from our army here at home . . . it does not seem that so very much more will be needed'.[90] What remains unclear is the nature of the 'design'; but from the tone of his remarks on this day and the next it seems a fair presumption that he was thinking of an expedition against Poland.

They proceeded now to vote on the two questions: how large ought the army to be? and where were the troops to be employed? As to the first question, six, including the Chancellor and Per Brahe, were clearly for a 'considerable' armament.[91] As to the second, the Danish option received last-ditch support, tentative from Magnus Gabriel de la Gardie, tenacious from Forbus and Wrangel;[92] while Arvid Wittenberg, though he conceded that danger was more imminent from the east, warned them that 'what a hard time we are like to have of it in Prussia we may well find out as long as we leave

[88] *RRP* XVI. 14–15.
[89] *RRP* XVI. 17.
[90] *RRP* XVI. 16–17; Hans Landberg, 'Decemberrådslagen 1654', p. 63.
[91] *RRP* XVI. 17, 21, 23, 24, 25. Contrast Hans Landberg 'Decemberrådslagen 1654' (pp. 53–4), who interprets the voting as showing reluctance to take the responsibility for war.
[92] *RRP* XVI. 17, 20, 22, 23.

the Danish side in uncertainty', and pointed out that this was their best chance to attack Denmark.[93] So much for Oxenstierna's reminders that they were not discussing war. The Chancellor, however, briskly demolished their arguments: the Danes would not willingly see a Dutch fleet in the Baltic (they proved ready enough to welcome one in 1656!); the Dutch could do little damage without the command of the Baltic harbours; it was in their interest to preserve Swedish friendship. He conceded that danger from Denmark was possible; but danger in the east was certain. Meanwhile, Sweden was in the happy position of having always on hand a stock of quarrels with Denmark which could be used as pretexts if the occasion demanded it; but would not always be as well supplied with them in regard to the east as at present. He invited them to consider the umbrage it would give in Germany if they were to attack Denmark now; 'but not to the same extent in regard to Poland, for no one will take it amiss if we look to our security at a time when our neighbours are so arrayed and stand on our frontiers with such forces'.[94]

This effectively disposed of Denmark: the Chancellor had finally changed his mind. As to the east, eight now thought in terms of Poland rather than Russia; though some still spoke of 'the Polish side', or 'the Polish-Russian war', rather than of 'Poland'. Six were for negotiation before action: most strongly Herman Fleming, who, though he admitted the need for arming, remained firmly in favour of peace, no doubt on economic grounds. Three noteworthy points appear in the course of the discussion: first, the strong support for Erik Oxenstierna's view that they are bound to use the chance against Poland; above all from Per Brahe, who now defines action against Poland as 'our most important consideration at this time', since 'we cannot engage in anything before things on that side are cleared up'. Secondly, the view expressed by some of those who favour war against Poland (or, indeed, against Denmark) that any such action does not represent the limit of Swedish policy: they are for settling with Poland (or Denmark, as the case may be) *first*: what comes after is not expressed, but it is possible to conjecture that some of them may have meant Russia. Lastly, a point raised by Christer Bonde, Wittenberg, and Per Brahe: the sensitiveness of the Dutch (among others) to the possibility of a Swedish seizure of Pillau.[95] Which suggests that despite Schlippenbach's *gaffe*, Pillau was seen, by responsible Swedish statemen, as a probable objective.

The Chancellor summed up the sense of the meeting – this time, in

[93] *RRP* XVI. 20.
[94] *RRP* XVI. 18–19
[95] *RRP* XVI. 18 (Bonde); 20 (Wittenberg); 24 (Per Brahe).

rather more accord with the actual course of the debate than on the previous occasion. There must be a 'considerable' armament. It must be directed against 'Poland' (not 'the east', or 'the Russo-Polish war'); and for these reasons: the danger was greatest on that side; controversies were in any case certain to lead to war on the termination of the truce; action against Poland would give less umbrage than any other; the chance offered was important and the prospects were good; and success would provide a basis for their security afterwards against *all* their neighbours. The practical application of their decision was to be left in the king's hands.

When they met on the following day they found themselves confronted with two new questions from Charles X. He asked whether, if Poland conceded the two main points in the old controversy – i.e. recognised his title to the throne, and abandoned all claims on Livonia – it would be expedient to demobilise the forces that had been raised; or whether it would not be better – and, indeed, whether the sums that had been expended upon them did not require – that Sweden should raise her terms, 'stretch the bow' tauter, and insist, first, on the 'satisfaction of the soldiery', and, second, upon an *assecuratio de non amplius turbando*.[96] So this, it seemed, was what Per Brahe's 'certain conditions' might mean; these were the concessions which 'would be of no great consequence to them'. It seems likely that the king had perceived that he might be faced with an awkward predicament. If the Poles gave way upon the two main points at issue, there might be no option but to use his mercenary troops against Russia, since he was in no position to pay them off. He was now trying to provide himself with an alternative which would enable him to avoid this conclusion. His question assumed (to the somewhat naive surprise of Gustav Bonde, who had been absent from the previous meeting)[97] that the recruiting of mercenaries was well under way. When Bonde persisted in asking whether foreign mercenaries were really necessary, he was firmly told that no sufficiently imposing force could be provided by the native militia alone: it was no wonder if Sweden, with her limited human resources, availed herself of an expedient which appeared to be essential even for populous France.[98] This matter thus satisfactorily disposed of, the Chancellor led the way in declaring his support for the king's implied proposals: among other reasons, because their acceptance might forestall the possibility that other powers (Russia, Brandenburg?) might appropriate 'what we might have our eye on'; and added that

[96] *RRP* XVI. 26.
[97] *RRP* XVI. 27.
[98] *RRP* XVI. 27, 29.

the supposition was that Charles 'should engage himself first in Poland'.[99]

Leijonhufvud and Gustav Bonde were then detailed to conduct the formal debate. Leijonhufvud's argument was short: he was in favour both of satisfaction and of *assecuratio*; the recruiting of mercenaries was inevitable; they could not afford to neglect this opportunity: 'If we miss it, we may never afterwards obtain such terms.'[100] Gustav Bonde, on his side, argued that it was enough if the old controversies were settled to Sweden's satisfaction; that any attempt to 'stretch the bow' might drive the Poles to make peace with the Russians, and afterwards to make common cause with them against Sweden. The right policy, he insisted, was to negotiate with Poland upon tolerable terms, and then to think about defensive measures against the Russian danger.[101]

At this point Erik Oxenstierna intervened with a new issue. There was news, he informed them, that the Cossacks might attack Prussia. In such a case the inhabitants might well apply to Sweden for protection. Ought it to be granted? If so, that was an additional argument for a large army, and hence for that satisfaction of the soldiery which the king had suggested. He had already, on the 8th, wondered whether Sweden ought not to be strong enough to give assistance 'if any should solicit our help'. This now became an explicit proposal.[102]

The danger to the peaceful inhabitants of Prussia (despite long memories of Bothe and Crachow)[103] could scarcely be considered very serious; if they needed protection, the nobility of royal Prussia were disposed to seek it from Brandenburg (which, to be sure, it was a Swedish interest to forestall), and the burghers of Danzig and other towns desired no protection from anybody – except the King of Poland. As to the Cossacks, an emissary from Chmelnicki, the Abbot Daniel, had been in Sweden since September 1654, offering an alliance *contra quemcunque* (including, therefore, Russia), and the Swedish government was still keeping this possibility open at the beginning of 1655.[104] It is unlikely that Oxenstierna believed in the imminence of Cossack marauders on the lower Vistula. But Lithu-

[99] *RRP* XVI. 26–7.
[100] *RRP* XVI. 28.
[101] *RRP* XVI. 28.
[102] *RRP* XVI. 8, 29.
[103] Herman Bothe had made a raid on Livonia in 1639; J. Ernst Crachow had made an incursion into Pomerania in 1643. The Swedes believed – or affected to believe – that both had the connivance of the Polish authorities: see, e.g. *RRP* XVI. 9, 100; *SRARP* v₂. 212–13, 216, 220.
[104] Kentrschynskyj, 'Ukrainska revolutionen', pp. 33–8.

ania was another matter. Refugees from that unhappy country had already sought shelter in Livonia, and had been received there; but protection acquired a very different political complexion if it were to be extended to discontented, vanquished, and half-treasonable magnates such as Janusz Radziwiłł, though the idea had been canvassed as long ago as 1648.[105] Gustav Bonde defined the issue with brutal frankness: 'To insist on *assecuratio* and satisfaction, and to offer protection, is nothing other than to embark on a new war.'[106] It is in fact difficult to believe that Erik Oxenstierna should have proposed this provocative measure on his own responsibility. It bears every appearance of being a deliberate stiffener of the already unacceptable terms implicit in the king's two questions, and it was in fact associated with those questions in the ensuing debate. In vain Gustav Bonde urged that experience from the Thirty Years War showed that Prussia and Livonia could not support such forces as were contemplated: his colleagues told him that he was mistaken.[107] And even he had admitted that it would be 'not undesirable' if they could get possession of Danzig:[108] economic imperialism and territorial aggrandisement, as he ought to have realised, were virtually inseparable. Bengt Skytte, less modestly, proposed as security the whole of Prussia; for Prussia was '*ocellus Maris Balthici*', a bastion for Livonia, and a barrier both to Poland and to Brandenburg.[109]

When the time came for voting, Per Brahe, though it was the convention that members should speak *juniores priores*, did not scruple to lend the support of his rank and authority to these attractive prospects by speaking first.[110] His message was plain enough: there must be a large army, including mercenaries; 'for the present' action must be against Poland; satisfaction and *assecuratio* must be insisted upon; there must be no demobilisation, partly for fear of the Russians, partly in order not to damage Sweden's reputation in the mercenary market; and finally protection should be given to all who asked for it, though care must be taken not to apply it in sensitive areas where it might give offence to the Russians – as, for instance, Dünaburg.[111] Herman Fleming, as before, was resolute for peace, and suggested that if satisfaction and *assecuratio* were to be insisted upon, it should be in cash:[112] an odd suggestion, for though satisfac-

[105] Carlson, *Sveriges historia*, I. 158 n. 1, Bengt Skytte to Per Brahe, 17 November 1648.
[106] *RRP* XVI. 33.
[107] *RRP* XVI. 30.
[108] *RRP* XVI. 28.
[109] *RRP* XVI. 30.
[110] To the annoyance of at least one of his colleagues: *RRP* XVI. 31.
[111] *RRP* XVI. 30–1.
[112] *RRP* XVI. 33.

tion of the soldiery must obviously be in cash, it is difficult to understand how money could provide *assecuratio*. But he added, with characteristic grasp of realities: 'Our circumstances are not now what they used to be. Better forget about protecting others than by doing so run into more difficulties.'[113] Gustav Bonde, arguing on the same side, urged that if after negotiations nothing better could be obtained than an acknowledgment of Charles's title and a renunciation of the Polish claim to Livonia, then they must make the best of it and act *coniunctis viribus* with the Poles against the Russians, 'who are the most formidable, and whom we ought to keep our eye on'.[114]

The majority was unresponsive to the arguments of Gustav Bonde and Herman Fleming. Skytte, eager for satisfaction and *assecuratio* in order to forestall 'others', his eyes fixed already on the coastlands,[115] was ready in his enthusiasm to extend Swedish protection to 'the whole of Poland'.[116] To refuse protection, thought Leijonhufvud, would be 'a great *lâcheté*'; to offer it, thought Jacob de la Gardie, was 'Christian and reasonable' – a judgment in which the Chancellor concurred.[117] And by twelve votes to four their opinion prevailed.[118] The Chancellor thus formulated their advice: we must have satisfaction for our outlay, and *assecuratio* as a guarantee of good faith. If the Poles would accept the Swedish terms, so much the better; but if not, they must be coerced by force of arms into accepting them. Protection must be extended to all who might seek it. 'What further action may be required is referred to His Majesty to decide as may be best and most serviceable for the realm.'[119]

We are left with two general impressions. The first, and strongest, is of the feeling of members that the weakness of Poland presented an opportunity – perhaps a fleeting one – not merely to extort a favourable solution to the old issues between the two countries, but also to obtain substantial cessions of territory. These are perceived (occasionally explicitly) to be the coastlands; which meant in fact annexations which must primarily look to royal Prussia.[120] The

---

[113] *RRP* XVI. 33.
[114] *RRP* XVI. 34.
[115] *RRP* XVI. 30, 33.
[116] *RRP* XVI. 33.
[117] *RRP* XVI. 34.
[118] *RRP* XVI. 30, 33. There were thus three abstentions.
[119] *RRP* XVI. 35–6.
[120] Kentrschynskyj's verdict ('Karl X Gustav', p. 65)'This is very different from the picture of the Swedish Council as a lot of booty-hungry warmongers . . . which has become standard in Polish historiography', is somewhat weakened by his earlier remark (p. 56) that (on 8 December) 'The Council members were not indisposed to allow the ever-victorious Swedish arms once more to try the fortunes of war against any suitable adversary, "provided that it is *cum honestate coniunctum*" '

danger from Russia, though they are well aware of it, is not seen as imminent, and care must be taken to avoid provoking the Tsar; though a war with Russia later on is by some clearly seen as possible, and by a few as the real objective to be aimed at. But for the moment, they have time – time to redress the deplorable consequences of the truce of Stuhmsdorf, time for further lucrative adventures, to include perhaps a port (or the control of a port) in ducal Prussia: the mention of Pillau reveals unspoken aspirations. The immediate enemy is clearly Poland. And this reawakened readiness to tread once more the path of imperial expansion gives rise to the second impression that the debates leave upon the reader: the fear that if they did not act quickly they might be forestalled.[121]

And so, pushed on by the king's enquiries, Per Brahe's urgings, and the Chancellor's ensnaring plea for protections, conscious of grave responsibility at a fateful moment, they came to decisions which, if the king and the Estates accepted them, could hardly fail to lead to an attack on Poland.

VI

It will be obvious that this account of the debates in December accords ill with Kentrschynskyj's thesis. The crucial difference, of course, concerns the Council's attitude to Poland; and here it is a matter not of a difference of opinion only, but (on occasion, at least) a simple matter of fact. Thus when Kentrschynskyj wrote that in the debate on 11 December 'The idea of an alliance with Poland against Russia comes out strongly', and that it is an idea 'which is put forward both by the king's spokesmen and several other Council members', it must at once be said that there is not a word recorded of the debate on that day to substantiate this. On the 12th, indeed, Gustav Bonde is for a settlement with Poland prior to facing Russia;[122] and later does indeed suggest an alliance; but to state flatly as Kentrschynskyj did[123] that the vote for a peaceful settlement with Poland *and* for securing its alliance against Russia was 'unanimous', and that 'many' spoke 'warmly' for it, does not accord with the record as we have it. The basic difficulty about his article is that it is somewhat vitiated by the author's consistent assumption of the truth of the thesis he was concerned to demonstrate: having laid it down

---

[121] Carlson, *Sveriges historia*, I. 37–8, 41, 45 and Edén, 'Grunderna för Karl X Gustavs anfall på Polen', pp. 25–6, 27, 34 had the same impression.

[122] *RRP* XVI. 28, 32, 34.

[123] Kentrschynskyj, 'Karl X Gustav', p. 63.

that Charles had already planned to intervene 'by force'[124] against Russian expansion, he took the debate between 'east' and 'west' as being really a debate on whether or not the Council should approve of 'the measures he had already taken against Russia'[125] – a view which assumed without proving that it was in fact against Russia that those measures had been directed. Thus his account of the Council meetings became in fact an attempt to provide support for his contention that Charles desired a Polish alliance by demonstrating that the Council was of the same opinion. But the Council's resolutions in reality neither confirmed this thesis nor confuted it. If they were accepted, they implied, perhaps, only one thing: that there would be a war within a reasonably short time. As to whether it was to be a war against Russia or against Poland they did no more than to give a strong pointer towards Poland; but this the king was free to ignore: the choice of victim was still his; the decision on policy lay in his hands. Kentrschynskyj's thesis might still prove the right one. But though the evidence from the immediately following period does seem to suggest that their resolutions in fact embodied the advice which the king had hoped to hear, that was not because they were at one with him in desiring a Polish alliance; it was because both king (probably) and Council (certainly) were for using the opportunity to regain – and expand – Sweden's grip on the coastlands.

VII

Two letters, of 23 and 24 December, from Erik Oxenstierna to Gustav Horn in Livonia, reveal how Charles saw the situation at the end of the year, and both accord well with the upshot of the Council debates of 7-12 December. On the 23rd Horn was informed that 'We have reasonable cause to secure the coastlands to us, and get in before all the armies swarm in there.' The policy of offering 'protection' which Oxenstierna had put forward on 12 December is expressly endorsed; and anxious Lithuanians are to be 'animated' to apply for it.[126] And on the following day Horn was provided with the first precise indication of the policy which the king had in mind. Sweden's prime interest, he was told, must be to settle the controversies with Poland this winter; or, if that should prove impossible, to arrive at a decision about appropriate measures, taking care in the meantime not to permit Russian encroachments inconsistent with Swedish interests. But it remained Sweden's greatest interest to

[124] Kentrschynskyj, 'Karl X Gustav', p. 54.
[125] ibid., p. 55.
[126] Kentrschynskyj, 'Karl X Gustav', p. 71.

shut out the Russians from the Baltic, and to prevent their obtaining a foothold in Kurland, since that would entail a threat to *dominium maris*, and the possible encirclement of Livonia.[127] Thus there was a 'prime interest' and a 'greatest interest': it was a question of priorities. This was effectively the conclusion which the Council had reached a week or so earlier. It might indeed prove that there was no essential contradiction between the one interest and the other: a quick settlement with Poland, by blackmail or by force, and the solid advantages which such a settlement might bring with it, might either facilitate an early and effective confrontation of the Muscovite, or it might (on the other hand) be sufficient to persuade the Tsar that Matveev's policy entailed less risk than Ordyn-Nashchokin's.[128] However that might be, the situation, from Sweden's point of view, had altered significantly in the preceding two or three months. Before November the recovery of royal Prussia had been a legitimate objective and a desirable prize, and since the preceding March Charles had been arming with (apparently) just that end in view; but by the end of the year the acquisition of 'the coastlands' (by which was meant not only royal Prussia) had become an urgent necessity. The unique opportunity to which reference had been made so often in the Council debates might prove as transient as it was tempting. In mid-December the king showed Chanut a letter indicating that Poland hoped for peace with the Tsar and a joint attack on Sweden afterwards.[129] The offering of 'protection' was a device which Frederick William of Brandenburg might use as effectively in royal Prussia as Horn was being exhorted to use it in Lithuania.[130] John Casimir's promiscuous appeals for aid had been directed, *inter alia*, to Vienna; and in Stockholm men had not forgotten the effect of Imperialist intervention in Gustav Adolf's Polish war. Worst of all, Dutch naval aid to John Casimir would involve both a challenge to Sweden's economic strategy and to her *dominium maris*. All these considerations contribute to the emphatic identification of the Polish question as Sweden's prime interest.

That being accepted, Charles's policy towards Russia followed as a natural consequence. It was a reasonable assumption (or at least, it was an assumption that he made)[131] that Alexis would not wish to have two wars on his hands at the same time; and that before he had finished with Poland – which might be very soon – there would be

[127] Carlson, *Sveriges historia*, I. 176.
[128] As Kentrschynskyj (p. 82) suggested.
[129] Carlson, *Sveriges historia*, I. 172 n.2.
[130] Kentrschynskyj. 'Karl X Gustav', pp. 84, 113.
[131] *Ibid.*, p. 79.

time to force a settlement on John Casimir without Russian interference. Every effort must therefore be made during this period to
preserve amicable relations with the Tsar. This was a delicate task,
for the Russian and Swedish armies stood on either side of the
Livonian–Lithuanian frontier, and it might be difficult to pursue the
policy of 'protections' without trespassing upon preserves which the
Tsar might regard as at least potentially within his sphere of
influence. The stream of orders which was despatched to Gustav
Horn vividly reveals the difficulty. Order and counter-order succeeded one another with bewildering frequency, as Charles vacillated
between the wish to strengthen the Swedish position in Livonia, and
fear that by doing so he might provoke a quarrel with Alexis, which
it was (for the present, at all events) essential to avoid. The test-case
was Dünaburg: on the one hand a probable Russian objective; on the
other a coveted position from which an attack upon Poland could be
launched from the north-east. In January he still seems to have had
no idea of any offensive action on this side: when Horn asked for
reinforcements, Charles enquired how many men he would require
'for defence'.[132] But from February onwards he was increasingly
preoccupied with the idea of taking Dünaburg: at times only if its
capture could be effected without offending the Russians; at times
regardless of Russian reactions, since here, at least, they must be
forestalled. But in general Horn's orders were to treat the Russians
with discretion and to keep them in good humour, if possible.[133]
These swiftly changing and confusing directives led eventually to
Horn's supersession, and that in turn to a controversy with the king
which Horn later carried on through the medium of Oxenstierna. At
the heart of the dispute was Charles's charge that Horn was too anti-
Russian, too eager to engage the good-will of the Poles[134] – an
accusation to which Horn replied that it was he who had acted
consistently throughout, and the king who had changed his mind,
but an accusation which must be given some weight in estimating
what the king's policy really was. But if the king's orders were
apparently self-contradictory, the explanation was probably simply
that he found it hard to make up his mind whether he could risk a
war with Poland until he was reasonably confident that he could do
so without involving himself in a war with Russia.

Kentrschynskyj's view was the converse of this. He summed up
his argument on Charles's plans in the early months of 1655 as

---

[132] *Ibid.*, p. 93.
[133] *Ibid.*, p. 95.
[134] *Ibid.*, pp. 125–30, for a full and careful examination of the correspondence and the
problems raised by it.

follows: 'From the beginning, Poland's role in these plans is that of an ally, not an enemy';[135] he believed that the assault on Russia which was the 'greatest interest' could not be undertaken safely until a secure settlement, and if possible an alliance, had been concluded with Poland; and hence he held that the main base in these months was Horn's army in Livonia, not Wittenberg's in Pomerania – partly because a strong Swedish presence there might discourage the Tsar from interfering before he was ready to deal with him; partly because it would provide reassurance, if not succour, to elements in Lithuania sympathetic to Sweden and disposed to see their salvation in a Swedish alliance. 'Protection', in this interpretation, was not an intolerably provocative attempt to subvert the loyalty of the subjects of a sovereign state, but a measure to cover them against a Russian invader. Kentrschynskyj's argument rested in part upon a draft letter, as from *riksdag* to *sejm*, which the king caused Erik Oxenstierna to draw up in January. That draft was, in effect, a simple plea to come back to the negotiating table without any preconditions being laid down, and it was indeed, as Kentrschynskyj rightly wrote, 'surprisingly moderate, muted, and encouraging'.[136] The letter was not in fact sent off until 3 March, when the Estates were on the point of meeting; but the fact that it *was* sent off might suggest that it was still thought to be relevant to the situation. In January there had been another development, which seemed to indicate that Charles was prepared to agree to the conduct of negotiations, not in Stockholm (on which the Swedes had previously insisted), but at some place in Livonia to be agreed upon.[137]

Kentrschynskyj considered that this constructive approach was wrecked by what he termed John Casimir's 'sabotage'.[138] As to this, there can be no difficulty in conceding that John Casimir's proceedings were dictated largely by his personal interests, and were violently at odds with the wishes of the Polish magnates.[139] But though John Casimir might be a devious character and a decidedly unsatisfactory king, he was intelligent enough to perceive the obvious, and in particular the fact that if Sweden entered the war as Poland's ally, the Swedish forces must fight on Polish soil – in Lithuania certainly, in royal Prussia if what were regarded as essential Swedish interests were to be taken care of. Kentrschynskyj himself put the point with force and candour: 'It is not very likely that Charles could expect that

---

135   *Ibid.*, p. 135.
136   *Ibid.*, p. 103.
137   *Ibid.*, p. 80 and n. 3.
138   *Ibid.*, p. 91.
139   *Ibid.*, pp. 88–91.

John Casimir should accept, without further ado, an offer of alliance on such onerous terms, when he could not even bring himself to abandon claims to what he did not possess';[140] and again: granted that the presence of Swedish armies on Polish soil was the natural conse-quence of any alliance, 'Whether Charles intended afterwards to take himself off elsewhere, must again remain an open question. And John Casimir must have wondered how it would be in this regard.'[141] Yes, indeed! If John Casimir did in fact sabotage the plan for an alliance, Kentrschynskyj provided him with ample justification for doing so.

However, the evidence for Charles's desire for a Polish alliance seems inconclusive, and the arguments Kentrschynskyj based upon it do not represent the only – nor, perhaps, the most natural – inter-pretation of it. For instance, when on 4 February Charles presented his demands to Morsztyn, they showed no deviation from the advice of the Council in December: he must have sole right to the title of King of Sweden, he must have his right to Livonia accepted without further controversy,*and* he must have royal Prussia as satisfaction for the soldiery and *assecuratio* for the future.[142] At the same time Oxen-stierna was reminded that time was running out, and that they were in danger of incurring 'tremendous expenses, if we do not immedi-ately engage the troops in action'.[143] Edén construed this to mean that he had come to the conclusion that 'barring Polish concessions which were improbable', he must 'take action' against Poland.[144] Kentrschynskyj was of a different opinion. But it seems on all accounts unlikely that Charles at this stage can have contemplated action against Russia. Amicable relations with Poland might con-ceivably (however improbably) be somehow arranged; but friend-ship must have its price – or its penalties. Åsard would hardly have agreed in considering the concentration of forces in Pomerania to be of as little significance as Kentrschynskyj did. Next, the question why Charles continued to tolerate John Casimir's exasperating pro-crastinatory tactics for so long can be answered equally cogently on the assumption that he preferred not to risk an attack on Poland until he had a clearer idea of how the Russians would take it, and of where the main thrust of their spring offensive could be expected: until as late as June he feared that their objectives would be Lithuania and

[140] *Ibid.*, p. 83.
[141] *Ibid.*, p. 85.
[142] *Ibid.*, p. 88. Morsztyn's report reached Warsaw in mid-February. Kentrschynskyj conjec-tured that the readiness of Polish senators to negotiate on the basis of Morsztyn's information suggests that there may have been some temperament of the terms, of which we have no record.
[143] *Ibid.*, p. 87.
[144] Edén, 'Grunderna för Karl X Gustavs anfall på Polen', p. 37 n. 1.

Prussia, and was unaware that they were concentrating, not at Velike Luki, but, around Smoleńsk and Brjansk.[145] And, not least, it was inexpedient to reveal himself as the aggressor before the meeting of the Estates: it proved difficult enough to carry them with him even after he was able to tell them of the conciliatory offer to negotiate without preconditions, and to cite it as an example of his readiness for a reasonable settlement.

When Charles spoke of a 'settlement' with Poland, what did he understand by that expression? If by this was meant a settlement short of war, there is very little to suggest that he seriously entertained the idea. The only traces of it in the first few months of 1655 are the draft suggesting negotiation without preconditions, and the concession about where those negotiations might take place. If the draft of January was seriously intended, why was its despatch delayed until 3 March? His inertness in pursuing this line contrasts forcibly with his virtually continuous efforts to conciliate the Tsar against the event of a war with Poland. The final decision for war came before any answer to the letter of 3 March had reached him.[146] A settlement with Poland meant one of two things: either a settlement enforced by war; or a settlement imposed at the negotiating table; in either case, a *diktat*. It is not conceivable that Charles would have receded from the demands which the Council had advised him to make: the satisfaction of the soldiery was not negotiable; the recovery and extension of Sweden's hold on the coastlands was essential to the policy of economic imperialism which Axel Oxenstierna had launched, and of which Erik Oxenstierna was the enthusiastic champion. Nor is it conceivable that the *sejm*, or any other Polish authority, would have acquiesced in those demands: a peace with Russia could be no worse. The January draft was a propaganda weapon held in reserve: on 3 March it was duly brandished at the appropriate moment.

Meanwhile the Abbot Daniel had been lingering in Stockholm as the emissary of Chmelnicki. Since the conclusion of the treaty of Pereyaslavl Chmelnicki's forces had been fighting side by side with the Russians against the Poles. Latterly, however, their collaboration had been a good deal less than satisfactory: the Ukrainian troops under Zolotarenko had refused to co-operate with the Russian commanders and had pursued operations on their own.[147] It was against this background that Daniel had been sent to Stockholm with an offer of an alliance *contra quemcunque*. But the offer was untimely; for

---

[145] Kentrschynskyj, 'Karl X Gustav', pp. 91, 100.
[146] The reply of the *sejm* did not reach Stockholm until 11 June: *ibid.*, p. 103.
[147] Kentrschynskyj, 'Ukrainska revolutionen', pp. 58–61.

Chmelnicki, despite Zolotarenko's display of independence, was not yet strong enough to face an open breach with the Tsar. Untimely also for Charles; for if the secret had leaked out that would have been a gross provocation of precisely the kind that he was anxious to avoid.

He would soon be revolving in his mind other uses for Chmelnicki. This emerges from Kentrschynskyj's discovery of fragmentary notes in the margin of a despatch from Harald Appelboom,[148] which were apparently intended to serve as the basis for minutes of a meeting of the Council of which we have no other record. It took place on 17 January. On the previous day Erik Oxenstierna had received Morsztyn's credentials: they authorised him to offer *negotiation* on the royal title and on Livonia, but only if Sweden would help John Casimir to recover the Ukraine and the areas of Lithuania which the Russians had overrun.[149] These were impossible terms; and the Council meeting was probably called to discuss their implications. The draft minutes contain three significant passages. In the first, the king is recorded as saying that if the Poles would negotiate before 'we let rip' the opportunity should be taken; and Sweden should therefore use the time available before the Russians finally disposed of Poland, either to negotiate *or* to 'obtain a solid *assecuratio*' – which was, in fact, the policy which the Council had advocated a month earlier. The second passage ran as follows, the speaker being, in Kentrschynskyj's opinion, the king:

It is not sufficient to get *assecuratio* and territory from Poland: but we must also gain the support of Chmelnicki, so that Poland gets little, and Russia nothing; and [so that] all the burden [of war] against Poland does not fall on us . . . Chmelnicki can be useful and do no damage. *Ergo* give him encouragement.[150]

And the final passage:

H.M. is of a mind to sound the Russian through the Greek [the Abbot Daniel] as to how he would react if we entered into war with Poland, if this can be effected through the Cossack Chmelnicki.[151]

Kentrschynskyj took these passages as confirming his view that Charles's policy was for a Polish alliance: 'Both from Charles's letters *and from his remarks during the Council debate of 17 January* [my italics] it appears with all possible clarity that what the king wants is not war with Poland but co-operation.'[152] But only the first passage

---

[148] Kentrschynskyj, 'Karl X Gustav', p. 76, and n. 15, where he points out that Åke Lindqvist had earlier noticed this draft.
[149] *Ibid.*, pp. 79, 86.
[150] Kentrschynskyj, 'Karl X Gustav', pp. 79–80.
[151] *Ibid.*, p. 80.
[152] *Ibid.*, p. 80. cf. his similar verdict in 'Ukrainska revolutionen', pp. 36–8.

can possibly bear this interpretation; and it ignores the fact that the second passage – whatever its real import – is irreconcilable with the third. The second passage can be construed as pointing to an alliance with Poland only on the assumption that Charles is seeking, in Chmelnicki, a partner in the dismemberment of the Republic. The bow is to be stretched still tauter; land and *assecuratio* are no longer enough; Poland must be so weakened, by Chmelnicki's gains and Sweden's operations on the coastlands, that not much remains of it: an arrangement which simultaneously (if all went well) would bar the way to Russian expansion. What sort of alliance was this? Was it conceivable that Poland would prefer such terms to a settlement with Alexis? The explanation of the conflict between the second and final passages easily suggests itself. For three or four months the Swedish government had had before it Chmelnicki's offer of an alliance *contra quemcunque*, and perhaps Abbot Daniel was beginning to press for an answer. At all events, what appears from the extracts which Kentrschynskyj retrieved is that the Council is discussing what they are to do about Daniel and his employer. How can they use him? There seems to have been no question of accepting an alliance *contra quem-cunque*: what we have instead are *alternative* suggestions thrown out by the king for the Council's comments. What those comments were, what decision was taken (if any), does not appear; but neither of the alternatives can be taken as a considered policy. Kentrschynskyj's discovery turns out to have been something of a mare's nest. Meanwhile, recruiting must continue: on 8 February Coyet in London was ordered to arrange for the raising of six to eight regiments of Scots, and to remind Leven of his offer to furnish a further two.[153] First things first.

VIII

The royal Proposition was read to the Estates by Erik Oxenstierna on 12 March.[154] It gave them a broad survey of the state of Sweden's relations with foreign powers, with the general conclusion that the situation, especially in the east, required the utmost vigilance.[155] On the 20th a meeting of the Secret Committee, at which the king was

---

[153] J. Levin Carlbom, *Sverige och England 1655–aug. 1657* (Göteborg 1900), p. 6.

[154] Two accounts of the proceedings at the *riksdag* of 1655 are available: one in the minutes of the Estate of Nobility, the other in the minutes of the Council. The former is much the fuller and more satisfactory, as might be expected: the Council minutes, besides being defective, with *lacunae* at critical points, on occasion conflate several of the king's interventions into a single paragraph; though they also have significant points of which the minutes of the Nobility make no mention.

[155] *SRARP* v₂. 195–206.

present, heard a more detailed exposition from the Chancellor. As to
Russia, he reported that though there had recently been provocations
from the Muscovite side, and though Sweden's trade had suffered
damage (by which he meant that the Russians had declined to grant
the privileges and concessions for which the Swedes had been pressing), these things did not constitute adequate grounds for a rupture.[156] On the contrary, the envoy who had been sent to Moscow at
the beginning of the year had returned on 5 March with a report so
satisfactory that it had been determined to send a full-scale embassy
to the Tsar without delay.[157] The war between Russia and Poland
had made it necessary to reinforce the frontiers 'and not leave everything at the enemy's mercy'.[158] Kentrschynskyj found it notable that
for the first time in decades the Russians were now termed
'enemy';[159] but it seems doubtful whether the word had all the significance he attached to it: in the Proposition, the reinforcement of
Livonia had been explained by the proximity of 'the main armies of
both',[160] and there could be other 'enemies' than Russia or Poland:
with reference to de Bye's treaty Oxenstierna had remarked that any
fleet of war in the Baltic must be either 'allied or enemy'.[161]

On the following day the king and Council met a committee from
all four Estates to discuss the international situation. The king is
reported[162] as saying that the procrastination of the Poles forces him
to arm, and comments that de Bye's draft alliance reveals Polish
intentions in the Baltic; though to be sure 'the attitude of the Russians bodes no good either'.[163] All this is missing in *SRARP*. Both
have the ironic remark that 'Poland and Moscow are equally dear to
me';[164] but *RRP* continues 'but when now we look at the circumstances, *causam*, [?] *ratio* dictates that H.M. should have . . . with
Poland'.[165] Any temptation to fill the *lacuna* by conjecturally supplying some such word as 'patience' is effectively negatived by what
follows: 'And besides, Poland is now in such a low state that it may
perhaps collapse... And so it would be a good thing, indeed *neces-
s[arium]* to avail ourselves of this opportunity'.[166] The continuation
in *SRARP* is different, but the conclusion is the same: 'the *qvaestio* is

---

[156] *SRARP* v$_2$. 207.
[157] *SRARP* v$_2$. 208: missing from *RRP*.
[158] *RRP* xvi. 83: missing from *SRARP*.
[159] Kentrschynskyj, 'Karl X Gustav', p. 105
[160] *SRARP* v$_2$. 200, 201.
[161] *RRP* xvi. 86.
[162] *RRP* xvi. 97.
[163] *RRP* xvi. 97.
[164] *SRARP* v$_2$. 219; *RRP* xvi. 97.
[165] *RRP* xvi. 97.
[166] *Ibid.*

this: are we to save them in order that their affairs, which are now in so wretched a state, may be amended – to our prejudice?: much better that we have a slice of his land than that someone else shall make away with it'.[167]

Although the decisive orders to Wittenberg in Pomerania did not come until 21 April, and though the invasion of Poland did not actually begin until 6 June, by 21 March Charles seems virtually to have made up his mind that Poland was to be attacked. The discussions in the committees concentrate on Poland; the Russian question occupies very little of their time; the Chancellor makes every effort to excite the patriotic indignation and the martial ardour of his hearers by raking up every grievance against the Poles, from Bothe and Crachow to Canasilles and de Bye. The response seems to have been at best tepid, though they find de Bye's activities disturbing; the prospect of acquiring 'a slice of land' awakes scarcely an audible echo; of the other members of the Council only Per Brahe makes a couple of unimportant contributions to the debate: the Estates are strikingly less bellicose and Gothic than the Council had been in December. There is a strong feeling that war with Poland is unjustifiable in terms of the truce of Stuhmsdorf. Bengt Skytte had raised this point in December,[168] but had found no one to listen; but now the Estates insisted on consulting the text of the treaty, and they found in Article XIX that it was there laid down that insoluble disagreements between the parties were not to prejudice the continuance of the armistice for as long as the truce remained in force.[169] Nor were they much more responsive to the argument that this was not a chance to be missed. Both Charles and Erik Oxenstierna had laboured the point that Sweden's military preparations were directed not only against Poland or Russia: they were 'of general application'; for among potential enemies against whom it was necessary to be prepared were not only the Dutch but also the Emperor, either or both of whom might come to Poland's aid.[170] The only argument to make any impression on the committee was the impossibility of maintaining the recruited mercenaries except by using them. Lars Kruus put it in a nutshell when, answering Bishop Laurelius, who had expressed the hope that the king would not make war for the sake of the title, he said: 'We have got the troops on our necks, and they may well eat up both you and me if they are not employed.'[171] –

[167] *SRARP* v$_2$. 219.
[168] *RRP* XVI. 10.
[169] *Sverges traktater med främmande magter* v$_2$. 340.
[170] *SRARP* v$_2$. 216, 223; *RRP* XVI. 87, 97, 99–100.
[171] *SRARP* v$_2$. 214.

a conclusion which had been predictable at any time since the previous autumn. In the end, with conspicuous lack of enthusiasm, they left the decision for peace or war, and the choice of enemy, wholly in the king's discretion.[172] Charles had got what he wanted; and the Secret Committee had shuffled off the responsibility on to his shoulders. For another two months he would pursue the same tactics which had so distracted Gustav Horn: the final instance was a letter sent to him on 30 March announcing the start of a war against Poland, which was to be forwarded to Moscow provided that the Tsar took no apparent 'umbrage' at the capture of Dünaburg; otherwise not.[173] And as Horn, almost to the end, was directed to shape his actions in accordance with Russian reactions, so Wittenberg in Pomerania was to shape his in accordance with Horn's reports, and with the state of Polish resistance.[174] But this delicate balancing could not go on indefinitely. On 12 May Coyet was ordered to announce to Cromwell the king's intention of invading Poland.[175] By June the need to employ the mercenaries – and perhaps too the fear that Frederick William of Brandenburg might forestall him in royal Prussia – forced Charles to delay no longer. By then the *riksdag* too could only acquiesce: on 15 June Erik Oxenstierna could report that they had 'categorically' approved an 'immediate' war with Poland;[176] and that decision duly appeared in the Resolution of the *riksdag* on 25 June.[177]

IX

On the whole, then, it seems impossible to accept Kentrschynskyj's contention that Charles's immediate objective was a Polish alliance. When in August 1655 Schering Rosenhane suggested it he seems to have taken no interest in the proposal; and even if he had done so, the price which Rosenhane proposed that Sweden should demand was not one which it was probable that John Casimir would be prepared to pay.[178] It is true that within six months or so of launching his invasion Charles appears to have given serious consideration to what might be seen as a variant of such a policy; namely, assimilation by means of a union of the crowns. But whatever plans he may have had

---

[172] *SRARP* v$_2$. 227, 318.
[173] Kentrschynskyj, 'Karl X Gustav', pp. 109–10.
[174] *Ibid.*, p. 110.
[175] Roberts, ed., *Swedish Diplomats at Cromwell's Court*, pp. 77, 82.
[176] *RRP* XVI. 209.
[177] Stiernman, *Alla riksdagars och mötens besluth*, II. 1, 233–4.
[178] Kentrschynskyj, 'Ukrainska revolutionen', p. 51

for installing himself on the Polish throne, or for obtaining recognition as hereditary prince (it might have been thought that one experience of that position ought to have sufficed him), they were shattered by the successes of the Polish guerrillas. They were succeeded – indeed, they had been preceded – by projects of partition whose insubstantiality (to give it no harsher name) was as a rule demonstrated within a very short time after their formulation; though as late as 1658 he was still devising ingenious solutions of this sort.[179]

What, then, of the thesis of the great parenthesis? Did Charles ever manifest any sign of a consistent long-term policy directed against Russia, as distinct from exploitation of conjunctures as they arose, and of improvisations to meet the needs of the moment? No doubt it is inherently probable that he retained throughout a conviction of the danger impending from Moscow. If there is an identifiable basis for Swedish policy after 1654 we must look for it in Erik Oxenstierna's letter to Gustav Horn of 24 December: the doctrine of the 'prime interest' and the 'greatest interest'. But though this may have continued to be accepted as a general principle, it cannot be said to have been applied with unvarying consistency either by the king or by his advisers. When in January 1656 Magnus Gabriel de la Gardie wrote to Charles advocating a peace with Poland and an attack upon Russia, the king dismissed his letter as an 'insolence'.[180] In April 1656, at a moment of near panic in view of the imminent arrival of a Dutch fleet in the Baltic, the Council was debating the possibility of making peace with the Tsar.[181] About the same time Bengt Skytte, now General-Governor of Estonia, was reacting to the disastrous news from Poland by urging an alliance with Russia as the only means of averting the overrunning of Livonia by Lithuanian guerrillas.[182] This advice Charles did in fact take: he indicated his willingness to accept French mediation, and he offered the Tsar a defensive alliance designed to safeguard their respective conquests in Poland.[183] Even when the game was obviously lost in Poland it was rather against Denmark than against Russia that he thought of directing his energies.[184] On 27 February 1657 he sent home a Proposition to be

[179] C. Adlersparre, *Historiska Anteckningar* (Stockholm 1822), v. 201; *RRP* XVIII. 27.

[180] Georg Wittrock, 'Valda brev till M.G. de la Gardie från fränder och vänner 1656–1678', *Historisk tidskrift*, (1913), p. 296.

[181] *RRP* XVI. 444.

[182] A.B. Carlsson, 'Sverige och den östeuropeiska krisen 1656. Ett betänkande af Bengt Skytte om den svenska politiken' *Historisk tidskrift* (1912), pp. 111–13.

[183] *Ibid.*, p. 117; cf. Carlson, *Sveriges historia*, I. 292 n. 2.

[184] Cf. Georg Landberg, *Den svenska utrikespolitikens historia*, p. 97.

laid before the various provincial meetings.[185] It was a moment when he was demanding extraordinary sacrifices from his subjects, and the Proposition was not sparing of what was apparently considered to be appropriate propaganda. But the propaganda was directed almost entirely against *Poland*:[186] relations with Moscow were mentioned almost incidentally; the Russian attack was blamed on the intrigues of John Casimir; a wish for reconciliation with Alexis was expressed; and though there was the usual reference to Russian faithlessness, the opportunity to play upon the traditional 'Russian Peril' was conspicuously neglected.[187] It is true that by March 1658 the king was still identifying the main danger as coming from Russia (and Austria), and was emphasizing that his concern was to prevent the crown of Poland from passing either to the one or the other;[188] but by now he clearly wanted peace with the Tsar. In January 1658 he was speculating upon the implications of such a peace: a joint attack on Poland, perhaps, with delicate problems of spheres of influence arising from it.[189] In March he wrote urgently to Biörenklou that he must have peace with Moscow, 'cost what it will';[190] and a month later it was with resignation that he constated that such a peace was apparently not to be had.[191] Douglas's *coup* in Kurland certainly represented the attainment of a long-coveted objective; and for one desperate moment Charles offered to abandon Prussia to the Tsar in exchange for a peace which would leave Kurland in his hands.[192] But when in December the truce of Vallisaari was at last concluded, he was glad enough to put the Russian question into cold storage for the next three years. The great parenthesis had ended in humiliation in Poland; in transient triumph in Denmark; and at last in a predicament graver than any that Sweden had faced since 1611. After it there was neither the will nor the capacity to resume the interrupted sentence.

For some historians the really consistent element in Charles's career was his determination to secure the coastlands and *dominium maris*, and by doing so to provide a solid base for those plans of

[185] For them, see above. pp. 66 ff.

[186] *SRARP* VI. 132–5, 140–2, 148–51.

[187] *Ibid.*, 145-6, 151. For 'the Russian Peril' see Kari Tarkiainen, *'Vår Gamble Arffiende Ryssen'. Synen på Ryssland i Sverige 1595–1621 och andra studier kring den svenska Rysslandsbilden från tidigare stormaktstid* (Studia historica Upsaliensia, 54) (Uppsala 1974).

[188] *RRP* XVIII. 27.

[189] *RRP* XVIII. 139.

[190] Adlersparre, *Historiska Anteckningar*, v. 185, 198.

[191] *RRP* XVIII. 35.

[192] *SRARP* VI. 291. At the same time he was telling the Estates that Bengt Oxenstierna and Schlippenbach had orders to offer to Poland the restoration of Prussia 'against reasonable satisfaction': *ibid.*, 290, 316.

economic imperialism which Axel Oxenstierna had laid down.[193] Up to a point this is plainly true, as his utterances on various occasions bear witness. Even when his fortunes were visibly declining he contrived to secure the insertion into the treaty of Labiau of secret articles which maintained Sweden's claim to the coastlands, including Semgallen, Samogitien, Kurland, and Polish Lithuania.[194] But though this might be a basic aim, it was intermittently and inconsequently pursued; the 'red thread' which Birgitta Odén saw running through his actions[195] was all too often crossed by other threads of a very different colour. In vain Erik Oxenstierna, in vain his generals, urged the speedy reduction of royal Prussia and Danzig; in vain Schering Rosenhane argued the desirability of a reasonably moderate peace which should give Sweden the coastlands, and thereby the larger hope of mercantile imperialism. As Georg Landberg remarked, his decision to press on with campaigns in inner Poland, rather than secure control of Danzig (which was not seriously tackled until May 1656, by which time it was too late) reveals the fact that Charles was attempting to pursue two policies at the same time:[196] on the one hand, the policy of acquiring the coastlands; on the other, a vaguely imperial vision directed towards establishing a Swedish authority deep into south-east Europe. This latter policy entailed such fantasies as a Swedish protectorate over the Ukraine:[197] which, if it could ever conceivably have been made effective, would no doubt have barred the way to Alexis, but would hardly have compensated for the loss of Riga. It led to the obstinate retention of Kraków in Swedish hands, long after it could have any meaningful part to play in Swedish operations. It was most strikingly illustrated by the terms of the treaty of Radnot; for that treaty allotted to Rákóczy, as part of his share in a partitioned Poland, Masovia, Podlachia and Podlesia – the very palatinates which Charles had earlier pronounced to be the indispensable hinterland to royal Prussia.[198] The decision to ally with Rákóczy was taken despite the fact that personal experience in an earlier war had convinced him that no reliance was to be placed on the fighting qualities of Tran-

---

[193] E.g. Georg Wittrock, 'Fördraget i Königsberg och des förhistoria', *KFÅ* (1921), p. 54; Fries, *Erik Oxenstierna*, p. 205; H. Landberg, 'Statsfinans och kungamakt. Karl X Gustav inför polska kriget', *KFÅ* (1969), p. 164.

[194] Georg Wittrock, 'Marienburg och Labiau', *KFÅ* (1922), p. 111.

[195] Birgitta Odén, 'Karl X Gustav och det andra danska kriget', *Scandia* (1961), p. 65.

[196] Georg Landberg, *Den svenska utrikespolitikens historia*, p. 95.

[197] Kentrschynskyj characteristically lamented that the best opportunity of establishing a protectorate (in 1653) had passed before Charles was in a position to take advantage of it: Kentrschynskyj, 'Karl X Gustav', p. 68.

[198] Sten Bonnesen, *Karl X Gustav* (Malmö 1924–58), p. 183.

sylvanian troops.[199] It alienated the Cossacks; it provoked Austria.[200] It was reached after confused debates with members of the Council, in what appears to have been a mood of desperate inconsequence; in which he could say '*Nescio an melius habere Cossacos et Ragozi amicos an vero Polonos*', and in which at one moment he was stipulating that he retain Kraków for the duration of the war and in the next was prepared to let Rákóczy have it after all, provided he paid for it in cash.[201] And though he also said that if he had to choose between the ability to succour Riga and a Transylvanian alliance he would choose the former, after much vacillation he chose the latter.[202] Charles had become trapped between his two inconsistent policies; and each suffered in consequence. Henceforward expedients must do duty for statesmanship.

By 1658 the vision of a Swedish sphere of influence in south-east Europe had been effectively dissipated (though in that year he renewed the Cossack alliance with Chmelnicki's successor),[203] and Poland could once again be viewed in the simpler terms of 1654. But by this time the necessity of splitting the coalition against him, and the pressing need for foreign gold, were shaking the bases of his original policy also. What mattered now was that neither Austria nor Russia should provide the successor to John Casimir on the Polish throne. On 4 April 1658, replying to a suggestion by Christer Bonde that the situation might be met by making the duc d'Anjou king, Charles went so far as to say that if that could be managed he had thought of handing over Prussia to France in return for a cash payment.[204] On the 22nd he was still stipulating for a peace which would leave him the coastlands and the tolls: 'Prussia, Kurland and Livonia, and the *survivance* in ducal Prussia, must belong to Sweden' – a pronouncement which was received by the Council 'with applause'.[205] In June he reverted to the idea of ceding the whole or part of Poland in exchange for money;[206] in November he was asking whether it would not be better to make peace by giving Prussia to Austria – a proposal which seems to have deeply shocked members of the Council.[207] Edén, it seems, was right when with classic under-

---

[199] Olofsson, *Karl X Gustav. Hertigen – Tronföljaren*, p. 92.
[200] For the background to the treaty see *Mémoires du Chevalier de Terlon pour rendre compte au Roy de ses négotiations, depuis l'année 1656, jusqu'en 1661* (Paris 1681), I. 1–49; and C. Wibling, *Carl X Gustav och Georg Rákóczy II* (Lund 1891), pp. 16, 28–36.
[201] *RRP* XVI, 735, 748.
[202] *RRP* XVI. 732; cf. *ibid.*, 734.
[203] Wibling, *Carl X Gustav*, p. 62.
[204] *RRP* XVIII. 27.
[205] *RRP* XVIII. 57.
[206] *RRP* XVIII, 75.
[207] *RRP* XVIII. 176–8; see above, p. 92.

statement he wrote that 'The field was wide open to the boldest mental experiments.'[208]

But this almost frivolously opportunist approach did on the other hand enable him to grasp immediately the possibilities presented by Frederick III's declaration of war. The battle for the Baltic trade which he had neglected to win in Poland should be transferred from the Vistula to the Sound; the Council decision of December 1654 should be reversed; the Danish, not the Polish option would prove the right one after all. *Dominium maris* would be assured; the long-enduring delusion of control of the Russia trade would become a reality – especially if Vardøhus kept watch on traffickers to Archangel;[209] though before the outbreak of the second Danish war this idea was considered only to be rejected, on the grounds mainly that '*invidia* would prove greater than the profits, and would in time do us serious damage'.[210]

Which brings us to a final point. Kentrschynskyj perceived Charles as inaugurating a new era in Sweden's foreign relations, as establishing new priorities which were long to be conventional wisdom. Henceforward Russia would be the mortal enemy. To this analysis there are two objections. In the first place, the inner consistency of Charles's policy seems open to question. There was an improvisatory, incalculable side to it; it could on occasion be the fruit of hasty decisions, the response to momentary impulses, which was not without its analogies in his tactical brilliance in the field: as Edén wrote, 'Charles X's war-policy was from the beginning marked by a reckless gambling, with varying odds, and this threatened its inner consistency.'[211] General principles of foreign policy could hardly be framed on such a basis;[212] and hence (to quote Edén once more) it could 'leave no fruitful heritage to posterity'.[213]

The second objection in part provides an answer to the first. If Charles laid down no sure base for a new system in foreign policy, he conformed well enough to the tradition he inherited. It is possible, no doubt, to look back upon him as the political ancestor of Charles XII, and this, it seems, is how Kentrschynskyj saw him; but we may also (and equally legitimately) look forward to him as the successor of Erik XIV, John III, and Charles IX. From 1560 to 1660 Sweden was confronted with three hostile neighbours; and in this situation it

---

[208] Edén, 'Grunderna för Karl X Gustavs anfall på Polen', p. 45.
[209] Odén, 'Karl Gustav och det andra danska kriget', pp. 88–94, 110–12.
[210] *RRP* XVIII. 47; cf. *ibid.*, 136.
[211] Edén, 'Grunderna för Karl X Gustafs anfall på Polen', p. 45.
[212] Cf. the concurring judgment of Birger Fahlborg: *Sveriges yttre politik 1660–1664* (Stockholm 1932), p. 2.
[213] Edén, 'Grunderna för Karl X Gustavs anfall på Polen', p. 45.

was prudent to be friends with at least one of them. Erik XIV would have chosen Russia, as Gustav Adolf and Axel Oxenstierna were to do; John III chose Poland; Charles IX made the mistake of fighting all three simultaneously. One conceivable method of cementing friendship was dynastic union. John III based great hopes on Sigismund's election as king of Poland; Gustav Adolf narrowly missed putting Charles Philip on the throne of the Tsars, and was himself for a moment a serious candidate for the Polish crown. Thus Charles X's idea of becoming king of a conquered and reformed Poland (and, later, Denmark) had at least precedent in its favour, however ill-judged it may appear: what he perhaps forgot was that all such previous ventures had turned out ill. So too in another respect one at least of his policies is entirely in line with a long tradition. The aim to recover and consolidate the coastlands, and the later interest in north Norway, stem from John III's hope of controlling the Russia trade, and from those numerous feasibility studies of the possibility of diverting the Archangel trade to Swedish-controlled Baltic ports, which occupied Swedish statesmen at frequent intervals from the 1620s onwards.[214] In short, from 1560 to 1660 the game was the same, the players were the same, the basic tactics unchanged. What was new was that Charles (to quote Georg Landberg) ventured upon 'a wide-ranging east-European imperialism, which did indeed include the domination of the Baltic, but did not stop even at the prospect of a protectorate over the Ukraine'.[215] It is true that successive kings had kept up intermittent contacts with the states and statelets of that region: an earlier Rákóczy had preceded Charles's lamentable client as a potential ally and tool; envoys from the Tatars of the Crimea had made their appearance in Stockholm from time to time, presenting tiresome linguistic and ceremonial problems; but neither Gustav Adolf nor any previous Swedish monarch had entertained ambitions as expansive and impracticable as those which animated Charles X.

After 1660 Swedish foreign policy became far more complex than it had been in the 1650s, as Fahlborg's five volumes amply demonstrate. New concepts such as the Balance of Power, old ones such as *libertates Germaniae* to which Charles had paid little attention, demanded decisions by the Regents and Council. The need for subsidies confronted them with hard choices: Holland or England? France or Holland?, and, most difficult of all, France or the Emperor? All this against the never-sleeping, latent hostility of Denmark. As to

---

[214] For these feasibility studies see *Ekonomiska förbindelser mellan Sverige och Ryssland under 1600-talet*, ed. A. Attman, A.L. Narotjinskij *et al.* (Stockholm 1978).

[215] Georg Landberg. *Den svenska utrikespolitikens historia*, p. 95.

Russia, the Peace of Kardis was followed by head-on diplomatic confrontations about its implementation, with tense moments when war seemed very near:[216] not until the conclusion of the treaty of Pljusamünde in 1666 did relations assume a less disquieting aspect.[217] But already before the Regency ended the situation was changing, both in Poland and in Russia. In Poland, the fear of a Habsburg or a Romanov on the throne was dispelled by the election of two *piasts* in succession; in Russia, factors over which the Regents had no control were making it apparent that the Tsar had sufficient preoccupations at home to deter him from any aggressive adventures: the revival of Tatar incursions; the revolt of Stenka Razin; virtual defeat in the long war with Poland, as manifested by that provision of the Peace of Andrussovo which gave the Poles the prospect of the recovery of Kiev; the *raskol*. With the death of Alexis in 1676 came a dynastic crisis reminiscent of the disorder which had followed the death of Ivan IV. And, after that, there was the long struggle against the Turk which was not to be concluded until 1699. Though the Regents never allowed themselves to forget about Moscow, it is difficult to believe that relations with Russia were now perceived as Sweden's 'greatest interest;.[218] After 1680 it is impossible: Charles XI's eye was fixed upon Denmark; the defences of Balticum were virtually left to take care of themselves. Not until Charles XII was forced to defend himself did Russia resume the place in Sweden's foreign policy which had been allotted to it in December 1654; only then did Sweden find a successor to Chmelnicki in Mazepa. It had been a long parenthesis.

[216] Birger Fahlborg, *Sveriges yttre politik 1664-1668* (Stockholm 1949), I. 57–60.
[217] *Ibid.*, I. 535–9.
[218] It may be noted that Fahlborg's vol. II has no mention of Russia at all.

IV

The Dubious Hand:
The History of a Controversy

I

Advent Sunday, 1718: by the Old Style, 30 November; by the New, eleven days nearer to midwinter. The time, around 9 o'clock in the evening, or a little later. The sun had set at three: and it is now a dark, cloudy, misty winter's night. The scene is outside the Norwegian border town of Fredrikshald, which Charles XII, intent on obtaining a Scandinavian equivalent for the lost Baltic provinces, is engaged in besieging as the first move in his second attempt to overrun Norway. The Swedish attackers, having stormed the outwork of Gyldenlöve three days before, have pushed their approach-trenches to a line roughly parallel with Fredrikshald's main defences, and are for the first time within effective musket range. There is much firing by all arms on the Norwegian side: from the main fortress of Fredriksten, and from two forts, Mellembierg and Overbierg, which lie somewhat further off to the Swedes' left. Though the moon has been risen for more than an hour, it is obscured by clouds, and will remain so for another hour or more; but the darkness is mitigated by the pitch-fires maintained by the defenders on the walls, and is fitfully illuminated by star-shells: there is light enough, perhaps, to alert the besieged to the fact that the Swedes are digging a new approach-trench running out towards the fortress at an acute angle from their front line; for Norwegian fire is concentrated on this area, and there are casualties among the diggers. In the old line, within a yard or two of the spot where the new line branches out of it, stands Charles XII, determined to see anything that is to be seen, and particularly concerned, no doubt, with the progress of the new approach-trench. He has his heels dug into the face of the trench, and lies on his left side; his head projects over the parapet: his body is almost covered, for though the trench itself is shallow (no more than a foot and a half), the parapet rises to perhaps four feet above ground-level. He wears a new uniform, put on for the first time that day; and on his head is a plain three-cornered hat of English felt – not, it would seem, sitting quite squarely on him; his cheek rests on his left hand, his left elbow is propped against the top of the parapet. There comes a projectile – of what kind, and whence, remains obscure. It kills him stone dead: the hand drops from the cheek, the head sinks into the collar, not a sound escapes him.

There are three certain eyewitnesses: three officers who at the moment of the king's death were in immediate proximity to him, standing in a little group at his feet. One was Colonel Maigret, the French engineer responsible for the technical direction of the siege; the second was a Balt named Friedrich von Kaulbars; the third was a young Swedish lieutenant, Bengt Vilhelm Carlberg, who had been in command of the men digging the new approach, and had returned to the old line within the previous six or seven minutes. Maigret and Carlberg each later left an account of what happened; and a third, anonymous, narrative may have been the work of Kaulbars: it is at all events the narrative of an eyewitness. Maigret and the Anonymous vividly remembered the sound of the impact: to Maigret it seemed to resemble the sound made 'when a stone is slung violently into mud'; to the Anonymous, the sound of striking two fingers smartly on the palm of the hand. Carlberg recorded no such recollection; but all three agree upon one point: that the shot passed through the king's head from left to right. It was a point of great significance; for the alignment of the Swedish trenches in relation to the defences, and Charles's posture at the moment of his death, were such that though a shot from the left might (or might not) be an enemy projectile, a shot from the right must almost certainly have come from within the Swedish lines.

At all events, the king was indubitably dead; and in the interests of morale in the army it was desirable to conceal that fact, at least for the moment. Carlberg was despatched to obtain a bearer-party; and when it arrived staff officers who had by this time collected wrapped the corpse closely in a cloak in order to conceal its identity. At this point there appeared another Frenchman, Adjutant-General André Sicre. Sicre was attached to Prince Frederick of Hesse, whom Charles XII had recently appointed *generalissimus* of the Swedish forces, and who in 1720 was to succeed him on the Swedish throne as Frederick I. Sicre now completed the business of concealment by placing his own ample wig on the king's head, and on top of it put his own richly braided cocked hat; it being known to all Europe that the king never wore a wig, and that his simple sartorial tastes did not extend to gold lace. Thus disguised, the corpse was removed by Carlberg and his bearer-party to headquarters at Tistedalen, not without a slightly macabre mishap on the way. Sicre now took the king's hat as evidence of his death – for the fatal shot had sliced a neat semicircle out of the lower brim – and with this bloodstained trophy made all speed to report to Prince Frederick at Torpum, some five miles away; whence he was despatched without loss of time to bear the news (and – probably – the hat) to the Governor of Stockholm.

II

So began a controversy which was to continue for almost two-and-a-half centuries, and which even yet has reached no agreed solution. In the course of time, and particularly since 1920, it has acquired many new facets and entangled a surprising number of disciplines, but the central issue is still, as it always was, quite straightforward: did Charles XII fall by enemy action, or was he murdered? It was a question which simply did not occur to the officers serving in the Swedish army on 30 November: to them – whatever their party affiliation or political principles – it seemed obvious that he fell to a shot from the enemy lines. The evidence of the three eyewitnesses was not known to contemporaries: it was to be half a century before excerpts of Carlberg's story become available;[1] nearly a century before Maigret's got into print;[2] while the narrative of the Anonymous had to await publication until as late as 1898.[3] The newswriters of the day did indeed publish so-called *Gazettes*, based on hearsay information picked up from private individuals, but none of these can be considered as official. The earliest of them, that of 10 December 1718, has by some historians been considered as reflecting what Sicre told the authorities on his arrival; but since it stated that Charles was killed by a shot from the right while attacking a fort – a combination impossible topographically except upon the psychologically incredible supposition that he was shot while running away – it seems unlikely that Sicre should have said anything of the sort. What he actually told the Governor of Stockholm is probably reproduced in a letter of the same date from that nobleman to Hugo Hamilton, in which it is stated that Charles was killed by a shot from the fortress (*sc.* Fredriksten), and that the bullet was a small one.[4] But of this private letter the generality had of course no knowledge: they were dependent on rumour, on tales brought home by returning

---

[1] First in Sven LagerBring's *Sammandrag af Swea Rikes Historia*, vol. IV, Part 3 (2nd Edn. 1786), pp. 115–19, where he summarises the narrative which Carlberg had shown him.

[2] In *Handlingar rörande Skandinaviens Historia*, III (1817).

[3] In *Historisk tidskrift* for that year.

[4] Cited in Nils Ahnlund et al., *Sanning och sägen om Karl XII:s död* (Stockholm 1941), p. 40. The nature of the various contemporary Gazettes is analysed in *ibid.*, pp. 53–62.

soldiers, on gossip influenced by the fact that Charles had miraculously survived such extraordinary dangers for so long that there was a feeling that it was somehow against the regular order of things that he should be dead at last. That feeling produced, in 1724–5, the familiar historical phenomenon of a Pretender, who alleged himself to be Charles, wonderfully escaped from the designs of his enemies;[5] and it engendered the no less familiar belief that the great king lay hidden in a grotto, ageless and eternally solicitous for his people's welfare, destined to return as a deliverer in Sweden's hour of need.[6] More important than such fancies, and longer-lived, was the suspicion of foul play. It began very early: in the versified funeral oration which Olof Rudbeck the younger delivered to the university of Uppsala in February 1719 the suspicion was clearly expressed;[7] and it seems to have established itself in many parts of the country at a very early date. Already before 1718 was out strange rumours had reached London.[8]

Not the least remarkable evidence of this climate of opinion is provided by the odd affair of Neumann's dream.[9] Melchior Neumann had been entrusted with the task of embalming Charles's body. On 14 April 1720 he dreamed that he was once more busy with the corpse; as he turned the king on his side, Charles seized his hand and said 'You shall bear witness to how I was shot'; and when Neumann asked whether he was shot from the fortress, the king answered 'No, Neumann; someone crept up on me' ('Es kom einer gekrochen'). On waking, Neumann noted down his dream in a quarto volume (now vanished) where it lay hidden until 1859, when a transcript of his narrative was made, sent to the historian Anders Fryxell, and published in *Historiska Handlingar* in 1864. As to Neumann's opinion on the question whether it was murder or accident, the only real indication is his statement that the shot came from the left; which of course leaves the question open. But there is much to suggest that the suspicions of others were very much on his mind.

A murder probably, though not necessarily, suggests premeditation and a motive: can any motive be discerned strong enough to explain a regicide? Some contemporaries thought so, and not a few

---

[5] A short account in S. Loenbom, *Historiska Märkwärdigheter Til Uplysning af Swenska Häfder*, I. 5–8 (1768); a full examination in Samuel E. Bring, 'Benjamin Düster – en falsk Karl XII', *Karolinska Förbundets Årsbok (KFÅ)* (1917), pp. 237–74.

[6] P. Wieselgren (ed.), *DelaGardiska Archivet* (Lund, 1841), xv. 36.

[7] LagerBring wrote 'Some murmurs indeed were heard, when Rudbeck mentioned the king's death, and said that it was not a Danish bullet, but some sort of explanation silenced them': *Sammandrag*, vol. v, part 1 (1779), p. 15.

[8] Ahnlund, *Sanning och sägen*, p. 61.

[9] Vilh. Djurberg, 'Om regementsfältskären Melchoir Neumann och Karl XII:s blessyrer', *KFÅ* (1913), pp. 117–19, 138–9.

historians have agreed with them. One motive, it is suggested, was dynastic ambition. By 1718 the question of the succession was becoming acute: Charles was unmarried and unlikely to marry; he declined to designate a successor; and his habitual indifference to danger might lead to his death in battle any day. In such a case there were two possible claimants. One was the young Charles Frederick of Holstein, son of Charles XII's elder sister Hedvig Sofia; the other was Charles's younger sister Ulrika Eleonora, who in 1715 had married that same Frederick of Hesse who was Charles's *generalissimus*. By entering into this marriage she had doubly compromised her claim: first, because Frederick was a Calvinist; and secondly, because the Norrköping Succession Pact of 1604 (and Charles XI's Testament also) had laid it down that in the event of failure of heirs male the throne should descend to the eldest princess 'who was unprovided for' – and after 1715 Ulrika Eleonora was no longer in that situation. The succession was an issue upon which Swedish politicians were divided; and in the last three years of Charles's life Hessian and Holsteiner parties struggled subterraneously for the ascendancy.[10] The Hessians saw with growing alarm the rise of Baron Görtz to a position in which he was entrusted with virtually supreme control of foreign and domestic policy; for Görtz was a Holsteiner himself, and the most formidable supporter of the Holstein cause. It was known that among the various expedients which he devised for extricating Sweden from her catastrophic situation was a project for a peace – or at least, negotiations for a peace – with Russia; to be sealed, perhaps, by the marriage of Charles Frederick with the Tsar's daughter, Anna. If such a marriage were to take place, it might be expected to entail Russian support for a Holstein succession in Sweden. To the Hessians, therefore, it seemed imperative that they should be prepared for the situation which might arise if Charles were killed in battle; and in May 1718 the Hessian Councillor Hein, acting on Frederick's instructions, drew up a memorandum for Ulrika Eleonora which was in fact a detailed plan for immediate action should the throne become vacant. Ulrika Eleonora was a good woman of limited intelligence, pious to the point of bigotry, and she was undoubtedly fond of her brother.[11] Nevertheless, she was convinced of her rights and determined to assert them – not so much for her own sake as with the intention of making way for her husband, to whom she was devoted. Frederick, who had married her as a

[10] Stig Jägerskiöld, 'Den hessiska politiken och den svenska tronföljdsfrågan 1713–1718. Några bidrag', *KFÅ* (1934), pp. 111–43.
[11] Walfrid Holst, *Ulrika Eleonora d.y. Karl XII:s syster* (Stockholm, 1956), pp. 146–52.

political speculation, was no less determined that that speculation should show the intended profit. At the beginning of November it seemed that the crisis they had feared might be upon them: the interrupted peace-talks with the Russians on the Åland Islands were resumed, with Görtz as Sweden's negotiator; on the 13th he started for Charles's headquarters to report; he was expected to reach them on 1 or 2 December, and the news he brought might be fatal to Hessian hopes. But he never got to Tistedalen. On 30 November Charles was killed; on the following day Frederick of Hesse effected Görtz's arrest. From the Hessian point of view it was certainly a remarkable piece of good fortune that at the crucial moment their most dangerous enemy happened to be within reach and at their mercy.

It was not long before the story became current that Ulrika Eleonora had suborned her brother's murder: it was a story which was widely believed until the middle of the next century. Nor was it long before those who credited it were ready to identify the assassin as Frederick's adjutant André Sicre. A Frenchman, a soldier of fortune, a Hessian agent, entrusted with bearing the news of the king's death to his sister – the recipient, rumour said, of a tangible token of her joy[12] – he seemed on general grounds a suitable candidate, apart from the unlucky accident that his name could be Latinised as *Sicarius*. More specific grounds appeared in 1723. Some time in the spring of that year Sicre fell seriously ill in Stockholm, and while (allegedly) in a state of delirium threw open the window of his room and called out 'like a man out of his senses, to doctors and surgeons, and through the window to all the people in the street, that he it was that had done the king to death'.[13] At about the same time a certain Schultz, formerly in the Swedish army but now practising as a dancing-master in St Petersburg, came out with a story that on an earlier occasion Sicre had confided to two named persons that he had shot Charles for a reward of 3,000 or 5,000 ducats. The named persons[14] denied all knowledge of any such confession; Schultz was arrested at the request of the Swedish government, and it was resolved to ask for his extradition; though when Schultz admitted that his tale had no other foundation than current rumour the Council decided that the matter was not worth pursuing further. But

---

[12] For these rumours, see Ahnlund, *Sanning och sägen*, p. 132, nn. 6–7.

[13] So Jöran Nordberg's *Konung Carl XII:s historia* (Stockholm 1740), here quoted after Walfrid Holst, *Fredrik I* (Stockholm 1953), p. 152.

[14] Or at least one of them: the other for the moment could not be found. For the Schultz affair see C. F. Palmstierna in Albert Sandklef et al., *Carl XII:s död* (Stockholm 1940), pp. 105–7; and Ahnlund, *Sanning och sägen*, pp. 123–6, which puts it in its proper perspective.

from King Frederick's point of view it was highly desirable to clear Sicre's name, if that were possible; and accordingly the Court Chancellor von Düben wrote to the Swedish ambassador in Paris, directing him to obtain from two French officers who were present when the king fell an account of what they remembered of the circumstances. One of these two officers was Maigret; the other, it appears, could not be found, and it is a matter of speculation whom they may have had in mind.

From Maigret's terse reply to this enquiry it is apparent that he had been asked, first, whether it was possible to suspect a murder; and further, his opinion of the rumours concerning Sicre. His answer was clear and decided: murder was absolutely impossible, since the projectile, which he described as about the size of a large pigeon's egg, must have come from a weapon too heavy for a man to carry. As to Sicre, Maigret shrugged that off by observing that presumably he was the victim of a campaign of slander. From Frederick's point of view this was satisfactory: but since Maigret's answer remained confidential (it was first published in 1817)[15] it had no effect on public opinion. For Sicre's confession was not forgotten: it formed one of the elements in the strange affair of Olof Dagström in 1728.[16] Dagström was an old soldier who had fallen into disgrace with Charles XII for dereliction of duty; he had become a religious fantast, and appears to have been unhinged; and he convinced himself that it was his duty to atone for his disobedience by bringing the king's murderers to book. He accordingly publicly denounced Frederick I as the inciter of Charles's murder by the hand of Sicre, and proclaimed Charles Frederick of Holstein to be the legitimate king of Sweden. The commission appointed to investigate the affair decided that he was a madman rather than a traitor, and shut him up in an asylum; but not before he had deponed to having seen a letter from the French secretary of embassy in Stockholm which had contained the statement that Charles had been shot at close range. Sicre, by now recovered, had been on the point of leaving for France when the affair blew up, and had to be tactfully persuaded to defer his departure, as being liable to misconstruction.

These accusations provoked literary repercussions. In 1723 Aubry de la Motraye had published the first (English) edition of his *Travels*, in which was included an account of the circumstances of Charles

---

[15] In *Handlingar rörande Skandinaviens Historia*, III.

[16] For the Dagström affair, and the alleged falsification of the record, see C.F. Palmstierna, in Sandklef, *Carl XII:s död*, pp. 116 ff.: a photograph of the supposed falsification appears opposite p. 96. For Ahnlund's refutation of the charge see p. 191 n. 125, below.

XII's death, collected from officers in the Swedish army.[17] In that edition Sicre had appeared simply as the man who lent his wig and took the news to Stockholm. But in the French edition of 1727 Sicre was given an emphatic alibi: he arrived on the scene, we are told, only *after* the king's death, which greatly shocked him. This information de la Motraye alleged that he had from an Italian engineer officer, Marquetti, who was present in the trenches.[18] By this time Sicre had returned to France; and Voltaire, then engaged upon his *Histoire de Charles XII* (1731), took the opportunity of consulting him. How far he accurately reproduced what Sicre told him must remain uncertain; but as it stands his account, too, can be interpreted as giving Sicre an alibi: according to Voltaire, Sicre was standing next to the king when he was killed, and the only other person present was Maigret.[19] Voltaire further informed his readers that Sicre insisted that the shot came from the *right*: de la Motraye had stated emphatically that the shot came from the *left*. Moreover, Voltaire gave the weight of the projectile as half a ship-pound – a weight which is certainly irreconcilable with murder, since (as in Maigret's version) the weapon that fired it could not have been manhandled, and which flatly contradicts Sicre's report in Stockholm that the bullet was a small one. Neither edition of de la Motraye (nor any of the three eyewitness accounts that have come down to us) mentions Sicre as being in the group of officers around the king. In the course of sharp polemical exchanges between de la Motraye and Voltaire – which turned on de la Motraye's very 'literary' account of Maigret's alleged remonstrances to Charles on the exposure of his person: an account dismissed by Voltaire as fabulous – the position was further confused, and Sicre's alibi blurred, by Voltaire's assertion in 1732 that Sicre had told him that he was *alone* with Charles when he was shot – a statement which is palpably untrue.[20] It is hard to resist the impression that de la Motraye and Voltaire, though they may have meant well, did Sicre no service. To have an alibi is useful; to have three alibis, not easily reconcilable with each other, is a misfortune. One can readily understand that Sicre, even if he were innocent, might well be anxious after the unfortunate events of 1723 to provide himself with one. But he had himself confused the issue from the

[17] Aubry de la Motraye, *Travels through Europe, Asia and into Part of Africa* (1732), II. 340–9. I was not able to consult the first edition.
[18] *Voyages du Sr A. De la Motraye en Europe, Asie et Afrique* (The Hague, 1727): the original French text is printed in Sandklef, *Carl XII:s död*, pp. 74–6.
[19] Voltaire, *Histoire de Charles XII* (pocket edn. Garnier-Flammarion, 1968), p. 237.
[20] Voltaire, Note LVII in *Notes sur les Remarques de la Motraye précédées du texte sujet des notes*, in *ibid.*, p. 251.

very beginning; for his report to the Governor of Stockholm that the shot came from the fortress agrees badly with his statement that the bullet was a small one: the general opinion of officers on the spot was that it was a canister-shot, and the wound on the left was by no means small. And Sicre had seen the corpse at close range.

However, all these inconsistencies and contradictions seem to have had little effect upon informed contemporary opinion. Sicre's delirium seems to have been pretty generally accepted as a sufficient explanation of his confession. Individuals here and there continued to believe that he was the assassin – Linnaeus was one; Tiburtz Tiburtius, whose improbable narrative we shall have to consider presently, was another – but by the time Voltaire's book appeared suspicion had largely died away. Even the supporters of the Holstein candidature abroad, and its former adherents at home, never attached much credit to the charge; and in 1727 both parties in the *riksdag* and the Secret Committee agreed in a generous grant of all his arrears of pay, including the period when he was disabled by sickness. He died in France in 1733, and it is said that he died in poverty; not before he had protested to Voltaire his horror at the accusations made against him. But though Sicre thus dropped out of sight, and though level-headed men might be disposed to forget him, that disastrous confession – or were there, after all, *two* confessions? – stuck in the popular memory; and there was enough uncertainty as to his movements on that fatal night, enough contradiction in what had already become public, and still more in what was to emerge in the future, to keep Sicre, in the minds of some future historians, among those to whom suspicion must attach.

III

The men of the Age of Liberty had contradictory views about Charles XII. On the one hand they abhorred his absolutism, demolished his emergency administrative machinery, and judicially murdered his minister. On the other hand they could not forget that he had spent most of his reign in fighting the national enemy, Russia, and was consequently to be considered as a patriot and a hero. Any murderer could therefore be regarded either as a traitor or a Brutus, according as internal or foreign politics might predominate in the feelings of the moment. Or, perhaps, according to party affiliation. The Caps, by conviction the party of peace, by necessity the *protégés* of Russia, could probably feel no great attachment to his memory, though even they would not have denied his extraordinary personal qualities. But they saw them as heroic attributes more appropriate to a Viking age than to their own.[21] The Hats, on the other hand, as the party anxious to reverse the verdict of the peace of Nystad by a war with Russia which would recover the lost Baltic provinces, could see Charles's policy as an example to be followed; and they did indeed believe that they were following it in their wanton and bungled attack upon Russia in 1741.[22] The Hats, moreover, were the lineal descendants of the old Holstein party, and not indisposed when it suited them to make things unpleasant for Frederick I – even to the extent of reviving the old insinuation that he had Charles's death on his conscience.[23] For though Sicre might be temporarily forgotten, the belief in murder was vigorously alive. In 1731 the clothes which the king had worn when he was killed were put on exhibition in Stockholm – one of the sights of the city inspected by foreign tourists, from Sir Nathaniel Wraxall to General Miranda – and his blood-stained right gauntlet perhaps gave substance to the belief – memorably enshrined in Anders Odel's *Sinclairsvisan* (1739), and not quite extinct at the end of the 1920s – that the king had seen his assailant, and had half-drawn his sword before he was shot, a story plainly irreconcilable with a shot from the right, except upon the supposition that Charles had eyes in the back of his head. In the mid-eighteenth century the view gained ground that he had been killed by a pistol shot – a musket being an unhandy weapon for lurking about with on a dark night, and a pistol being the ordinary armament of every officer. The theory involved difficulties; for a pistol-shot, if it was to be effective, would have required such short range that Charles's face would have been scorched and pitted. No such disfigurement had been noted, and was indeed expressly denied by some who had seen the corpse.[24] But by the early fifties Anders Johan von Höpken was recording that there were those who believed

[21] A point of view well represented by the Cap sympathizer Olof Dalin: see Nils Dyberg, *Olof Dalin och tidsideerna* (Uppsala 1946), p. 78. For Cap pamphlets censuring Charles's strategy and tactics, and comparing him unfavourably with Peter the Great, see A.S. Kan, 'Ryssland och de rysk-svenska relationerna i ljuset av den svenska publicistiken från frihetstiden och den gustavianska tiden', *Scandia* (1980), p. 167. And for the whole question, Karl-Gustaf Hildebrand, 'Till Karl XII-uppfattningens historia. I', *Historisk tidskrift* (1954), pp. 359–60.

[22] Nevertheless, the prominent Hat Anders Johan von Höpken could write in his *Memoirs* that he was 'a wretched king, an incomparable fighter, a miserable strategist and general, a hero fit for "the Old Goths" ... but in the present day, when war has become a science and demands something more than a knowledge of how to kill people, to be considered only as dauntless and courageous': *Riksrådet Anders Johan von Höpkens skrifter*, ed. Carl Silfverstolpe (Stockholm 1890), I. 13. For a judicious weighing of Charles's character against his policies, see the anonymous 'Facta till Revolutions-Historia under Konung Carl XII:s Regering ... ', *Handlingar rörande Skandinaviens Historia*, VII (1819), which seems to have been written between 1743 and 1751.

[23] Holst, *Fredrik I*, p. 225.

[24] *Riksrådet och Fältmarskalken m.m. Grefve Fredrik Axel von Fersens historiska skrifter*, ed. R.M. Klinckowström (Stockholm 1867), I. 6–7.

that these telltale traces had been skilfully eliminated: an achievement, one may think, that would have taxed the cosmetic art of a Californian mortician.[25]

Höpken personally was neutral on the question of how Charles met his death: 'a riddle', he wrote, 'and likely to remain so'; which is notable, since he was in a better position than most men to form an opinion. For on 12 July 1746, between five and six o'clock in the morning, he was one of a select party of three which witnessed the first exhumation. It was carried out in connexion with a shifting of the royal tombs in the Riddarholm church: the motive remains conjectural, but the inspiration is said to have come from the future Queen Lovisa Ulrika, who seems to have believed in murder, was perhaps anxious to have that belief confirmed, and was quite malicious enough to hope that an exhumation would provide results embarrassing to 'old Pan' (her disrespectful nickname for Frederick I).[26] However that may be, the examination of 1746 was superficial and altogether lacking in expertise. But their report made one important statement:[27] the shot came from the right. And to this conclusion they were almost certainly led by the fact that the hole on the right side of the skull was smaller than that on the left; for it was generally accepted by contemporaries that a bullet's exit-hole was always larger than its entry-hole. So it seemed that Sicre (and Voltaire) had been right after all: a small bullet, a shot from the right. Perhaps in order to spare King Frederick's feelings the report was not published until 1768, by which time Frederick had been dead for seventeen years; but when it did appear it was accepted as giving final confirmation of the theory of murder, and that verdict was not upset for another ninety years – certainly not by the second exhumation of 1799, which was carried out simply to satisfy the curiosity of Gustav IV Adolf as to whether David Krafft's portrait of the king was really a good likeness.[28] It seems very probable that it is to the report of 1746 that we must attribute the inspiration of various more or less incredible accounts which appeared in the succeeding half-century or so: for instance, that of the lackey Pihlgren, printed in 1773, with its narration of conspiratorial whisperings round Frederick's dinner-

[25] *Riksrådet Anders Johan von Höpkens skrifter*, ed. Silfverstolpe, I. 14.

[26] Holst, *Fredrik I*, p. 248. The evidence for her interest in the subject is strengthened by the strong possibility that it was at her instigation that the lackey Pihlgren set down his demonstrably erroneous account of the events of 30 November 1718, and by the possibility that she may also have been behind the equally erroneous reminiscences of Ture Gabriel Bielke: for them, see below, note 31.

[27] It is printed in [C.G. Gjörwell], *Anmärkningar i Swenska Historien* (Stockholm 1782), pp. 54–5.

[28] For Gustav IV Adolf and Charles XII see Sten Carlsson, *Gustav IV Adolf* (Stockholm 1946), pp. 86–7.

table, and its story of Charles's tight grip upon his half-drawn sword;[29] or the tale which was told to Nathaniel Wraxall by Hans Henrik von Liewen in 1774, which has Charles killed by a pistol-shot from the right while asleep: von Liewen was aged fourteen in 1718, but half a century later he could still clearly remember that the sound of the fatal shot was different from all the other miscellaneous detonations which were occurring at the same time.[30] Ture Gabriel Bielke, however, whose narrative was published only in 1817, posited no such nice discrimination: at the time of Charles's death, it appears, the enemy had not loosed off a shot for several hours, and this curious suspension of activity was broken only by the single shot which laid the king low.[31] This was a view of the situation which would certainly have surprised Carlberg, who, as we remember, had been marching up and down the new approach exhorting the diggers, exposed to a pretty intense fire. But it is remarkable that the publication of Carlberg's narrative in full in 1803, and again in 1816,[32] seems to have had little or no influence upon contemporary opinion, despite his clear statement that the shot came from the left. As far as the reading public and Swedish historians were concerned the report of 1746 had settled the issue once for all. In the school textbooks of the first half of the nineteenth century Charles was pronounced to have been murdered, and Ulrika Eleonora was loaded with obloquy as the inciter of fratricide.

By an appropriate and perhaps necessary coincidence, the publication of the report of 1746 was very soon followed by the appearance of a new suspect to fill the place once occupied by Sicre. This time it was no foreign soldier of fortune, but a native Swede and a person of some importance. Major-General Carl Cronstedt had served all through Charles XII's wars, and served with distinction. He was present at Narva, captured at Perevolotschna, contributed decisively to Stenbock's victory at Gadebusch, was severely wounded in Stralsund. His special branch was the artillery, and his special invention a device whereby much more rapid fire was attained by attaching the

---

[29] Printed in S. Loenbom, *Uplysningar i Swenska Historien*, (Stockholm 1773), I. 99–102.

[30] Nathaniel W. Wraxall, *Cursory Remarks made in a Tour through some of the Northern Parts of Europe* (1775), pp. 147–8. According to Ahnlund (*Sanning och sägen*, p. 111, n. 1) he was not in the trenches at all.

[31] Printed in Carl Hallendorff: *Studier öfver den äldre Karl XII:s historiografien* (Uppsala 1901), I. 97–8. This detail, and the statement that Charles was asleep, with his head resting on both arms, seems to come from the alleged letter of the French secretary of embassy, quoted by Dagström at his examination, the record of which Bielke may well have seen. For Bielke's possible connexion with Lovisa Ulrika, see Palmstierna, in Sandklef, *Carl XII:s död*, p. 150; for Pihlgren's, Loenbom, *Uplysningar i Swenska historien*, I. 99 ff., where it is stated that the original MS is in Lovisa Ulrika's collection. Query: how did Loenbom get hold of it?

[32] In *Handlingar rörande Skandinaviens Historia*, I. 177–95.

charge to the cannon-ball. Charles XII thought highly of his services and abilities, and in 1717 entrusted him with the reorganisation of the Swedish artillery; he was in command of the guns at the siege of Fredrikshald; and on 3 August 1718 he was created a baron. As to party politics, he was a Hessian; on more general issues he seems by 1718 to have come to the conclusion that it was essential to make peace, if anything were to be saved from the wreck.

For the suspicion which fell on Cronstedt it would seem that he had mainly himself to blame. In Fredrik Axel von Fersen's *Historiska Skrifter*, written some time during the 1780s but first published in 1867, he recalled that Cronstedt himself had told him many years after 1718, that some three weeks before Charles's death he had predicted that the king would not outlive the year. The only reason he could assign for this idea was that when preparing by prayer and meditation to take communion at the end of October he had had a sort of revelation.[33] He seems to have made no secret of his experience, nor to have refrained from repeating his prediction. By 1736 it was sufficiently common knowledge for the historian Jöran Nordberg (who had been entrusted with writing the official history of Charles XII) to incorporate it into his account of the events of 30 November: in this version the generals entreat the king to take some rest and not to go to the trenches; Charles refuses to listen to them; and on his departure Cronstedt 'is said to have observed to the others: "he who wishes to see the king alive sees him now for the last time." '. This passage, however, Nordberg suppressed when his book was published in 1740.[34] Nordberg's anecdote may be true or not; but at least it does not appear that in Cronstedt's lifetime it affected his reputation or caused him embarrassment. His advancement after Charles's death was not perhaps what might have been expected: Ulrika Eleonora, it seems, did not approve of him; but in 1740 he was appointed President of the College of War, and he continued to hold that office until his death at the end of 1750. He was given a state funeral of quite unusual pomp and splendour;[35] and Olof Dalin – a member of the order *Awazu och Wallasis*, which was dedicated to celebrating Charles's memory – in his glowing funeral oration provided him with what was perhaps intended as a deliberate refutation of any slanderous aspersions.

[33] *Fredrik Axel von Fersens historiska skrifter*, I. 5–6.
[34] For Nordberg's 'suppressed passages', see Carl Hallendorff, *Studier öfver den äldre Karl XII:s historiografien*, I. *Bidrag till frågan om publicerandet af Nordbergs Konung Carl XII:s historia* (Uppsala 1899).
[35] See the description in P. Wieselgren (ed.), *DelaGardiska Archivet* (Stockholm 1841), XV. 215–19. Cronstedt was in 1748 made a Commander of the Order of the Sword and a Knight of the Order of the Seraphim: *ibid.* IX. 144.

But if rumour left Cronstedt unscathed during his lifetime, it played havoc with his character after he was dead. At some time between 1751 and 1759 Fersen heard a story to the effect that on his deathbed Cronstedt had sought the ministrations of a famous Pietist divine named Tollstadius, and to him had confessed that he had employed a certain Major Magnus Stierneroos to kill the king; that he had personally loaded the blunderbuss which Stierneroos was to use; and that it was at that moment hanging on the wall of his chamber. Fersen, who knew Tollstadius well, asked him about it; and Tollstadius 'on his oath' assured him that the story was wholly untrue, and that Cronstedt had said no such thing.[36] Not everyone, however, was on Fersen's intimate footing with Tollstadius, and Fersen's account, as we have seen, did not appear until 1867. In the meantime the story took root; it spread; it engendered interesting mutations. One such appeared in Büsching's *Wochentliche Nachrichten* in 1776. In this version Cronstedt was alleged to have proclaimed himself the murderer at a dinner-party in 1750, to have displayed to his fellow-guests objects filched from Charles's pocket, and in an access of Sicre-like frenzy to have attempted to throw himself from a window into the street below.[37] Archdeacon Coxe, diligently noting down what he could pick up on his tour of northern countries in 1779, recorded that he had heard 'in general' that Cronstedt had confessed to loading a *pistol* with which Stierneroos had shot the king from behind; that Tollstadius had made a memorandum of the confession, which was preserved in the archives; adding for good measure that Stierneroos had also in his last illness confessed to his crime. Coxe rounded off his account of deathbed repentances with the report that it was still believed by some that Frederick I, too, 'raved' on his deathbed, and expressed 'great contrition and compunction'. And by way of indicating his view of just how much credit was to be attached to stories of this sort, Coxe revealed that he had been told by his friend the botanist Philip Miller that F.E. Fabrice, the Hanoverian minister in England, had confessed that Charles XII had been murdered by *him*: a feat the more remarkable since at the time in question it was a demonstrable fact that Fabrice was in London. All in all, Coxe's summing-up of the position does credit to his qualities as a historian: 'until positive proofs', he wrote, 'not merely drawn from flying reports and uncertain anecdotes, are established, we ought undoubtedly to lean on the side of candour and humanity, and we ought not to credit surmises so injurious to

[36] *Fredrik Axel von Fersens historiska skrifter*, i. 6.
[37] I was not able to see this version: this summary is derived from Palmstierna, in Sandklef, *Carl XII:s död*, p. 156.

characters otherwise without reproach'.[38] After Coxe's second visit to Sweden in 1784 his scepticism grew even more pronounced: anecdotes concerning Cronstedt's confession and Frederick's remorse, he considered, were probably void of foundation: the root of the matter was 'the natural propensity of mankind to attribute the death of an extraordinary person to extraordinary causes'; and 'those who have once framed an hypothesis will imperceptibly warp all events to its support' – an observation which was to be verified more than once in the future, and which might have been read with profit in 1940.[39]

However that might be, it would appear that it was not only once that Cronstedt found his conscience clamouring to discharge itself of its burden, nor that Tollstadius was the only confessor to whom he turned. At some time not earlier than 1808 an individual not otherwise known to history made a note of a conversation which had taken place in 1794, in the course of which it transpired that Cronstedt, being seriously ill, had sent for his parish priest, Magnus Asplind (who, unlike Tollstadius, was not available for comment, having died in 1772), and to him revealed that he had shot the king himself. By way of assuaging his remorse he had asked Asplind to remove from his sight the portrait of Charles XII which happened to be hanging in his sick-room. And Asplind too made a memorandum of his confession which was said to have been found among his papers at his death.[40] If so, it has escaped the attention of researchers.

Thus it is pretty clear that in the half-century after 1750 there had grown up a flourishing crop of miscellaneous anecdote as to the part played by Cronstedt and Stierneroos in the business. But there was, as yet, no hard written evidence to go on. It was not until 1837 that Per Wieselgren, to whom had been entrusted the task of printing selections from the vast collection of manuscript material preserved in the archives of the de la Gardie family at Löberöd, produced in the ninth volume of the series the evidence that was wanting.[41] What he printed was a note by Jacob de la Gardie, dated August 1799, which embodies the Cronstedt–Tollstadius–Stierneroos tradition, much as Fersen had heard it forty years earlier, except that the weapon now hung in Stierneroos's house, and that Cronstedt twice sent Toll-

[38] William Coxe, *Travels into Poland, Russia, Sweden, and Denmark* (1784), II. 352–63. Coxe also read Pihlgren's narrative; and in Göteborg, which he visited a month after Carlberg's death, was informed that Carlberg 'constantly asserted that the wound was given by a musket or pistol'.
[39] *Ibid.* (4th edn. 1792), II. 95–9. For an appreciation of Coxe as a historian see P. Fritz, 'Archdeacon Coxe as Political Biographer', in *The Triumph of Culture: Eighteenth Century Perspectives*, ed. P. Fritz and D. Williams (Toronto 1972), pp. 211–18.
[40] For the Asplind story, see Palmstierna, in Sandklef, *Carl XII:s död*, pp. 142–3.
[41] Wieselgren (ed.), *DelaGardiska Archivet* (Lund, 1837), IX. 128–68; XIV. 162–87.

stadius to urge Stierneroos to confess. It incorporated also the statement that Stierneroos was paid 500 ducats for his trouble, from some
source unknown.[42] But what distinguished de la Gardie's note from
all previous information was that it purported to reproduce a document written by Tollstadius himself, discovered among his remains
after his death. The document itself had unfortunately disappeared;
but it was said to have been seen by Baron Malte Ramel, who had
either made a note of it, or caused a note to be made of it, from
memory; and it was this note, preserved among Ramel's papers in
the de la Gardie archives, that Jacob de la Gardie had copied.[43]

So the Tollstadian document turns out to be a copy from memory,
taken by someone not definitely identified, who may or may not
have been in a position to recognise Tollstadius's handwriting; and
this copy is known to us only in a second copy by somebody else,
and is vouched for on hearsay some eighty years after the supposed
original was written, and in the face of its alleged author's categorical
denial of the whole story. But Wieselgren believed implicitly in its
authenticity, and on at least one occasion had alluded to it in com-
pany; with disconcerting results. For among those who heard him
was Ture Funck, who was a half-brother of one of Cronstedt's
grandsons, and who received the information with a heated denial.
The so-called Tollstadian document, Funck explained, was a
forgery; and it had been perpetrated, if not by Gustav III himself
(who at the time of Tollstadius's death was aged four), then at least
by his direction, in order to provide a colourable pretext for retract-
ing the promise of a donation to Cronstedt's heirs. Gustav III, one
may think, was not the man to bother to invent elaborate pretexts for
failing to fulfil a promise; and in fact the Funck family grievance had
other origins of a less sinister kind.[44] At all events, Wieselgren (right
for once) brushed Funck's objections aside: even if the document had
been a forgery, it could have hoped to succeed only if it were *a priori*
plausible; but of course it was *not* a forgery: he had no doubt that
Cronstedt, 'the cleverest loader in the army'[45] (whether of cannon,
musket, or pistol did not appear) prepared the fatal shot. The question Wieselgren now asked himself was: Who was behind all this? He

[42] A bargain price, as Nils Ahnlund was later tartly to remark, for a regicide.
[43] Wieselgren (ed.), *DelaGardiska Archivet*, IX. 157 n.
[44] Wieselgren (ed.), *DelaGardiska Archivet* IX. 131–2, for Wieselgren's encounter with Funck.
Funck's grievance against Gustavus III is noted also by Coxe, *Travels*, (4th edn) II. 97–8, where
he adds that two years later Gustav altered his opinion, and 'voluntarily gave the commission
to the same person, candidly alleging that he had been mistaken, and that he was now
convinced Cronstedt had no share in the king's assassination'. For the real explanation of
Funck's grievance, see C.F. Palmstierna, in Sandklef, *Carl XII:s död*, pp. 160–70.
[45] Wieselgren (ed.), *DelaGardiska Archivet*, IX. 157.

was not satisfied with the easy solution. Frederick I, no doubt; but what dark forces were manipulating Frederick I? To any attentive observer of the international situation the answer at once presented itself: Cardinal Dubois. The murder of Charles XII was designed to forestall a Russo-Swedish action, directed in general against the Quadruple Alliance, whose first objective would be a Jacobite restoration in Scotland. In this *coup* the two Frenchmen, Maigret and Sicre, had their allotted parts to play. It was their business to keep Charles's officers away from him while the murder was committed by Stierneroos. And that murder, he reasoned, was carried out *within* the trench, *before* Charles's head appeared over the parapet: hence the king's half-drawn sword. And when the deed was done, the assassins lifted the body into position on the parapet, waited for the moment when a convenient enemy shot should fall near it, and then cried 'The king is shot!' The honest but credulous Carlberg was thus imposed upon, the eight or ten members of Charles's staff who now had been permitted to gather near him were deceived likewise, the habitually sinister proceedings of the French achieved their objective, and the Hanoverian succession was saved.[46]

There was no doubt an element of truth in Wieselgren's analysis of the implications of Charles's death for the international situation, but the evidence he adduced to prove French complicity would hardly bear such a construction. It was not long before he was sharply called to account. In 1846 the Danish historian C. Paludan-Müller, having fought his way through the jungle of *DelaGardiska Archivet*, took it upon himself to subject Wieselgren's scenarios to a critical examination in an essay entitled 'Er Kong Carl den Tolvte falden ved Snigmord?' ('Did Charles XII die at the hand of an assassin?') which was published in the Danish *Historisk Tidsskrift* for that year. Wasting little time on Wieselgren's gallophobe fantasies, Paludan-Müller directed his main onslaught upon the Tollstadian document; and if one bears in mind that at the time he was writing Fersen's memoirs were still unpublished, and the Asplind story lay unknown in the Uppsala University Library, it must be conceded that he managed to deal a telling blow to the belief in its authenticity. He pointed out the vague and derivative nature of the evidence; he noted errors which Tollstadius would not have made; and above all he insisted that in no circumstances would Tollstadius have violated the secrecy of the confessional (and he might have added that such a violation is made still more incredible by the fact that if it occurred, it occurred while Stierneroos was still alive: Fersen heard the story between 1751 and

[46] For this remarkable reconstruction of events, see Wieselgren (ed.), *DelaGardiska Archivet* IX. 159–60; XIV. 8–10.

1759; Stierneroos did not die – loaded, like Cronstedt, with honours and preferments[47] – until 1762). Paludan-Müller then proceeded to deal with another point which Wieselgren had made much of: the distribution by Frederick of Hesse of 'gratifications', immediately after Charles's death. It so happened that 100,000 *dalers* had just been received at Charles's headquarters: money urgently needed to pay the troops. Frederick unhesitatingly used this supply to secure – or confirm – the support of the most important army officers, the gifts (or retainers) being graded, on the whole, according to rank. Wieselgren had printed the list of donations,[48] and had drawn attention to the fact that Cronstedt had received 4,000 *dlr* – or just five times as much as any other major-general: a discrimination surely of sinister significance. Paludan-Müller had no difficulty in blunting the edge of this innuendo from Wieselgren's own figures; which showed that Charles Frederick of Holstein – Frederick's rival for the throne – had been given 6,000 *dlr*, that two leading supporters of the Holstein cause had received 12,000 and 4,000 *dlr* respectively, and that if the gratifications were (as Frederick alleged) 'for difficulties endured', then Cronstedt, in command of the artillery in a difficult terrain and in mid-winter, had probably endured more than most of his colleagues, and really deserved his reward. He might have added, if he had pursued the matter further, that in the decades after 1720 the government took the line that these gratifications were to be considered as advances which the recipients were now due to repay; and they did in fact extort repayment in almost all cases. The most conspicuous case in which they failed was that of Carl Cronstedt, who was able to show that what he had received was acknowledged at the time to be a 'gift and reward', already promised by Charles XII in recognition of exceptionally meritorious services.[49] Paludan-Müller was also the first man to make one other observation of some importance: namely, that Charles must have been in the trench for several hours before he was killed (he arrived soon after 4, and was not killed earlier than 9); and that this fact may well explain, for instance, the discrepancy between de la Motraye's account of Maigret's remonstrances to Charles upon the exposure of his person, and Voltaire's rejection of that account as fabulous: their respective informants may have had different moments in mind.

Paludan-Müller may have savaged the Tollstadian theory, but he

---

[47] Stierneroos was made Commander of the Order of the Sword, with Grand Cross, in 1748, and promoted General of Cavalry 1755: Wieselgren (ed.), *DelaGardiska Archivet*, IX. 145.

[48] Wieselgren (ed.), *DelaGardiska Archivet*, IX. 134, 139.

[49] For Cronstedt's successful struggle against the demand for repayment see Palmstierna, in Sandklef, *Carl XII:s död*, pp. 136–40.

certainly did not kill it. Within a year of the publication of his article Evert von Saltza came forward with a new version.[50] In this Tollstadius insisted that two members of the Council of State be present as witnesses to Cronstedt's confession; and Cronstedt, by a confusing inversion of roles, confessed that *he* had shot the king with Stierneroos's weapon. Von Saltza subsequently produced at least three alternative accounts, each differing from the others, and one of them eliminating Tollstadius altogether.[51] More interesting, perhaps, was the deposition of Ture Cederström and two of his sisters in 1862.[52] They were descendants in the third generation of Cronstedt's elder brother Gabriel; and they offered to affirm on oath (though nobody seems to have thought it worth while to take them at their word) that their father had told them that his mother, Gabriel's daughter, was present at Cronstedt's deathbed, and that the dying man bade the attendants remove from his sight the weapon he had lent to Stierneroos. Of Tollstadius there was this time no mention. The story makes Cronstedt die in the wrong place (as Asplind had also done), and there were other difficulties, but the Cederströms stuck to it valiantly: it is not every family that can boast a regicide, and they were not disposed to jettison theirs.

IV

Despite this family piety, despite von Saltza's enviable fertility in anecdote, by the middle of the nineteenth century the attention of those interested in the problem had shifted: shifted away from a concern about the identity of a murderer to the larger question as to whether it was a murder at all. The change of emphasis was primarily due to Paludan-Müller's translator, Georg Swederus. Paludan-Müller had indeed argued warmly against murder; but since he accepted the result of the exhumation of 1746 – namely that the shot came from the right – he could sustain his argument only by shifting the topography as though it were a stage-set, and the Swedish translation was accompanied by a running fire of footnotes in which Swederus patiently corrected his author's misconceptions, though he wholeheartedly accepted his conclusion. It was Swederus who initiated the demand for another exhumation, less cursory and more competent than that of 1746. The demand was not met for

---

[50] Evert von Saltza, *Familjeanekdoter och minnen från barndomen*, ed. Nils Sjöberg (Stockholm 1912), pp. 28–9.

[51] For von Saltza's anecdotes see Ahnlund, *Sanning och sägen*, pp. 161–2; and Palmstierna, in Sandklef, *Carl XII:s död*, pp. 166–7.

[52] Palmstierna, in Sandklef, *Carl XII:s död*, p. 173.

another thirteen years; and it was mainly owing to pressure from the historian Anders Fryxell (no friend, incidentally, to Charles XII, but conceivably not unwilling to exculpate the aristocracy) that permission was at last given for the third exhumation, that of 1859.

It took place on 31 August of that year; was conducted by a professor of surgery, a professor of anatomy, and a court physician; and it seems to have occupied no more than a single day. They reported that the shot that killed the king came from a distance, was probably a musket or cannon-shot, and that it came from the *left*. Their proceedings were not only limited in scope and duration; they were besides open to grave methodological objections: the final report differed, both by alterations and additions, from the notes taken on the spot at the time of the examination; and they got themselves into absurd mensurational tangles about the dimensions of the wounds through mixing up decimal and non-decimal measurements. In so far as they were correct in their conclusions, it seems hardly unfair to say that they were so by accident; and if they had not been men of unimpeachable scientific integrity a hostile critic might suspect that they fiddled the result.[53] It is more likely, however, that they were unconsciously influenced by the climate of opinion in which they worked. The nature of that climate appears plainly from the debate of their report at the meeting of the Swedish Medical Association on 1 November, where the very pertinent criticisms of Dr Liljewalch (in a minority of one) were simply brushed aside. Not without reason could he describe the purpose of the investigation as apparently being

to wipe out from Svea's escutcheon, if that be possible, the stain of blood which vicious party animosity, insidious malice and unpardonable credulity have so contrived to implant into the mind of the public that the conviction of regicide has not only become a folk-legend, but has also secured a place as an established *truth*, in our most widely used textbooks.[54]

The exhumation, in short, was to be the Swedish nation's *Ehrenrettung*; and as such it handsomely fulfilled the hopes of those who had pressed for it.

This new climate of opinion had begun to set in as early as 1772, with Gustav III's revolution. Gustav admired Charles, partly as a stage hero in a splendid battle-play – the sort of part he saw himself as playing in 1788 – partly because 1772 implied a historic revenge for 1719. It was in accordance with this view that he rehabilitated

[53] For criticisms of the 1859 investigation, see Algot Key-Åberg. *Om Konung Karl XII:s banesår* (Stockholm 1918), pp. 10–12, 19–21; and the devastating account in Sam Clason, *Gåtan från Fredrikshald* (1941), pp. 21–39.

[54] Clason, *Gåtan från Fredrikshald*, p. 24.

Görtz and restored the family fortune to his heirs. Gustav IV Adolf identified himself with Charles as the type of righteous man struggling with iniquity. The first Bernadotte extolled him, perhaps by way of propitiating the public. For, apart from the views of the monarchs, there had been a perceptible shifting of opinion in Charles's favour, and a corresponding shift in approach to the problem of his death.[55] It found expression among the late Gustavians: the Anjala conspiracy and the murder of Gustav III predisposed them to see the events of 30 November 1718 as the work of the aristocracy. To Jonas Hallenberg, for instance, whose five volumes on Gustav Adolf (1790–6) are a landmark in the historiography of the subject, Charles's murder was part of a general pattern: Charles X, Charles XI, and Charles XII had all fallen victims to the same dark forces. G. A. Silfverstolpe's *Lärobok i svenska historien (Textbook of Swedish History)* (1805) stated bluntly that Charles had been killed by 'that vengeful party' which had earlier sabotaged his policies.[56] Although the anonymous author of 'Facta till Revolutions-Historia' had already in the mid-century laid heavy stress on internal discontents, and had retailed a story of aristocratic plots,[57] it was not until the Gustavian period that the theory of a constitutional rather than a dynastic motive really began to emerge; to survive, as a minority opinion – the poet Atterbom, for instance, believed that the assassins were men 'pregnant with the Age of Liberty' – until it was forcefully argued in the twentieth century.[58]

The loss of Finland in 1809, which could be considered either as the justification or the condemnation of Charles's policies, produced an upsurge of patriotism which coincided with the rejection by the new Romantic school of literature of all the chiselled classicism of which Leopold was the last great defender. The Romantics revived the old enthusiasm for the Ancient Goths; a revival signalised by the foundation in 1811 of the Gothic League: the new generation found in their forefathers a source of poetic inspiration. As to Charles, they were fascinated by his personality, though they showed small enthusiasm for his policies. Tegnér's *Kung Karl den unge hjälte (King*

[55] Among the broad masses of the Swedish people there was of course no such shift: for two and a half centuries their view remained unaltered. Charles was a national hero, and the controversies of the learned affected them not at all.

[56] Hildebrand, 'Till Karl XII-uppfattningens historia' pp. 367–8. Hallenberg might have added Ulrika Eleonora to his list: popular rumour had it that she had been poisoned: Holst, *Ulrika Eleonora* p. 312. The anti-aristocratic attitude appears also in the historian E. M. Fant: Emerik Olsoni, 'Karl XII:s-gestalten genom tiderna', *KFÅ* (1956), p. 206.

[57] 'Facta till Revolutions-Historia under Konung Carl XII:s Regering', *Handlingar rörande Skandinaviens Historia*, VII (1819), pp 223–38, 243–4.

[58] Gustaf Jacobson, *Från Geijer till Hjärne, Studier i svensk historieskrivning under 1800-talet* (Stockholm 1945), p. 175; Olsoni, 'Karl XII:s-gestalten genom tiderna', p. 206.

Charles, the youthful hero) did homage to the king's character in lines imprinted on the memory of every schoolboy. The historian Erik Gustaf Geijer – though he blamed Charles for the catastrophe of 1809 – hymned his heroic virtues in lines only less famous than Tegnér's, and by proclaiming the fundamental identity of interest of King and People in the face of Aristocracy implicitly rejected the ideology of the Age of Liberty. In the years after 1815, something akin to the idealistic, romantic nationalism of the *Burschenschaft* sprang up in Sweden; and by the 1840s the undergraduates of Uppsala were making that seat of learning – and, indeed, the whole of Sweden – ring with proudly patriotic choruses.[59] A little later, the Liberals added their voices: for them Russia was the natural enemy, not only for the usual historical reasons, but also as the great oppressive despotic power, the enemy of national self-determination and freedom. At a great popular gathering in 1862 on the anniversary of Pultava, the rhetoric of Polish, Hungarian, and Italian orators confirmed that they had correctly identified their adversary. When the Crimean War came in 1856 Oscar I made pertinacious attempts to associate Sweden with the anti-Russian alliance. And in 1859, a bare two months before the third exhumation took place, the throne passed to Charles XV, who in his person seemed fitted to reflect the feelings of the time: chevaleresque, impressively martial – at least, to the extent of brilliant uniforms, dashing horsemanship, and glittering reviews – immensely popular (even with Norwegians), he was believed by some to be destined to reverse the verdict of Nystad and stand conqueror upon the ruins of St Petersburg. For the first time it occurred to the Swedes that they had no statue of Charles XII.[60] In 1868 that omission was repaired. And since this was the temper of the age the obstinate family traditions of a few aristocratic houses such as the Cederströms appeared as what perhaps they were: lingering echoes of eighteenth-century Whiggery. For most other people, the national honour had been vindicated; and there was little disposition to undertake any further probe into an unsavoury subject.

But the verdict of 1859 was not to enjoy as long a period of undisputed authority as that of 1746. It was precisely in the late fifties – from 1856 to 1859 – that Anders Fryxell published the four volumes of his *Berättelser ur svenska historien (Tales from Swedish History)* which covered the reign of Charles XII. Though deplorably

[59] The second verse of the immortal *Studentsång* (words by H. Sätherberg, music by Oscar I's second son, Prince Gustaf) is a prime example of the *genre*.

[60] For Charles XV, see Sven Eriksson's admirable biography, *Carl XV* (Stockholm, 1954). For popular belief in his mission to reverse the verdict of Nystad, Anna Hamilton Geete, *I solnedgången* (Uppsala, 1911), II. 306. For the statue and its antecedents, see Nils F. Holm, 'Poltava-minnet och tillkomsten av Carl XII:s staty', *KFÅ* (1977).

uncritical, they provided the most comprehensive condemnation of Charles's policies that had so far appeared in Sweden, and they were to have an influence greatly exceeding their intrinsic value. It was doubtless significant that the critics of the day totally ignored them – though they had been ready enough to pronounce excoriating verdicts on the preceding volumes, and would repeat them on the volumes that followed.[61] But the critics could neither ignore nor condemn F.F. Carlson, whose magisterial seven-volume history of Sweden under the Palatine dynasty also began publication in 1856.[62] It was a narrative as readable as Macaulay (whom Carlson admired), impeccable in its use of a wide range of sources, and its general view was clearly hostile to much of what Charles XII stood for. For a generation Carlson's authority made the stance which Fryxell had adopted a historically respectable attitude: an attitude which would later be referred to as 'the Old School'.

Carlson, and his contemporary Malmström, represented the impact of Ranke on Swedish historiography, which in the half-century that followed the exhumation of 1859 developed critical approaches and more sophisticated techniques which could hardly be expected to leave the slapdash conclusions of 1859 unexamined indefinitely. In the case of Charles XII a dividing-line between old, often emotional, attitudes (whether for or against) and new approaches, which should be more detached, more scientific, but at the same time more understanding of his age in its own terms, was drawn by that great public figure and historian Harald Hjärne at the end of the century. Hjärne insisted that nothing less than systematic, co-ordinated research, conducted without preconceptions, based on foreign as well as Swedish material, seeing the problems in a European as well as a Swedish perspective, would serve to put the history of Charles's reign on a satisfactorily firm basis.[63] And it was in response to this demand that *Karolinska Förbundet* (The Caroline Association) was founded in 1910, and in that year started the publication of its annual volume, *Karolinska Förbundets Årsbok*, still vigorously alive three-quarters of a century later. From the stimulus to research provided by Hjärne, there took shape the so-called New School of Caroline historians. Their view of Charles XII tended in almost all respects to be far more positive (and also better based) than

[61] Olsoni, 'Karl XII:s-gestalten genom tiderna', p. 220.

[62] F.F. Carlson, *Sveriges historia under konungarne af pfalziska huset* (Stockholm, 1856–84). Carlson did not live to carry his work down to 1718: it was continued in an eighth volume by his son Ernst Carlson, but even this stopped at 1711.

[63] Harold Hjärne, *Svenskt och främmande* (Stockholm 1908), pp. 107–46. which reprints his essay of 1897. Hjärne himself, incidentally, came to take a relatively positive view of Charles, and may in that respect also be considered the father of the New School.

the old; and in particular the military historians – Artur Stille, Carl Bennedich – argued strongly for a reappraisal of Charles's strategy and tactics. The fruits of their work appeared in 1918–19 in two monumental collective volumes.[64] And it was scarcely surprising that in this climate of lively historical debate the decision should have been taken to undertake the fourth, and, it was hoped, the final exhumation of 1917.

This time everything was carefully prepared, every scientific precaution taken, much technical expertise enlisted. They were able, in part, to reconstruct the defects on either side of the skull by fitting fragments of bone together; they carried out X-ray examinations and chemical tests; they made trigonometrical measurements of the presumed line of the shot through the head; and a supplementary investigation established that the hat which Sicre had carried to Stockholm, though it had shrunk a little, had once fitted Charles's head. And after taking enormous pains the team of experts presided over by Professor Algot Key-Åberg pronounced their verdict.[65] They reported that the shot came from the *left*: that its course through the skull was more or less horizontal if Charles's head was erect at the moment of impact; that the projectile that killed him was a spherical object of either iron or lead, with a diameter of between 18 and 20 mm;[66] that it had high momentum when it struck him; but that they saw nothing to suggest that it was fired from very short range. It was no part of their task to give an opinion as to whether the evidence pointed to murder or to enemy action; and in fact they carefully avoided doing so. But their last finding seemed to rule out a pistol-shot. On the other hand it did not rule out murder by a musket-ball. It was not their business to offer opinions as to whether the visibility was good enough for a murderer with a musket, twenty or twenty-five yards away, to see his target and to risk a shot: they were not marksmen or meteorologists. Nor were they historians. Their report consequently left a number of issues open, and some critical questions unsolved. The exhumation of 1917, therefore,

---

[64] *Karl XII. Till 200-årsdagen av hans död (Charles XII. On the bicentenary of his death)*, ed. S.E. Bring (Stockholm 1918); and *Karl XII på slagfältet. Karolinsk slagledning sedd mot bakgrunden av taktikens utveckling från äldsta tider (Charles XII on the battlefield. Caroline warfare viewed against the background of the development of tactics from the earliest times)*, ed. Carl Bennedich, I–IV (Stockholm 1918–19), which was in effect (or at least in intention) a triumphal vindication of his military decisions.

[65] Algot Key-Åberg (ed.), *Karl XII:s banesår* (Stockholm 1917). The essence of this bulky volume is conveniently distilled in Algot Key-Åberg, *Om Konung Karl XII:s banesår. Föredrag på Karolinska Förbundets sammankomst den 30 november 1917* (Stockholm 1918).

[66] This measurement was subsequently narrowed down to precisely 19.5 mm. on the basis of the diameter of the hole in the hat-brim: though the crown of the hat had shrunk a little, it was assumed that the brim had not.

despite the impressive authority of those who conducted it, in fact proved the beginning and not the end of the controversy: in the next quarter of a century it raged more fiercely than ever before. And the first area in which it developed was in regard to the narrative sources.

V

In the 1920 volume of *Karolinska Förbundets Årsbok* Samuel E. Bring published a long article which for the first time presented historians with a critical edition of the basic texts: that is, of the letter of Maigret and the narratives of Carlberg and the Anonymous.[67] Bring's analysis proved to be a serious challenge to the authority which had hitherto been ascribed to them. All three, he believed, were written to order, at the request of Frederick I, with the object of countering the suspicion of murder. All three, therefore, were tainted sources; and the general belief among historians that Carlberg, at any rate, was an honest, truthful, and impartial witness required some modification. Bring based his estimate of Carlberg's credibility on a passage in the autobiography which he wrote in May 1777 (at the age of eighty-one), where he mentions having handed over his narrative 'on orders from an Exalted quarter': this event Bring dated to 1723 or soon after.[68]

As to Maigret, in Bring's view he was obviously concerned to whitewash his compatriot Sicre. There remained the problem of identity of the Anonymous, which had never been subjected to a really critical examination since its first publication in 1898.[69] The obvious candidate was Kaulbars: known, from the accordant testimony of Maigret and Carlberg, to have been one of the little group of three who stood at the king's feet; a Balt, moreover, which might explain a few Germanisms in the spelling of the text. The difficulty was that in two places the writer refers to 'Kaulbars', though in general using the first person singular or plural. Bring decided that the document before him was an original, and not (as had been suggested) a translation; that the writer was certainly on the spot; that he was not identical with any person named in his narrative; that the MS was written on Danish paper of the eighteenth century, commonly used in Sweden; and that it could be dated to the 1720's or early 1730s. He considered all the other officers known to be in the neighbourhood, rejected all of them for good reasons, and

---

[67] Samuel E. Bring, 'Bidrag till frågan om Karl XII:s död', *KFÅ* (1920), pp. 196–225.

[68] The text of the narrative which has come down to us, as Swederus had pointed out, is certainly datable to the years 1768–75, and represents the revision of a lost original.

[69] In *Historisk tidskrift* (1898), pp. 259 ff.

eventually came up with a certain Bengt Anders Burguer (another Balt), who very conveniently proved to have died in March 1726, thus providing a useful *terminus ante quem* which fitted in nicely with the idea that the narrative was to be connected with Frederick I's attempt to collect supporting evidence for Maigret's letter of 1723. It was unfortunate, however, that Bring was unable to find sufficient material in Burguer's handwriting to make a comparison with the text possible; and he frankly admitted that Burguer's signature looked nothing like it.

Bring's article, though it represented a historiographical advance, was not so immune to objections as the contemporary silence might lead one to suppose. In the first place, there is really very little in Maigret's letter to suggest that he was concerned to whitewash Sicre.[70] There is no attempt to give him an alibi, there is not even an explicit testimonial as to character.[71] The letter is brief, businesslike, strikingly free from irrelevances, silent upon many of the writer's own actions (by no means to his discredit) which are known to us from Carlberg or the Anonymous; and it probably intends no more than it says. As to Carlberg, Bring's hypothesis is not the only conclusion that can be drawn from the evidence. It is much easier to believe that the 'Exalted quarter' is not Frederick I trying to cover the traces of his crime, but that acquisitive bibliophile Gustav III trying to obtain an interesting manuscript for his library.[72] And as to the Anonymous, Bring's identification of him with Burguer seems insecurely based. It rests, first, upon Ture Gabriel Bielke, who in his *Hågkomster af Karl XII* mentions a certain Börje (otherwise unidentified) as accompanying Maigret and other officers to the trenches, and on the identification of this 'Börje' with Burguer;[73] and secondly, upon the fact that the real Burguer was one of the five officers ordered to escort the king's corpse to Uddevalla, the presumption being that the selection was made from officers who had been on the spot when Charles was shot. That may be so; but another of the five was Kaulbars. And that Kaulbars might at the beginning of his narrative have referred to himself in an official third-person style,

---

[70] The only direct mention of Sicre is the statement that 'Sicre passa et me demanda ce que le Roy faisoit [i.e. up there on the parapet], je luy respondit que ce n'estoit pas moy qui l'auoit placé, Sicre s'en fut . . .'.

[71] All he says is 'Ceux qui en accuse la personne que vous marquez ont apparement des raisons pour tacher de la persuader au peuple'.

[72] Bring's argument depends, first, on construing *aflemna* (usually translated 'hand over, deliver') as equivalent to (say) *nedskriva* ('write down'); and secondly on interpreting Carlberg's statement that he wrote his narrative *strax* ('immediately') after Charles's death to be capable of meaning 'in 1723 or soon after' – i.e. five years later. Both points seem to be very dubious.

[73] See Bielke's 'Remarque' in Hallendorff, *Studier öfver den äldre Karl XII:s historiografien*, II. 97.

and subsequently lapse into a more natural first-person narrative, is hardly a decisive reason for rejecting his authorship.[74]

Nevertheless, Bring's article inaugurated a period in which there was clearly more disposition than had existed for many years to take the case for murder seriously. The next historian to do so was Lauritz Weibull, a member of one of those academic dynasties (the Hildebrand and Boëthius clans provide other examples) which are so typical of the university scene in Sweden. Weibull had been appointed to the chair at Lund in 1919, after a struggle of exceptional rancour even by Swedish academic standards. For he and his school challenged the traditional approaches and accepted orthodoxies of Swedish history in many areas, from the middle ages onwards. By the mid-century they would dominate Swedish historiography. In furtherance of their general view that the historical Establishment was in need of a sharp jolt, they started in 1928 the journal *Scandia*, which was to some extent a deliberate reaction against the long-unchallenged monopoly of *Historisk tidskrift*; and on the inside of the front cover of its early numbers they flung out a defiant declaration of intent which denounced the assumption by historians of 'national, political or religious attitudes', and promised to wage war on research which 'deals in loose presumptions or rests on the shifting sands of romantic hypothesis'. Swedish historians soon became divided into the new Lund–Göteborg school, on the one hand, and the old Uppsala–Stockholm school, on the other: it was to some extent a battle of South *versus* North, the North being represented most typically by the formidable figures of Nils Ahnlund and Bertil Boëthius.[75] And it was in *Scandia*, one year after its foundation, that Lauritz Weibull contributed a random shot to the skirmish over Charles XII's death.[76] It was a spirited, provocative, and rather summary argument which has not worn well.[77] Weibull started from two assumptions: first, that the so-called *Gazette* of 10 December 1718 was a semi-official publication which represented what Sicre told the authorities in Stockholm; and secondly, that Görtz's successful conclusion of the negotiations on the Åland Islands made a *coup* imperative for the Hessians. Unfortunately neither of these assump-

[74] Colonel Stenflycht, the undisputed author of notes on the campaign of 1718, writes in the third person. See the excerpt quoted in Ahnlund, *Sanning och sägen* p. 38; though Ahnlund does not make this point.

[75] The clash between the schools is perhaps best exemplified in the debate of 1950: on the one hand Erik Lönnroth's 'Är Sveriges historia oföränderlig?' ('Is Swedish history unalterable?'), on the other Bertil Boëthius's 'Behöver vår historievetenskap lägga om sin kurs?' ('Does our historiography need to change course?'), both in *Historisk tidskrift* for that year.

[76] 'Carl XII:s död', *Scandia* (1929).

[77] Which has not prevented its republication in a collection of essays by various hands on Charles XII: see *Historia kring Karl XII*, ed. Gustaf Jonasson (Stockholm 1964).

tions has turned out to be true.[78] But on this basis Weibull unfolded a history of guilty collaboration and connivance in which the Stockholm authorities, Sicre, Maigret, de la Motraye, and even Voltaire all combine to exaggerate the danger of Charles's position, the intensity of enemy fire, and the zeal of officers to persuade the king to take cover. For Weibull, the primary sources are even more unreliable than for Bring; for in his view the Anonymous is simply Maigret supplementing his original letter by an amended and more circumstantial account at the behest of the Stockholm court. The anonymous relation is thus not an original, but the translation by a German-speaker of a missing French original, whose existence is (to say the least) highly conjectural: it is simply Maigret II. Though he would have none of Bring's theory that Carlberg wrote his narrative as part of a campaign in 1723 to collect appropriate testimony, Weibull held that he wrote it 'after long and ripe consideration', and that it was meant to be a refutation of Maigret I and Maigret II, though how either should have been known to Carlberg is not explained.[79] And finally, his attempt to argue that the king was not in fact exposed to hot fire from the enemy is refuted, not only by all three primary sources, but by the journal of the Norwegian commander in Fredriksten.

In *Scandia* for the following year another Lund historian, Sture Bolin, in the course of a wide-ranging article, returned to this problem. Unlike his immediate predecessors, he saw no sign of tendentiousness in Carlberg, and would have none of Bring's contention that his narrative was written at the instigation of Frederick I; but he concurred with Weibull in believing that the Anonymous was in fact Maigret II: Maigret's original reply having been drawn up (he considered) 'with notable nonchalance'. This would seem to entail the assumption that the anonymous relation had in fact been directed to the same address as in the case of Maigret I – though if that had been the case one might reasonably have expected it to have the same archival provenance.[80]

---

[78] See above, p. 148 and below, p. 191.

[79] Equally remarkable is his statement that Voltaire must have known of Maigret's letter of 1723: this seems on all counts impossible. Voltaire does indeed say that Charles lay with half his body above the parapet, but it is a long jump from this to explaining how it could come about that he had access to a confidential letter preserved in Sweden.

[80] Sture Bolin, 'Kring Carl XII:s död, *Scandia* (1930). Bolin argues for Maigret's authorship of the Anonymous on the general ground that the differences between them show them to have been complementary, and the omissions in the Anonymous to have been tendentious; and more particularly because Ture Gabriel Bielke in his *Hågkomster* says that Maigret had his hands under the king's feet, while the Anonymous says that *he* performed that office – from which we are to infer (most improbably) that Bielke read the anonymous relation, and knew

And with that, the critical analysis of the sources came for the moment to an inconclusive halt, and was not to be resumed for another decade. But Bolin's article gave impetus to a renewed examination of the problem along two quite different lines. On the one hand, he reopened the long-suspended question of Sicre's part in the affair; and on the other, he made a tentative approach to the linked problems of Charles's position when he was shot, and the probability of his being shot from long range, and more particularly from Overbierg. Finally, he recurred to the suggestion with which Key-Åberg had concluded his lecture on the findings of 1917; namely, that it was high time to institute a thorough topographical-ballistic investigation, with especial attention to the location of the trenches[81] – questions to which the experts of 1917 had, by the very nature of their brief and the strictly medical skills which they commanded, naturally given no attention. And it was along these lines that the most vigorous researches of the 1930s were conducted.

As to Sicre, the anecdotalists and family tradition-bearers had never fallen wholly silent, though latterly there had been a tendency to confuse an already confused picture still further by grafting on to the ordinary accusation details borrowed from the Tollstadius story.[82] And in 1930 what was probably the last of these eighteenth-century fantasies was published by Sixten Dahlquist in *Karolinska Förbundets Årsbok.*[83] This was a narrative of the experiences of one Tiburtz Tiburtius, a strong-minded parson whose qualifications as a witness are sufficiently attested by the fact that on 30 November 1718 he was aged 12 and many miles from the scene of action.[84] At a later stage, however, he became domestic chaplain to Axel Banér, and in that capacity heard a good deal of loose talk over dinner, notably a story (attributed to Schering Rosenhane) to the effect that Sicre met Charles as he was leaving the trenches, and in effect lured him back to his death. Schering Rosenhane's own account of 30 November, it need hardly be said, gives no support whatever to this suggestion.[85] But, apart from the table-talk, Tiburtius had a lively imagination of

that it was the work of Maigret: see Bolin, 'Kring Carl XII:s död, pp. 155 and n. 2, 160 n. 2, 167, 169, 180 n. 1.

[81] Bolin 'Kring *Carl XII:s död*, p. 183; Key-Åberg, *Om Konung Karl XII:s banesår.* p. 35.

[82] Thus in 1892 Baron N. Kaulbars was reported to have written an article in *Russkaya Starina* retailing a family tradition that Charles had been murdered by his 'private secretary' Sicre, with a weapon which he had borrowed from Kaulbars for the occasion. Summarised in *Historisk tidskrift* (1892) under the heading 'Ännu en gång Karl XII:s död'.

[83] Sixten Dahlquist, 'Till belysning av frågan om Karl XII:s död', *KFÅ* (1930), pp. 134 ff.

[84] For Tiburtius and his strong-mindedness in general see Sixten Dahlquist, *En kämpagestalt under Frihetstiden. Tiburtz Tiburtius 1706–1787* (Stockholm 1964).

[85] 'Utdrag utur General-Majorens, dåvarande Ryttmästarens, Baron Schering Rosenhanes Dagbok', *Handlingar rörande Skandinaviens Historia*, IV (Stockholm 1817), p. 311.

his own, not enervated by the lapse of half a century since the events
he described: Sicre, it appears, was not mad at all, but was shut up by
the authorities on the pretext of insanity in order to keep him out of
the way; was subsequently smuggled out to Hesse-Cassel; and was
there given an estate, on which he lived in perfect sanity ever after. It
would not have been worth retailing this confection, if its editor had
not taken a great part of it quite seriously, and on his own account
contributed the suggestion that Sicre may in fact have confessed on
his deathbed (in Hesse, presumably) to the ubiquitous Tollstadius.[86]

By the 1930s, all the same, the delphic pronouncement of the
experts of 1917 – that the bullet came with high velocity, but that
there was no particular reason to suppose that it was fired at very
short range – was coming to be considered with some scepticism: in
December 1928 a certain W. Carlgren, in a letter to the press, had
asserted that Algot Key-Åberg had confided to a colleague that he
personally believed in a shot at close quarters; and in the same year
the amateur historian Anton Nyström had made the same assertion
'on his honour'.[87] These allegations are not in themselves incredible:
in his lecture on the findings of 1917 Key-Åberg had been very
careful to state that in view of the 'colossal' damage to the skull a shot
at short range was possible; and he defined such a shot 'in the true
sense of the term' (*i egentlig mening*) as a shot which left traces of
powder on the skin; adding that the skin after 200 years would not
necessarily show such traces.[88] However that may be, the time was
clearly ripe for a re-examination of the whole mass of rumour,
insinuation, and family tradition which had sprung to life in the
eighteenth century, and which seemed once more to be putting out
rank shoots. The task was undertaken by the historian C.F. Palmstierna, who in a lengthy article in *Historisk tidskrift* for 1939 discharged it with great thoroughness, if not always (one may think)
with discrimination:[89] it is not difficult, reading between the lines, to
perceive that he was already committed to the theory of murder. He
was the first historian to take account of the Asplind version of
Cronstedt's alleged confesssion; he cleared up the business of

[86] Dahlquist, 'Till belysning', p. 140.
[87] See Palmstierna, in Sandklef, *Carl XII:s död*, p. 183.
[88] Algot Key-Åberg, *Om Konung Karl XII:s banesår*, p. 32. It may be noted, however, that
Key-Åberg's son, who acted as his secretary during the investigation, in his only published
contribution to the controversy refrained from either refuting or confirming the allegation:
Hans Key-Åberg. 'Karl XII:s dödsskott', *Svenska Läkaretidningen* (1941).
[89] C.F. Palmstierna, 'Mordryktena kring Fredrikshall', *Historisk tidskrift* (1939), pp. 362–
417. There are some very dubious conjectures on pp. 371–2; and the suggestion that the
exhumation of 1746 may have been prompted by von Liewen appears to be based on the
ground that Hårleman (one of the exhumers) married von Liewen's sister two years later (!):
p. 404; C.F. Palmstierna, in Sandklef, *Carl XII:s död*, p. 150.

Frederick's 'gift and reward' to Cronstedt; he unravelled the circumstances which lay behind Ture Funck's attempt to father the Tollstadian document on Gustav III; and though he extended his charity
to a number of questionable sources, he drew the line (for the
moment) at Tiburtius. He also offered the suggestion that the
Anonymous was really the second of the two French officers to
whom the enquiry of 1723 had been directed,[90] and made the point
that although the anonymous relation does indeed refer to Kaulbars
in the third person, it refers to Maigret in the third person also, so
that the objections to Kaulbars's authorship apply with equal force to
Maigret's.

Palmstierna's most significant contribution, however, was on the
question of motive. Here he recurred to the view of some of the
Gustavians; arguing that the most likely motive was not dynastic,
but was to be sought in war-weariness, despair of military success,
hatred of the absolutism, and a determination on the part of the
aristocracy and the senior civil service to seize the opportunity of the
king's death to carry through a constitutional revolution which had
been in contemplation for at least the preceding five years, and which
awaited only a 'fortunate accident', a 'beneficent shot', a 'bullet with
the king's name on it'[91] for its launching. Towards this conclusion he
may possibly have been impelled by an article by Stig Jägerskiöld
which had appeared a few years before;[92] for Jägerskiöld, printing
material from the Hessian archives, had made the dynastic theory
almost untenable. He had shown that since 1715 Frederick had *feared*
Charles's death, as an event unfavourable to his chances; that in
Hessian circles it was suspected that Görtz encouraged the Norwegian campaign in the hope that a lucky bullet might clear the way for
a Holstein succession; that Hein's memorandum of May 1718, with
its programme for action if Charles should be killed, had been preceded by similar plans in 1715, and was not therefore necessarily
related to the issue of the Åland conference; that Frederick in fact
hoped that Charles would make peace with the Russians, or at least
make peace with somebody; and finally that what the Hessians and
Ulrika Eleonora really feared was not, after all, the Holstein rival,
but an attack on the absolutism by the constitutional opposition – an
attack which they were not yet prepared to meet. The effect of this
demonstration on Palmstierna remains uncertain: what is certain,

---

[90] But this leaves unexplained why it should have been thought necessary to translate the
presumed French original into slightly Germanised Swedish: this had not been done for
Maigret.

[91] Palmstierna's fantastic explanation of this familiar expression is in 'Mordryktena', p. 367.

[92] Stig Jägerskiöld, 'Den hessiska politiken och den svenska tronföljdsfrägan 1713–1718.
Några bidrag', KFÅ (1934), pp. 112–43.

however, is that he now saw the most likely candidate for regicide as Cronstedt rather than Sicre. He did indeed give the evidence against Sicre some attention, and he conceded (though he did not for the moment pursue) the possibly sinister implications of an erasure in the record of proceedings against Dagström, which Bolin had already pointed out,[93] but the main thrust of his argument centred on Cronstedt, and the crucial point in it was not all the old stories with which we are already familiar, nor even his contention that there is no smoke without fire and that two discrepant versions of a tradition do not negative the assumption that there is a real source common to them both: essential to his case is the attempt to show that Cronstedt was really in touch with, and in sympathy with, the peace-party, or the party of constitutional revolution. Unfortunately, it cannot be said that Palmstierna produced much more than vague indications pointing in this direction. But this solution to the problem of motive might well explain why the men of the Age of Liberty preferred to think in terms of blaming Frederick I and Ulrika Eleonora. And one final point emerged, inconspicuously enough, from Palmstierna's article: the suggestion that the sound of impact which Maigret and the Anonymous recorded was not, as they supposed, made by the bullet hitting the king's skull, but was the sound of its impact on stone after passing through the king's head.[94] It was a suggestion which was to play no small part in the great controversy of 1940.

Meanwhile the topographical-ballistic investigation for which the report of 1917 had called was at last making progress. The question was of obvious importance in assessing the possibility of murder. If, for instance, it could be shown that the king was not within range of musket- or canister-shot from the enemy positions, murder was an almost inevitable conclusion. On the other hand, murder depended, not only on such factors as the possibility of seeing the king's head in the prevailing conditions, and on the risk a murderer would run of being seen – factors quasi-subjective, and very difficult to assess – but also on quite objective considerations such as the relation of the terrain to the ascertained line of the shot through the head, and the possibility presented to a potential murderer of firing a shot (standing or lying) which would comply with that line. From the outwork of Gyldenlöve the ground fell away in the direction of the fortress, and the trench in which Charles stood (the so-called Old Line, in contra-distinction to the New Line whose digging Carlberg had been supervising) traversed this slope, more or less parallel to the Nor-wegian defences. One of the first points to be determined, therefore,

[93] Bolin, 'Kring Carl XII:s död', p. 175. n. 2.
[94] Palmstierna, 'Mordryktena', p. 376.

was just where on this slope the Old Line was sited. And the answer to that question must be reconcilable with the nature and extent of the wound: if the trench were high up on the slope, a murderer, firing uphill from a lying position, would hit the king in a line rising more sharply than was actually the case; if on the other hand the trench were on the more level ground at the bottom, the pitch-flares on the wall would give a better chance of a certain shot (but also a greater risk of being seen). The topographical-ballistic investigation, in short, reopened the medical question, and transformed it into a *forensic*-medical question.

Successive Norwegian officers stationed in Fredriksten had for more than thirty years occupied themselves – with the benevolent encouragement of the Norwegian military authorities, who may well have felt that their time was less than fully occupied by their routine duties – with the problem of the location of the trenches. It was a problem which might not appear too difficult, since in 1723 the Norwegian commandant had erected a monument on the supposed spot of Charles's death. But that monument not only bore an offensive inscription which caused the godly Christian VI to demolish it in 1730; it was also generally recognised to have been in the wrong place. Another, equally questionable, was put up in 1788; and thereafter monuments sprouted like mushrooms: by the 1930s investigators had no less than seven sites to choose from. The first excavations had been made by the Norwegian Major-General Raeder; who in a dip at the bottom of the slope found what had certainly been a trench (though an improbably deep one) which he pronounced to be the Old Line, and on that basis had plotted a conjectural course for the New Line also. Both were much nearer the fortress than had hitherto been supposed; and both – on the basis of the line of the shot and the presumed visibility from the pitch-flares on the walls – made murder conceivable.

However, doubts about Raeder's lines emerged when the area on which he had plotted his New Line was drained, and no trace of a trench was found.[95] In June 1930 a commission led by the Swedish military historian Major Gustaf Petri visited the site at the behest of the Caroline Association, and made investigations across Raeder's New Line which produced (as expected) no result. Meanwhile one of Raeder's successors in Fredriksten, Major Finn Backer, had been tackling the problem by way of an exhaustive analysis of all contemporary maps; and on the basis of his report the Norwegian Mili-

[95] For what follows see Finn Backer, 'Karl XII:s dödsted', *KFÅ* (1936), pp. 214–92, and also what is in effect an introductory note to Backer by Gustaf Petri, in *Historisk tidskrift* (1934), p. 289.

tary History Department, in conjunction with Petri and the Swedish experts, agreed that Raeder's lines were impossible, as being irreconcilable with the best maps, and also for tactical reasons.[96] A joint Swedish-Norwegian pronouncement accordingly officially declared Backer's line to be the right one, explaining rather glibly that the original trenches had been very shallow and that in the succeeding centuries the ground had been so much disturbed that a negative result for Backer was only to be expected. And Backer's line was fairly high up on the slope.

At this point the discussion began to be bedevilled by a number of confusing questions arising out of Carlberg's narrative. First, Carlberg's estimate of the distance from the Swedish lines to the fortress. He had put it at around 200 *alnar*. But the Swedish *aln* is reckoned at 59 cm; the French *aln*, on the other hand, at 118 cm. It was arguable that since the siege was directed by French engineers, and since Carlberg was an engineer himself, it was the French *aln* that he intended: clearly much might depend on which one preferred.[97] Secondly, Carlberg wrote of his going 'down' the trench to fetch General Schwerin after Charles's death, and of Schwerin's coming 'up' to the king: was he using these expressions in a topographical or military sense (going 'down the line', 'up to the front')? Thirdly, in what direction was Charles's head turned when he was hit? Could any projectile from the fortress have hit him on the left? The men of 1917 had laid it down that the line of the shot was horizontal *if* the king's head was erect. But Carlberg tells us that his left hand supported his cheek: if he was hit in that position, the apparently horizontal line of the shot must in fact have been *rising* slightly – a conclusion hard to reconcile with a shot from the enemy, but reasonable if we posit a murderer firing a musket at (say) 25 metres from somewhere not too far off down the slope.

It was the 'down' and 'up' problem that worried General Bruusgaard, the next Norwegian to occupy himself with the question.[98] Bruusgaard insisted that Carlberg's 'down' and 'up' simply

---

[96] Mainly on the ground that it is known that breaching batteries were to have been brought into action on the following day, operating on the Swedes' right flank (against which they were expecting a sortie, and on which they had massed some troops): it would have been impossible to bring up the guns to the right of Raeder's line, but 'a sort of a road' round the side of Gyldenlöve made that possible if Backer's line were taken: Backer 'Karl XII:s dödsted', pp. 257–8.

[97] Backer, 'Karl XII:s dödsted', pp. 256–7. The best Norwegian-Danish maps gave the range as 187.5 metres (and it is reasonable to suppose that their gunners got it right), so that perhaps this element of confusion mattered less than might appear.

[98] Chr. Bruusgaard, 'Undersøkelse og funn 1936–1937 vedrørende Carl XII:s løpegraver og dødsted ved Fredriksten. I førbindelse dermed stående betraktninger over kongens dødsmåte', *KFÅ* (1939), pp. 15–30.

did not fit Backer's line. But they *did* fit topographically, if that line were shifted about 20 metres forward. Acting on this idea, he started digging; and in due course he found what he believed to be the stone foundation of the monument of 1788. With the aid of a contemporary map which gave the distance from various points of the fortress to the monument of 1723, he dug again, and sure enough found the foundations of that monument also. Both monuments had admittedly been wrong in regard to Charles's position; but Bruusgaard argued that they were likely to have been right to the extent that both lay *somewhere* in the Old Line. All one had to do, then, was to plot a line connecting them, and excavation would confirm that conclusion. Bruusgaard therefore dug; and it did. He found clear evidence of a trench, in two places; it seemed to have been filled in with stone; and it contained bits of old iron of a type which was (perhaps) used in 1718. His conclusion was that the range was such as to make it perfectly possible for Charles to have been hit by musketry or canister from the fortress; and his discovery of a hitherto unknown (and now vanished) bastion of the fortress on its east front effectively disposed of the objection that no shot from the fortress could possibly have hit the king on the left. His arguments were supported by the report of two State geologists – one Swedish, one Norwegian – who in an exceptionally categorical pronouncement declared that Bruusgaard's line was the right one, and that all other suggested lines were geologically impossible. This was decisive: on 4 December 1937 the heads of the Military History Sections of the Swedish and Norwegian General Staffs issued a joint statement accepting Bruusgaard's findings, declared the question of the siting of the trenches to be 'definitely closed', and the Norwegian War Office authorised the appropriate corrections on its maps.[99] The controversy, on this front, seemed over. Yet there remained two nagging questions. One was the rising line of the wound. The other was the stone filling of Bruusgaard's trench. Immediately after the Swedish withdrawal the Norwegian defenders came out and hastily filled in the Old and New Line, apparently with the spoil left behind by the sappers. Their intention was to fill in the whole Swedish trench-system; but on 4 December 1718 their work was stopped by frost. It was not resumed until 1728, when it was completed by filling in the trenches with stone. An important question for Bruusgaard then was, did the work of 1728 include a more thorough treatment of the Old and New Line? Were they, too, now filled with stone? The official Norwegian narrative of the work of 1728 can be interpreted

[99] *Ibid.*, p. 23-5.

one way or the other, and has been so interpreted by Bruusgaard's critics and defenders.[100] The point is essentially a semantic one, which even Scandinavians find it hard to determine; but it is clear that Bruusgaard's theory is seriously affected by the answer.

Meanwhile some progress had been made on a different though related question. At an early stage of their investigations Petri and his colleagues had felt the need of the assistance of an expert in forensic medicine. In 1931 they had enlisted Dr Gustaf Hultkvist, eminent in his profession, and eminently qualified to advise them. By 1937 Hultkvist felt himself in a position to publish what he was careful to describe as an interim report.[101] It contained much interesting matter not immediately relevant to the problem he was considering (among other things, the novel suggestion that Sicre's 'fièvre chaude' is to be explained as a passing attack of *delirium tremens*),[102] but on the nature of the wound his opinions were clear and decided. The investigation of 1917 had already explained that when a projectile passes through the spongy mass of the brain it sets up a hydrodynamic wave which in effect produces an explosion inside the skull: Hultkvist, concurring in this opinion, objected that any musket-ball hitting the head with high momentum would have produced an explosion far more shattering than had in fact been the case.[103] The experts of 1917 had made perfunctory experiments by firing at two museum crania – one empty, the other filled with gelatine; and the latter of these had almost totally disintegrated. Hultkvist dismissed these attempts as worthless: a dry and brittle specimen from a museum was no basis for estimating what happened to a living head. He proceeded therefore to construct cylinders whose composition and behaviour under

[100] The Norwegian text runs: 'og ellers i det øvrige alle fientlige approcher bleven tilkast og opfylt med store sten' ('and otherwise and in general all enemy approaches were dismantled and filled with great stones'): for a discussion of the difficulty see Sandklef, *Carl XII:s död*, pp. 199–200, and Tor Holmquist, 'Löpgravarna vid Fredriksten', *KFÅ* (1944), pp. 170–1. The geologists had reported that the trench was filled 'with moraine-material and stones'.

[101] Gustaf Hultkvist, 'Skottet vid Fredrikshald, De preliminära resultaten av en ballistisk-medicinsk undersökning', *Svensk Tidskrift* (1937), pp. 612–41.

[102] *Ibid.*, p. 618.

[103] One of the difficulties lay in the absence of case-histories of shot-wounds through the head, especially by musket-balls. There was a literature on musket-ball wounds (see e.g., Sir Charles Bell, *A Dissertation on Gun-shot Wounds* (1814)), but in the nature of the case army surgeons were concerned to describe wounds they could treat: shots through the head were for the undertaker. A Berlin professor had offered some guidance to the men of 1917; but the only published authority Hultkvist could find was a treatise by a Belgian, one Medinger (1923), who had conducted experiments by firing into boxes packed with flesh; but Hultkvist found that the formulae Medinger derived from these grisly researches produced impossible results. Hultkvist noted that in general the bones round the temple are less resistant than might be expected: a remark supported (though he did not make this point) by the opinion of 1917 that Charles's bones seem to have been thinner than normal in a man of his age: Algot Key-Åberg. *Om Konung Karl XII:s banesår*, p. 23.

fire came as close as possible to what might be expected in the real thing;[104] and at these he directed musket-fire at various ranges, with gunpowder of varying composition, and with charges of various sizes. And he reached the conclusion that an eighteenth-century musket with a standard eighteenth-century charge of 16 grams, fired at a distance of 25 metres from its target, gave a maximum impact-velocity of 450 metres per second (if the powder were dry), and a minimum of 310 m/s (if the powder were damp, as it was likely to be on 30 November 1718); and even at the minimum velocity would have caused far more shattering damage than was to be observed in Charles's skull. He found, moreover, that he could cause comparable damage at very much lower impact-velocities than the men of 1917 had postulated: indeed, the small size of the hole on the right led him to propose a velocity of as little as 100-150 m/s – a speed so low, that the skin on the right side had time to stretch before penetration.[105] How, then, to account for the great size of the hole on the left side? Maigret had said the projectile was as big as a pigeon's egg: Voltaire, that it weighed half a ship-pound; de la Motraye had stated the size of the hole, first as three fingers broad, and then as four; all of which suggested that the dimensions of the hole were not to be attributed to its enlargement during the process of embalming. The obvious answer, it seemed to Hultkvist, lay in the hat: in that semicircular snippet which the bullet carried forward on its course, and which greatly increased the effect of its impact. Nobody, it appears, had thought of this before.

Hultkvist accordingly reached the following firm conclusions: that it was impossible, from the extent of the damage, to assume an impact-velocity of 300–400 m/s – which ruled out a musket-shot from (say) 25 metres; that a shot from the main fortress was entirely possible, especially in view of the fact that canister from three-pounder guns often consisted of musket-balls; that a shot from Overbierg, given the extreme range (554 m), was only an outside possibility, though it could not be entirely dismissed; and that the sound of the impact of a shot from any part of the fortress (although not of a shot at close range) would not have been masked by the noise of the gun.

[104] He took some pains with them: his cylinders were made of sheet-lead surrounded by hard plaster, and clad in tanned sheepskin; inside they were filled with melted fat which had been allowed to stiffen for forty-eight hours.

[105] After the passage of the ball the elasticity of the skin caused it to contract, so that it showed a hole which was actually smaller than the diameter of the bullet: we know this from the report of 1859 – partly from the drawing which was then made, partly from the note made by one of the investigators that the hole in the skin on the right-hand side was the diameter of a little finger.

The controversy thus seemed to have reached a reasonably satisfactory conclusion. The criticisms of the original sources could be considered to have cancelled each other out; the king's position had been demonstrated to be within range of enemy action; the wound in the head had been shown to be of such a nature as to exclude a shot from a murderer, given the necessarily shortish range which the extremely restricted visibility must have imposed. It was all very reassuring. With the exception, perhaps, of that unlucky matter of the hat. For what, one might ask (though nobody in fact did), had happened to the snippet of felt? Neumann had made no mention of it in his report on the embalming; the investigators of 1917 had indeed looked for it, but they had not found it, nor any trace of it.[106] Obviously, then, it must have passed through the skull ahead of the bullet. But if so, just as it had caused damage on the left-hand side bigger than might have been expected, so (one might suppose) it would have affected the wound on the right. That neat circular hole in the skin on the right-hand side which had been observed in 1859, a hole no bigger than a little finger: was that, too, reconcilable with Hultkvist's snippet? Nobody, it seemed, was anxious to raise this awkward question, just as nobody was anxious to press the problem of the rising line. Enough was enough; and the defenders of Sweden's honour, propped up by Bruusgaard on the one hand and Hultkvist on the other, could sleep securely in their beds. But in 1940 came a rude awakening.

VI

The *Intendent* of Varberg Folk Museum, Dr Albert Sandklef, in the course of making collections of the folklore of his hinterland, had become especially interested in folk-tales concerning the life – and particularly the death – of Charles XII. Dr Sandklef held the view that oral tradition in general had great value as a source of history, being less liable than written records to subjective distortion; a view which would no doubt command more support now than it did then. The traditions about Charles's death were of various types: some were simply to the effect that the king was 'hard' – that is, vulnerable only to bullets with magical properties; others asserted that he had in fact been killed by such a bullet, variously described as a bullet of silver, or a button from his own coat. Sandklef found what he considered to be a significantly high concentration of such traditions in the provinces through which the Swedish regiments

<hr>

[106] Algot Key-Åberg, *Om Konung Karl XII:s banesår*, p. 24.

marched on their way home after Charles's death. They occurred very notably around the villages of Öxnevalla and Horred, situated on the Västergötland-Halland boundary, where he collected no less than seventeen of them. And here the tradition had a specifically local interest. For all the tales which he noted down around Öxnevalla included the point that after the king had been shot, a soldier from the village picked up the fatal bullet and took it home with him: five of the seventeen added the information that the soldier who picked up the bullet was also the man who shot him; but to this remarkable detail Sandklef gave no credence.[107] Sandklef had known in general of this local tradition for some years: a certain August Carlson (since dead) was recorded as having deponed in 1922 that the Öxnevalla soldier had boasted of his find, had been warned by the local parson to throw it away, and had in fact, in the parson's presence, thrown it into the gravel-pit at Deragård; of which circumstance the parish clerk had made a memorandum, now lost.[108] And in 1939 an old man aged 99 had supplied the name of this hitherto anonymous soldier: Nordstierna.

On 25 May 1932 – a date almost as important in this controversy as 30 November 1718 itself – Dr Sandklef received a visit at his museum from a certain Carl Hj. Andersson, the blacksmith in Horred. He brought with him what seemed evidently to be a kind of button: a spherical metallic object furnished with remnants of an appropriate eye for sewing purposes. The exterior was of brass, sheathing a filling which proved to be lead; the surface slightly flattened at the end opposite to the eye, and bearing a gash on one side consistent with collision with some jagged rock. This button-like object Andersson had found upon his garden-path after it had been spread with fresh gravel. And the gravel had come in a load from Deragård gravel-pit. Andersson was familiar with the local tradition, was a literate man, and was not unacquainted with the general controversy about Charles's death. It did not take him long to draw the appropriate inferences, and to persuade himself that he had made a find of historic importance. Nor did it take him much longer to persuade Sandklef of it also. Sandklef told himself that the damage to the button was caused by its hitting a sharp stone at the back of the trench after passing through Charles's head; and it was this impact which Maigret and the Anonymous had both so vividly described. It was certainly notable that there should have been no ricochet – if

---

[107] Sandklef, *Carl XII:s död*, pp. 233–4.
[108] Sandklef also heard a variant which made the soldier discard it in the swampy thicket near to the gravel-pit, on the ground that it gave him bad dreams: *ibid.*, p. 243.

there had been, the soldier would not have been able to retrieve the button from the trench; but the natural explanation must be that the stone had been covered by a thick layer of moss. The button itself was certainly very unusual: indeed, Sandklef believed it had no fellow in Sweden. He accordingly made enquiries abroad. An official at the Louvre reported that it appeared to be of oriental origin; the Director of Topkapîserail Museum in Istanbul 'had the impression' that it might be Turkish. The question then was: had Charles XII any Turkish buttons? And the answer was that he had. A line-and-wash drawing of him by Axel Löwen, 'executed in Turkey', shows him with buttons on his waistcoat which bore a fair resemblance to the object on the blacksmith's garden-path. There remained the problem of how an assassin could contrive an opportunity to possess himself of this indispensable projectile. But this was no problem at all; for it is a well-established fact that on the morning of Advent Sunday 1718 Charles XII ordered that he be provided with 'an entirely new uniform': the old one, we may suppose, would not have been inaccessible to any enterprising murderer. And, by the way of final confirmatory detail, the regimental muster-rolls revealed that the soldier who lived on the local military allotment (*torp*) at that time was indeed named Nordstierna. The case seemed complete; tradition had been vindicated. Charles had been murdered by a magic bullet in the shape of one of his own buttons; it had been picked up by Nordstierna, thrown away into Deragård gravel-pit, rediscovered by the blacksmith, and was now safely removed to the reverent custody of Varberg Folk Museum.

Sandklef first publicly proclaimed the new gospel in two broadcasts, on 6 and 20 April 1940. It very soon became apparent that he did not lack for disciples. Already in 1934 an enterprising journalist named Friedlander had scented a scoop in Öxnevalla, had interviewed the blacksmith, and in 1938, in the Sunday edition of a Göteborg newspaper, had published a colourful version of the discovery of the magic button. Among those who read the Sunday papers was a Lieutenant Nils Strömbom. Strömbom was having doubts about the validity of Bruusgaard's siting of the Old Line, and was investigating the trench-system outside Fredrikshald on his own account. After reading Friedlander's article he wrote to Sandklef and suggested that they pursue their investigations together. This was duly agreed upon, Sandklef's function being to act as Strömbom's photographer. In March 1939 Strömbom gave a lecture on his researches to the Historical Society of Stockholm University. That lecture was attended by Palmstierna, and seems to have stimulated him to write the article in *Historisk tidskrift* which appeared later in the year.[109] Finally, a Dr Sam Clason, by profession a gynaecologist, was moved by Sandklef's broadcasts to propose collaboration in a series of ballistic experiments, the versatile Sandklef this time participating as marksman, while Clason drew the appropriate medical inferences. For Clason was as sceptical of Hultkvist's analysis as Strömbom was of Bruusgaard's trenches; and all three – Palmstierna, Strömbom, and Clason – saw Sandklef's magic button as providing unlooked-for support for conclusions to which each was already tending.[110]

The upshot of all this was the publication in the autumn of 1940 of a collaborative volume, *Carl XII:s död,* to which all four contributed. Of Sandklef's chapters no more need be said, except to note that he was rash enough to travel outside the area of his own discipline: his discussion of the sources was an uncritical mixture of Weibull and Bolin; he attacked Hultkvist in terms which might well be resented; and his treatment of Bruusgaard was not only ironical but derisive. And it was the tone no less than the substance of his contribution which would bring retribution presently. Each of the others had something new to offer. Least significant was Palmstierna's contribution, an expansion of his article which was not an improvement. It accepted, more uncritically than before, all the dubious testimonies of the eighteenth and nineteenth centuries (including, incredibly, that of Tiburtius); it contained loose conjectures and illogical deductions;[111] and to one unkind critic it resembled rather the address of a prosecuting counsel than the summing-up of a judge. It did however include one new family tradition, this time from one of Carlberg's descendants: a great-granddaughter who had died at an advanced age in 1890, and who maintained that her father had always said that Charles had been shot by Cronstedt. And it also contained a revelation which attracted considerable attention: a conjectural reconstruction, under ultra-violet rays, of the erasure in the record of the proceedings against Dagström,[112] which provoked Palmstierna to denounce those proceedings as a nefarious attempt by Frederick's agents to suppress a statement that Charles had been shot at short range. Unfortunately, the effect of this revelation seems to have been to confuse Palmstierna's mind, and perhaps the minds of his collaborators also: certainly a reading of *Carl XII:s död* leaves the impression that the authors were never quite sure (and perhaps did

---

[109] See above, p. 173, n. 89.
[110] For all these prolegomena, see A. Sandklef, *Kulknappen och Carl XII:s död* (Lund 1941), pp. 12–15.
[111] Sandklef, *Carl XII:s död*, pp. 100, 110, 112, 118, 152, 156, 173.
[112] See above, p. 50; Sandklef, *Carl XII:s död*, pp. 118–21.

not greatly care) whether the responsibility lay with Cronstedt and the constitutionalist conspirators (to the list of whom Palmstierna now rashly added the name of Field-Marshal Rehnskiöld), or with Sicre and Frederick I. It was at all events clear that they had by now forgotten, or chose to ignore, the arguments of Stig Jägerskiöld.

More interesting was Strömbom's chapter on the trenches. Strömbom had the idea of using the engineers' work-diaries to reconstruct the process of digging the approaches. Those diaries carefully recorded how many 'paces' of trench were dug by the sappers each night; and Strömbom believed that by using this information and comparing it intelligently on the spot with the actual topography it would be possible to plot the line of the trenches on a modern map with a fair measure of accuracy. Backer in his time had pointed out the risk of error in such a method;[113] but if there were risks, Strömbom was prepared to take them. By using this technique he was able to fix the Old Line in a low position, some 125-130 metres distant from the nearest point in the fortress: very close, in fact, to where Raeder had put it in 1898. Strömbom accordingly declared emphatically that Raeder had been right all along, and that Bruusgaard was certainly wrong. At this point, however, he quitted the relatively firm ground of observation and measurement. To the already long list of conspirators he now added the Swedish map-makers, who had all, it seemed, tacitly agreed to shift the positions of Overbierg and Mellembierg on their maps in order to give plausibility to the story that Charles had been hit by canister-shot from one of them;[114] he embraced the Tollstadian theory as unreservedly as Wieselgren had done; and in a separate chapter he struggled hard to provide acceptable explanations of certain difficulties about the magic button. There was, for instance, the awkward fact that for Nordstierna to have picked it up, it must have failed to ricochet; there was the still more awkward fact that in one diameter it was a full millimetre too big to fit any Caroline musket; there was the baffling question of where Nordstierna was standing when Providence dropped the fatal bullet at his feet: certainly nowhere near Charles XII. Strömbom could only urge that in 1716 Charles XII had ordered a consignment of muskets of rather larger calibre, which the button would have fitted; though he confessed that he could not prove that they had ever been delivered.[115] Still, the idea fitted in well with the story of

[113] Backer, 'Karl XII:s dödsted', pp. 253–4: problems arise from the fact that the work-diaries include cross-trenches and all angles; also that lengths are measured on the ground and not on the map, and this is very uneven country.

[114] Sandklef, *Carl XII:s död*, p. 316.

[115] In fact, the order was cancelled before any deliveries were made: Tor Schreber von Schreeb. 'Några vapenhistoriska reflexioner med anledning av boken "Carl XII:s död" '*KFÅ*

Stierneroos's blunderbuss. And as to Nordstierna's position, the best Strömbom could do was to locate him in a trench running back obliquely from the right flank of the Old Line; and to explain that the noise which Maigret and the Anonymous heard was the sound of the button's impact upon a mossy stone on the inside of *this* trench. Which took some believing. For on the basis of Strömbom's own map, Maigret and Nordstierna must have been distant from each other not less than 50 metres.

Lastly, there was Dr Clason's chapter on the wound. In one respect it was the most substantial part of the book, and the only part of it which had a real impact on future research. Clason was as dissatisfied with Hultkvist's cylinders (which he disrespectfully terms 'phantoms') as Hultkvist had been with the museum crania of 1917. He wanted tests on real flesh and blood; and (in the absence of volunteers) did the best he could with the heads of recently slaughtered sheep and calves. He took care that at least some of the sheep should be provided with a double layer of felt, and a sweat-band, to simulate the hat's resistance to penetration in Charles's case. At them Sandklef, under Clason's direction, fired a Caroline musket with charges varying from 2.5 to 12 grams of powder. And it was found that in every case a musket-ball left traces of lead – even if only minute traces – which could be picked up on X-rays. Now the very careful X-ray examination of 1917 had shown no traces of lead, or of a lead salt. The inference was inescapable, and it has not been seriously challenged; the shot cannot have been an ordinary musket-ball, for musket-balls were made of lead. Two possibilities remained: either it was an iron shot (canister, falconet); or it was a special projectile. Clason caused replicas of the button to be made, and with them pursued his experiments. And he found that with a charge of 9 grams (impact velocity 300 m/s) he achieved a small exit-hole almost identical with that which had been observed in 1859. He was no ballistics expert, as was shortly to be made plain, but he argued that an *iron* shot was almost impossible: for an iron shot to penetrate the hat and the skull, he calculated, an impact velocity of about 225 m/s would be necessary; and he did not believe that the guns of the fortress (still less those of Overbierg) could have attained this. His argument on this point was to run into trouble shortly; but he had decisively altered the terms of this part of the debate. Henceforward a musket-ball was virtually ruled out. Yet there were two points about his demonstration which must provoke comment. One was

(1941), pp. 201–4. And Cronstedt's 'blunderbuss' (*studsare*) is impossible, since these weapons were usually rifled, not smooth-bore, and a rifled barrel would have left traces on the button: no such traces were found.

his admission that it was *conceivable* that a lead bullet at very high speed might in fact carry all the splinters with it and leave none behind: a point which does not seem to have been pursued. The other, much more awkward, was the fact that he never used the regulation charge of 16 grams. His demonstration was based on a reduced charge; his conclusion presupposed a specially reduced charge to fit the special effects of a special projectile. Reduced, one may ask, for what reason? And the only answer appeared to be that the assassin used 9 grams instead of 16 in order to hoodwink Dr Hultkvist, two hundred years later.

VII

Carl XII:s död was a publishing success: within a few weeks a second edition was called for. But though the man in the street might read it as a sensational story, or as a welcome distraction in those grim times, it was received by most of those competent to judge it with cries of outrage. Their reaction was not only critical, it was also emotional; and this imparted a disagreeable tinge of acrimony to the controversy which now developed. It is not difficult to understand why this should have been so. On 30 November 1939, while the Caroline Association was holding its annual commemoration of Charles XII's death, the Soviet Union invaded Finland. In March 1940 Molotov informed the Swedish minister in Moscow that Russia would demand from the Finns the frontiers set by Peter the Great:[116] it was a poignant reminder of the humiliating peace of Nystad, to which Charles's death had been the prelude. Swedish public opinion was virtually unanimous in its strong support of Finland; considerable material aid was provided by the Swedish government; Swedish volunteers served in the Finnish army. The cause for which Charles XII had fought became again for a moment a cause which enlisted the sympathies of the overwhelming majority of the Swedish people; and the idea that he had fallen for a Swedish bullet (or even button) became – intelligibly, if illogically – repugnant. There was worse to come. On 9 April 1940 Hitler overran Denmark and began the conquest of Norway. Sweden now faced the gravest crisis she had confronted for a century and a quarter: between Sandklef's first talk on 6 April, and his second on 20 April, the Swedish army was increased from 85,000 to 320,000 men; at the end of the month the Swedish government was expecting a German invasion within a matter of hours.[117] It never came; but what did come was a wearing

---

[116] W. Carlgren, *Swedish Foreign Policy in the Second World War* (English edn. 1977), p. 41.
[117] Carlgren, *Swedish Foreign Policy*, pp. 60, 62.

war of nerves which required cool heads in the government, and – not least – high morale in the nation. In this situation, with Sweden in total strategic isolation, it was not remarkable that the memory of Charles XII should be felt by many as an inspiration, a focus for patriotic endeavour, an example of determined resistance in circumstances not so very dissimilar, the symbol of Sweden's will to survive; and that there should have been hot resentment at the slur upon his memory which a theory of regicide might seem to carry with it. Hence it was that Major Hugo Uddgren, in a lecture to the Historical Society of Göteborg, could say 'For our army it is not a matter of indifference whether Charles XII died the death of a soldier, or fell by the bullet of an assassin'; hence it was that a writer in *Svensk Tidskrift* could attack the Dramatic Theatre in Stockholm for putting on a performance of Strindberg's *Carl XII* on 30 November 1940, with the comment that such a production 'hardly suggests that the managers of the theatre feel much solidarity with the demand in this country for the rousing of the nation and for moral rearmament'.[118]

There was also in certain circles a strong feeling of distaste at the manner in which the new theory had been proclaimed to the world. The mass media was not regarded as an appropriate vehicle for the advancement of serious research: for Palmstierna to publish his work upon the Dagström erasure in the glossy *Vecko-journalen* under the caption 'Detective-work on Charles XII's death' was bad enough; to launch the button in a couple of broadcasts was worse; to disseminate the theory in what its enemies called 'the hyaena press' was worst of all. It was not surprising that Sandklef should have been in great request as a lecturer to local historical societies; but to his critics he seemed to be carrying on a sort of Midlothian campaign. There was sharp criticism, too, when the button was exhibited in Varberg Museum, with security precautions appropriate to (say) Alfred's Jewel, and a legend which seemed to assert the Nordstierna theory as an established historical fact. *Carl XII:s död* was felt to be an attack by amateurs upon the professionals. The Establishment bristled. A gynaecologist was taking it upon himself to teach an expert in forensic medicine his business; a subaltern was rejecting the agreed verdict of the Historical Sections of the Swedish and Norwegian General Staffs, and ignoring the labours of two eminent geologists as though they had never been; a folklorist was challenging the historians on their own ground. It was this, perhaps, which really stung Professor Nils Ahnlund; for Ahnlund was the very embodiment of the histori-

---

[118] I take these examples from Sandklef, *Kulknappen och Carl XII:s död*, p. 29. Strindberg's great play represented Charles XII as a tragic figure and a broken man.

cal Establishment: 'One of the Eighteen' of the Swedish Academy; a member also of the Royal Academy of Letters, History and Antiquities; editor of *Historisk tidskrift*. It would be wrong to suppose that Ahnlund undervalued oral tradition as a historical source;[119] but he insisted that as far as possible the ordinary standards of historical criticism should be applied to it. It was not sufficient to be referred to a tradition simply by the number it bore in the Varberg collection: he wanted to know the name of the informant, and he wanted the opportunity to hear the tale for himself. But on these points he got no satisfaction from Sandklef, who told him that he was obviously ignorant of the fact that among folklorists the rule was never to disclose the names of informants without their permission. Thus to some extent the ensuing squabble was a clash of disciplines. But even though this be granted, Sandklef was certainly uncommonly evasive. When Ahnlund, writing as secretary of the Swedish Historical Association, asked for excerpts from Sandklef's material, he was told that it was doubtful if that would be possible, since the collection had been moved from Varberg on 12 April to a safer place inland. When Ahnlund induced the Royal Academy of Letters, History and Atiquities to request the loan of material in Sandklef's *private* collection, Sandklef refused on the ground that he was still checking it.[120]

The Caroline Association commissioned a volume which should examine the new theory on a scientific basis; carefully explaining that *as* an Association it expressed no view on the question. As editor of this volume it selected Professor Nils Ahnlund. The outcome was the publication of *Sanning och sägen om Karl XII:s död (Truth and legend on Charles XII's death)* which appeared, in pretty brisk time, in 1941. It contained chapters by Stig Jägerskiöld and Gustaf Hultkvist; but four-fifths of the book came from Ahnlund's pen. Jägerskiöld's chapters were devoted partly to rehearsing the matter of his article; but also to an examination of what the international situation really was on 30 November 1718. Charles's intentions in regard to the negotiations with Russia – and Görtz's also – are obscure; but Jägerskiöld argued persuasively that neither of them intended those negotiations to issue in a final result at that stage; that in fact no agreement with the Russians was reached at the Åland conference; and that in the autumn of 1718 a Russian marriage for Charles Frederick of Holstein was scarcely discussed. Less convincingly, he maintained that Frederick and the Hessians (who had their own representative on Åland) knew all this: there was thus nothing in the

---

[119] As is clear from Ahnlund's article, 'Folktradition som historisk källa', *Historisk tidskrift* (1926), especially pp. 351–3, 363.

[120] Sandklef's account of all this is in his *Kulknappen och Carl XII:s död*, pp. 19–24.

situation, as it might appear to them on 30 November, which could have operated to overcome that fear of Charles's death which Jägerskiöld had demonstrated to be their consistent attitude. Hultkvist's contributions were less impressive and more bad-tempered. In essence, he simply reiterated his view that impact at high velocity was inconsistent with the nature of the wound; though he now conceded that 225 m/s was a conceivable maximum.[121] A misguided attempt to simplify the medical argument for the lay reader produced more confusion than it removed. Clason was handled with some acerbity: an 'inexpert' investigator who committed the elementary error of making the muscles of the temple twice their actual thickness, and assumed a patronising tone not warranted by his status in the forensic-medicine field. Clason's point about lead splinters was shrugged off;[122] as also his use of sheep: Hultkvist, it now appeared, had used horses' heads in 1931, had rejected the results as untrustworthy, and had not thought it worth while to mention them. The button was treated with contempt; and the support it had enlisted was attributed to 'humanity's psychic need of the mystic and the magical':[123] an explanation which to be sure may not have been wholly without substance.

Between these skirmishing actions on either flank, Ahnlund delivered a massive frontal offensive. Unlike Sandklef, he was wise enough to steer clear of medical, ballistic, and tactical questions which his training did not fit him to assess; but within the limits he prescribed for himself and the time at his disposal it was a remarkable performance. And it was truly devastating: by the time he had finished with it the button-theory might seem to have been as badly battered, and as incapable of ricochet, as the button itself. As a historian, he saw it as his first task to reexamine and reappraise the primary sources and the literature. Bring, Weibull, and Bolin had indeed tackled the sources, but they had failed to reach agreement on them. Palmstierna had attempted to deal with the literature and the traditions; but his article had been more of a conspectus than a

---

[121] Clason, curiously enough, had fixed 225 m/s as the necessary – and unobtainable – *minimum* for an iron shot from the fortress.

[122] There was nothing new, said Hultkvist, in Clason's conclusion that the bullet could not be lead: the men of 1917, on the basis of the negative X-ray evidence, must have reached that conclusion: Ahnlund, *Sanning och sägen*, p. 239. If they did, they did not say so: they explicitly said 'iron or lead'.

[123] *Ibid.*, p. 259. The button was slightly flattened opposite the eye: Strömbom had explained this as being caused by a wooden ramrod. Hultkvist, contending that no wooden ramrod would have been strong enough to produce this effect, had a replica of the button made and achieved the flattening by getting the porter at Karolinska Institutet to sling it on to the granite steps: a demonstration which (perhaps rightly) he seems to have felt to be beneath his dignity to conduct in person.

serious analysis, and his chapter in *Carl XII:s död*, taken as a whole, could hardly bear critical examination. Ahnlund was thus the first historian to apply the standards of historical criticism to *both* these areas. He was also the last; and the absence of any serious challenge to his conclusions may perhaps be taken as indicating that historians in general accepted them as valid. As to the three primary narratives, he was perhaps by this time entitled to pass over in silence Bring's theory that they were all commissioned by Frederick I; at all events, he saw no trace of tendentiousness either in Maigret or in Carlberg; and he firmly identified the Anonymous as Kaulbars.[124] His analysis of the early *Gazettes* demonstrated that neither had an official, or even a semi-official character; and that all arguments based on that assumption stand on untenable ground. His dissection of de la Motraye and Voltaire produced, among other things, the point that Sicre cannot have been Voltaire's only informant; but he agreed that both were concerned to give Sicre an alibi.

This brought him to the problem of the suspects; and here he was confronted with what was in effect a comprehensive clearing-up operation. He performed it with unmistakable gusto. First, as to Sicre. He was able to show, from the Journal of Charles Frederick of Holstein's Gentleman-in-Waiting, F. W. von Bergholz, that the Holsteiners treated the accusations against Sicre as mere malicious rumour; he produced good evidence that Sicre's delirium in 1723 was not feigned; he pointed out that the man who moved the Diet to treat Sicre generously in the matter of arrears of pay was General Dücker – a Holsteiner who as it happened was one of those who believed Charles XII had been murdered. Passing on to Palmstierna's reconstruction of the erasure in the proceedings against Dagström in 1728 – a reconstruction which had been hailed in the popular press (as Ahnlund noticed, with frigid distaste) as a 'feat of detection' – he observed merely that Palmstierna's emendation was highly conjectural; that it had the disadvantage that it was impossible French;[125] and that in any case the difference in meaning between the original

---

[124] Mainly because there was no other reasonable candidate. Ahnlund noted that at the Diet of 1723 Kaulbars apologised for his imperfect Swedish: in later life he spoke and wrote it perfectly. This would suggest that the anonymous narrative must have been written well after 1723, since apart from a couple of inadvertent Germanisms its Swedish is irreproachable. Ahnlund pointed out, however, that the handwriting does not seem to be that of Kaulbars, and suggested that the narrative might have been dictated. In politics, it would seem, Kaulbars was if anything a Holsteiner: Ahnlund, *Sanning och sägen*, pp. 79–86, 94.

[125] The version in the official report read: 'il semble que le Roi a été au but [*sc.* bout] du fusil quand it a été tué'; Palmstierna's reconstruction ran: 'il semble que le Roi a été à vue basse de ce [*sic*!] qui l'a tué'. (Though if the French of the man who wrote the minutes was bad enough for him to write 'but' for 'bout', it may have been bad enough for him to write 'ce' instead of 'celui'.)

and what had been superimposed upon it was so fine that not much could be read into it: certainly not enough to justify the outraged indignation with which Palmstierna had celebrated his 'discovery'. And so dismissed the affair, as he was to dismiss so much else, in the name of common sense; removing – as it might seem for ever – Sicre from the list of suspects. It was a result which accorded well with Jägerskiöld's elimination of the dynastic motive.

This matter disposed of, Ahnlund could move on to attack the tangled zareba of eighteenth-century legend and family tradition. It fell before his sickle in swathes: Pihlgren, Liewen, Asplind, Hultman, Tiburtius were swept out of the arena of serious historical discussion; and the lively imaginations of Evert von Saltza were exploded by allowing his various versions to confront one another. The testimony of the Cederströms, however, was less vulnerable: here rebuttal rested only on a presumption.[126] And as to the Carlberg family tradition, Ahnlund was driven to take refuge in generalities. But as might have been expected he had a field-day with the Tollstadius legend: most of what Paludan-Müller had said, and a great deal that he had not, was urged against the authenticity of the document with a force and irony which there was no resisting, and which incidentally finally interred the story of the half-drawn sword. Ahnlund was mistaken, however, in his triumphant claim that by annihilating the Tollstadian document he had dealt the button-theory a mortal blow.[127] Certainly its adherents were faithful followers of Wieselgren; but it was by no means the case that their arguments necessarily depended upon Tollstadius: Nordstierna did not need Tollstadius to create him, and it was possible to believe in murder without suspecting Cronstedt. What mattered was the circumstances in which the button had been discovered; the reliability of the recordings of local tradition; and a few peripheral matters such as Charles's 'Turkish' coat.

Ahnlund began by making a clear distinction between the two types of tradition which had become entangled in this case. The first was the tradition that Charles was 'hard', and that he had been killed by a magic bullet or button. The second comprised various traditions regarding the finding, concealing, throwing away, and ultimate recovery of the projectile. Traditions of the first type, it was not difficult to show, were fairly common in many parts of Sweden, and

---

[126] The family tradition was that Cronstedt's confession on his deathbed was made in the presence of his niece: Ahnlund's retort was that she could hardly have been present, since her own mother died on the same day: Ahnlund, *Sanning och sägen*, p. 160.

[127] 'the acceptance of this document lies near the very heart of the historical thinking which directs and governs this most recent contribution to an old controversy':*ibid.*, 171.

in some cases were localised by making the murderer a local man: the high concentration around Öxnevalla was to be ascribed simply to Sandklef's laudable diligence as a collector. Very different were traditions of the second group, which Ahnlund called 'finder-traditions'. These were localised not merely to Öxnevalla, but to the blacksmith in person. Ahnlund could find no trace of their appearance, independently of Andersson, before the historic find of the button.[128] And various versions, if not directly traceable to personal contact with Andersson, appeared to have developed after the report of his find became public property. Others showed clear signs of literary influence.[129] Ahnlund pointed out that Andersson gave inconsistent accounts of the date of his find, contradictory versions of the provenance of the historic load of gravel, and a variety of locations for where the button was thrown away. He was able to show that the nonagenarian informant who in 1939 had supplied Sandklef with the name 'Nordstierna' had in 1935 given another version of his story (unknown to Sandklef) from which all the details of the 'finder-tradition' were absent; and he had information that the old man had had a protracted visit from Andersson on the day before Sandklef went to interview him. The most damaging blow to the finder tradition, however, came as a result of researches which (at Ahnlund's behest?) Miss Stina Christensson, an officer of the West Swedish Folklore Museum, and herself a native of Öxnevalla, had conducted in January 1941. She had interviewed twenty-eight residents in Öxnevalla aged between 51 and 87; and she had found that twenty-six had never heard of the soldier from Öxnevalla before Andersson picked up the button, and that no one before that date had heard of his taking the button home from Frederikshald and subsequently throwing it away. She was also able to examine the informant whom Sandklef regarded as his most valuable witness. And by him she was assured that though he had for many years known the story that Charles was killed by one of the buttons from his coat, he had never heard the story about the Deragård gravel-pit until the news of Andersson's find got about.[130]

After this, there was not much to be said. But Ahnlund took the opportunity to point out that the revelation that there actually was a

---

[128] To this the information of August Carlsson in 1922 (above, p. 182) might be an exception; but as Sandklef had made clear, the story came *not* direct from Carlsson: it was Andersson, reporting Carlsson. Ahnlund noted, however, that the Varberg accession-catalogue shows *no* accessions concerning Charles XII's death for the period 1920–33. We must presume that we have here to do with one of the (inaccessible) notes in Sandklef's private collection.

[129] Including, of course, the Tollstadius–Stierneroos tradition. There were articles on Charles's death in the widely read *Göteborgs Handels- och Sjöfartstidning* in 1931 and 1934.

[130] Ahnlund, *Sanning och sägen*, pp. 209, 206.

Nordstierna living near Öxnevalla need cause no great surprise, since for half a century all the successive soldiers who were allocated to that particular allotment were by convention given that surname; which was hardly likely to have been forgotten. And finally, he dealt with the 'Turkish button' – not that he attached any importance to whether it was really Turkish or not.[131] However, in the interests of historical truth he felt bound to point out that Axel Löwen's portrait was painted, not in Bender, but in Stralsund; that in any case it showed bullet-shaped buttons, not on Charles's coat (as tradition demanded) but on his waistcoat; that it was well attested that he always wore his coat buttoned up to the chin, so that the common soldier in his army was unlikely to be familiar with the appearance of his waistcoat-buttons; and lastly that Sandklef's assertion (in one of his broadcasts) that Charles was so fond of these particular buttons that he had them transferred from one uniform to another was mere fanciful speculation.[132] And with this short excursion into the history of costume he closed the case for Clio.

Ahnlund had been careful to disclaim any intention of impugning anybody's *bona fides*, and he lost no opportunity of expressing his thanks to Palmstierna for the information with which that gentleman had voluntarily supplied him; but as he frankly acknowledged his treatment of the finder-tradition was certainly polemical in tone, and it is pretty clear that he believed Sandklef to have been betrayed by the collector's enthusiasm, and a good measure of wishful thinking, into an uncritical acceptance of highly dubious material. He noted that Andersson was described by one of the supporters of his theory as 'a person of singularly lively imagination';[133] and he probably considered that this was a considerable understatement. For him, it is clear, the whole affair was a spectacular and irritating example of what can happen when amateur local historians and parochial patriots get the bit between their teeth. It was only natural that Sandklef should see it rather differently; and before 1941 was out he had published his reply.[134] To what he regarded as a spiteful and libellous attack on his reputation he retorted with unpleasant insinuations and what could only be construed as a threat of legal action.[135]

---

[131] *Ibid.*, p. 227.

[132] A supposition difficult to reconcile with the fact that Charles is said to have worn out his clothes about once a week. In a short Appendix to *Sanning och sägen*, Barbro Göthberg-Edlund produced what she contended was virtually a twin to Andersson's button. She had consulted a button-making firm in Prague about it; the answer was inconclusive, and her demonstration appears to be inconclusive too.

[133] Ahnlund, *Sanning och sägen*, p. 219.

[134] Sandklef, *Kulknappen och Carl XII:s död*.

[135] *Ibid.*, pp. 36, 38: 'If need be, the accusations will be rebutted in another *forum*.'

He was indeed able to score a small success by quoting the opinion of metallurgists that both the lead core and the brass mantle of the button suggested that it was not of Swedish origin;[136] but this was the only ace in his hand, and unfortunately it was in a minor suit. For the rest, he could only fall back upon reiterated assertions that Charles was not in a particularly dangerous position; that visibility was adequate for a murderer to risk a shot (but not, it would seem, to be at any risk of being observed); and that Bruusgaard's trench might indeed be *a* trench, but it was not the Old Line: it was rather the so-called *faux-attaque* – a theory irreconcilable with the position allotted to the *faux-attaque* by his collaborator Strömbom. Above all, that the Deragård tradition, and other local traditions about bringing home the bullet, antedated Andersson's find: a contention which appears to have rested in part on notes in his private collection. He had no reply to Miss Christensson's statistics about the opinion of twenty-eight Öxnevalla inhabitants; and two attempts to get his star witness to repudiate his disastrous evidence to her failed entirely, the witness finally taking to the fields in order to escape badgering (a manoeuvre which proved vain).[137] And in the end, after two hundred pages of argument, he virtually conceded most of the points Ahnlund had been making. He disclosed that Andersson was cognizant of the Tollstadius – Stierneroos tradition in 1931, though he did not appear to see the implications of that statement.[138] He admitted that a tradition-bearer might rationalise what he had heard, and include the rationalisation in his transmission of the tradition; that the tradition that Charles could be shot only with his own buttons 'logically' demanded a murderer, who might be supplied because he was 'logically' necessary; that Nordstierna, though he existed, might not have been telling the truth; and that the story he told would not have had 'sufficient dramatic life' to exist 'for two centuries', if in addition it had not been spiced with the story of how the button was thrown away.[139] Nevertheless, he did not perceive that he had in fact capitulated. On the last page of his book he promised that once the war was over he would seek a matching button 'inside and outside Europe', that he would institute spectroscopic analysis of brass and

[136] *Ibid.*, pp. 159–69.

[137] *Ibid.*, pp. 113–22. Sandklef's explanation of this unfortunate man's exasperating behaviour was that his family, and especially his wife, wanted no more publicity: after his fourth interrogation he may well have shared that view.

[138] The journalist who wrote the article about the button in *Göteborgs Tidning* for 27 November 1938 had visited Andersson in 1934, and had then found in his possession a copy of *Göteborgs Handels- och Sjöfartstidning* for 21 February 1931 which contained an article on the Tollstadius–Stierneroos theory.

[139] Sandklef, *Kulknappen och Carl XII:s död*, pp. 178, 185, 188, 189.

lead from different ages and regions; and that he would publish the results of his enquiries. No such publication seems in fact to have appeared. But in a defiant final paragraph Sandklef announced his attention of continuing to exhibit the button at Varberg, with an inscription even more categorical than that which it had hitherto borne.[140]

Dr Sandklef might nail his button to the mast; but his collaborators seemed to be more ready to follow Nordstierna's example and look for a convenient gravel-pit. Palmstierna maintained a discreet silence; and though Strömbom produced new maps in an attempt to buttress his old argument, he steered well clear of the button.[141] Dr Clason, smarting under what he considered to be the unsportsman-like[142] tactics of his assailants, was concerned only to correct Hult-kvist's errors, and to answer the criticisms of the historians of firearms and the experts in ballistics. Hultkvist's essential argument had been that the size of the exit-hole is determined by the speed of the bullet: low speed gives a small hole, high speed a big one. This Clason refused to accept. The small hole in the skin on the right-hand side which the observers of 1859 had noted was generally agreed to have been made possible only by the skin's elasticity. But the tanned skin which had covered Hultkvist's 'phantom' had had no elasticity at all; Hultkvist had never obtained an exit-hole smaller than the bullet; and his shooting-tests therefore provided no basis for his argument. What Hultkvist ought to have done was to estimate the head's resistance; and that meant, in fact, that he should have reconstructed the line of the shot through the skull. It was to this point that Clason devoted the major part of his book. The ordinary historian is in no position to question the validity of his arguments, which are intricate, highly technical, and probably fully intelligible only to an anatomist; but his conclusions are clear enough. Clason believed that the bullet did not hit Charles squarely at right-angles; that it may well have made a small ricochet inside the skull; that it had in consequence much less of the brain to thrust aside, so that the hydrodynamic wave was much less than Hultkvist had supposed; and therefore that a shot at relatively short range was entirely poss-

[140] Ibid., p. 205.
[141] Nils Strömbom, 'Kartmaterialets utsago om löpgravarna vid Fredriksten. Några nya bidrag', KFÅ (1945). Only one military expert was prepared to consider Strömbom's line as at any rate a possible hypothesis: Erik Zeeh. 'Kartmaterialet och frågan om det svenska löpgravs-systemet samt Carl XII:s dödsplats', KFÅ, (1942). Strömbom's theory was finally quashed, after an exhaustive examination, by Tor Holmquist: 'Löpgravarna vid Fredriksten', KFÅ (1944), pp. 161–210.
[142] He complained that Hultkvist's criticism contained 'en rikhaltigare förekomst av dylika vetenskapliga "fouls" ': Clason, Gätan från Fredrikshald, p. 15.

ible. And he established one other point of some significance: namely that a careful examination of the trigonometrical and radiographic material in the report of 1917 makes it clear that the line of shot was not, as the final report stated, horizontal if Charles's head was erect: even in that case the line of the wound rose by as much as 5 mm. And if, as seemed to be the case, he was leaning his head on his left hand, the inclination of the line of the wound to the horizontal would be increased by as much as 5 to 7 degrees: a result which presented real difficulties for the theory of a canister-shot from the fortress, except upon the supposition that at the moment of impact Charles had, unnoticed by observers, momentarily leant his head over to the right.

On the ballistic side of the question the controversy had by this time been reduced to a quite narrow compass, thanks to Clason's argument from lead splinters. It had become apparent that Charles owed his death either to iron canister-shot, or to some sort of special projectile: which did not necessarily mean the button. What was at issue was whether the king was within range of canister from any part of the defences; and whether (if he was) the wound was reconcilable with such a shot. The most substantial military criticism of *Carl XII:s död* was therefore directed to answering at any rate the first of these questions in the affirmative. Captain H. Jentzen had no hesitation in doing so.[143] Having demonstrated that Clason had done his calculations of muzzle- and impact-velocity incorrectly, he felt able to assert that there was no ballistic obstacle to the king's being hit by canister from Fredriksten. The Curator of the Army Museum, Lieut.-Colonel Th. Jakobsson, went a good deal further. He pointed out that besides the ordinary cannon there had existed 'strengthened' cannon with substantially greater range; that 6-pounder guns (probably strengthened) were known to have been in Overbierg; and that Charles was therefore within effective range of *all* parts of the defences (which made it easier to explain his being hit from the left). It was unfortunately the case that canister-balls for a 6-pounder usually had a diameter much too big for the wound; but Jakobsson had found examples with a diameter of as little as 22.4 mm., and robustly concluded that there were 'strong reasons' for supposing that in the 200-odd canister known to have ben fired by the defenders there had been a few balls of a calibre within the limits laid down in 1917.[144] He

[143] H. Jentzen, 'Inbillning och verklighet, diskussion angående boken om Carl XII:s död. Ballistiken', *Ny Militär Tidskrift* (1941).

[144] Th. Jakobsson, 'Kritisk granskning av i boken "Carl XII:s död" lämnade vapenhistoriska uppgifter', *KFÅ* (1941).

had forgotten, it would seem, the precise figure of 19.5 mm., as established by the hole in the hat.

But if he had forgotten it, Dr Clason had not. In his reply to his critics he would have none of any attempts to stretch the diameter beyond 20 mm. Frankly admitting earlier errors in calculation, and replying to Jentzen's criticism of his use of Medinger's formula by pointing out that the formula used by Jentzen was more antiquated and even less applicable, he concentrated upon two main points. His first was the impossibility of a canister-shot from Overbierg or Mellembierg. He did not dispute the increased range of Jakobsson's strengthened guns, but he made the valid point that this was at least partly offset by the increased windage when they fired canister rather than cannon-balls. Secondly, he questioned the validity of the rather vague suggestion that canister might contain balls small enough to fit the dimensions of 1917. This necessarily plunged him into the morass of Swedish weights and measures; for the energy of the ball on impact, and the damage it could inflict, were directly related to its weight, and this in turn to the size of the gun as measured in pounds.[145] But upon the basic question of just how much an (artillery) pound weighed there was the wildest disagreement: Clason stated it variously at 491, 496, 509, or 'in round figures' 500 grams; Jakobsson at 340 grams for iron balls and 425 for lead. One has the impression that Clason succeeded in confusing himself, as well as the reader, in traversing this tangled country.[146] However, he emerged with one hard fact: that though there did in 1704 exist canister-balls of 2.25 lod (which meant a diameter of 21 mm), a scrutiny of the estimates and reports concerning ammunition-supply for the artillery department of the College of War for the years 1682–1717 revealed no canister-balls of less than 2.25 lod. And a diameter of 21 mm was more than Clason was prepared to tolerate. Indeed, he rejected the whole supposition of the use of smaller-sized balls as packing: the very detailed contemporary textbook of artillery practice on which he relied gave no support to the idea. And on this point it seems undeniable that his research was more thorough, and his arguments more convincing, than those of his military critics. Nevertheless, he was prepared, with curious inconsequence, to consider the hypothesis of a canister-shot from Fredriksten (but not

---

[145] A canister packed with ball was taken to weigh the same as a cannon-ball. Cannon-balls were weighed in (artillery) pounds: a 6-pounder gun took cannon-balls weighing six (artillery) pounds. Each ball in a canister weighed as many lod as the cannon-ball weighed (artillery) pounds; and 32 (or sometimes 30) lod were reckoned to the (artillery) pound: Clason, Gåtan från Fredrikshald, pp. 132–42 for the full and careful explanation.

[146] The impression is strongest on pp. 142–3, where the argument does not seem to fit the table of weights and dimensions.

from the forts) as an open question:[147] an indication, perhaps, that this was ground upon which he did not feel himself at home. All the same, he pressed for a rigorous and impartial enquiry into the size, weight, availability, and ballistic properties of canister-shot.

The need for an enquiry of this kind was almost the only point on which Jakobsson and Clason were in agreement; though Jakobsson, with a juster appreciation of the priorities, was content that it should be postponed; the times were too serious for energies to be diverted to 'a problem which – after all – is as unimportant as this'.[148] But by an odd irony it was precisely at this moment that the long controversy was given a final and most unexpected twist, and a twist which seemed to make their dispute totally irrelevant. This was nothing less than a serious attempt to revive the theory of a shot from the right. It came from Hans Key-Åberg, son of that Algot Key-Åberg who had produced the report of 1917.[149] With its hail of exclamation-marks and deluge of italics it made a strange appearance in an otherwise sober professional journal. But it had two challenging points to make. The first rested largely on the opinion of a foreign expert who preferred to remain anonymous. This expert held that experience from 1914–18 showed that defects tended to be larger in exit-holes than in entry-holes (back to the eighteenth century!); and he was inclined to think that the report of 1917, which had rested mainly on the bevelling effect visible in those portions of the defects which they were able to reconstruct, might perhaps have gone further than the evidence warranted, since so much of the skull was missing. Key-Åberg's second point rested on the evidence of the hat. Existing portraits of Charles with a hat showed clearly that its button was on the right-hand side, not the left; and the wear on the hat caused by his raising it in salute confirmed that evidence. And since the hole was on the same side as the button, it too was on the right; which meant that the shot came from the right also. These points had already been made by the indomitable Dr Liljewalch in 1859, but had then been brushed aside. And Ahnlund himself, as Key-Åberg did not fail to point out, had written (in what may have been no more than an inadvertence) that the hole was on the right.[150] Clearly, much depended upon whether the historians of hats confirmed the not too extensive evidence from portraits. Realising this, Key-Åberg tried to have it both ways: if (which he did not believe) the button was after all on the left, then there were two possibilities: either Charles was

[147] Clason, *Gåtan från Fredrikshald*, p. 90.
[148] Jakobsson, 'Kritisk granskning', p. 198.
[149] Hans Key-Åberg, 'Karl XII:s dödskott', *Svenska Låkerefidning* (1941) pp. 1,729–69.
[150] Ahnlund, *Sanning och sägen*, p. 40; Hans Key-Åberg, 'Karl XII:s dödsskott', p. 1,769.

wearing his hat back to front (perhaps in order to get a wider field of vision); or somebody, at some time, had moved the button from its original place on the left, affixed it to the hat above the entry-hole on the right, and then turned the hat round; all this with intent to mislead.[151]

These remarkable conjectures (which assumed the theory they purported to prove), coming on top of an inaccessible anonymous expert, and conveyed in a style which made Sandklef's appear a model of classical austerity, probably prevented Key-Åberg's article from being taken seriously. Clason's book was already in proof when it appeared; but he managed to deal trenchantly with it in an appendix:[152] his most telling point was that the expert necessarily had his information at second hand; that it was impossible to tell whether that information was complete; and that it was apparently based on the presumption of a lead bullet. It was not until 1950 that Key-Åberg's theory was given careful consideration. It came in an article by Tor Holmquist which appeared in *Karolinska Förbundets Årsbok* for that year.[153] Holmquist was no medical expert, and admitted that he could do no more than record his impression of the medical debate; but this did not prevent him from reaching conclusions which were, perhaps, unexpected. He found the strongest argument for a shot from the left in the fact that the noise of the impact was not masked by the sound of the discharge. He conceded that a canister-shot from Fredriksten had been shown to be ballistically possible; but he pointed out that though Clason, with his special projectile, had succeeded in obtaining an exit-hole comparable to that observed in 1859, Hultkvist with his iron ball had never managed it. All in all, he was disposed to think that the grounds for a shot from the left, though strong, were no longer incontestable. The observers of 1859, after all, had seen bones on the right bent inwards, though they had vanished by 1917.

Algot Key-Åberg, before the investigation, had said that the drawings from 1859 suggested an entry-hole on the right. The phrasing of the 1917 report suggested that its framers had not expected the result at which they arrived. Holmquist therefore concluded that the wound on the left still lacked any satisfactory explanation as an entry-wound, but was certainly explicable as an exit-wound. And summed up: 'in our time [a shot from the right] has been considered

---

[151] Hans Key-Åberg, 'Karl XII:s dödsskott', p. 1,769.

[152] He had already confuted Key-Åberg's pharmaceutical conjectures about the embalming procedure in *Svenska Läkaretidningen* (1941), p. 1,949.

[153] Tor Holmquist, 'Dödsskottet år 1718. Reflexioner kring skottriktningen', *KFÅ* (1950), pp. 111–46.

more of a paradox than a hypothesis. A revaluation is beginning to break through.'

There were two other pieces of evidence in support of a shot from the right. The first was the statement in the report of 1917 that the skin around the wound on the right had the appearance of having been bruised, rather than of a laceration: a point which had been forgotten in the subsequent debate.[154] The second was the evidence of R.F. Lynar, who saw the hat as early as 1731, and noted that it was 'etwas gerissen' on the right side, but intact on the left.[155] Other considerations, of a more general nature, might also be urged: a shot from the right makes it easier for a murderer to escape observation, since the officers in the trench were not likely to be looking to their rear; and Carlberg – much the most likely observer, since he was patrolling up and down the New Line – must necessarily have had his back to the trench for half the time. It solved also the problem of visibility: the king would be silhouetted against the pitch-flares on the fortress. And it solved the problem of the line of the shot. But though all this is true, the hypothesis (apart from all other objections) runs into grave difficulties in regard to the hat. If indeed the button was on the right, that hole 'the size of a little finger' which observers in 1859 saw on the right side is none the less inconceivable as an entry-hole: Hultkvist's snippet rules it out.[156] A shot from the right is reconcilable with the evidence of the hat only on the supposition that the projectile had no hat-brim to penetrate before it entered the skull, and that it hit the hat on the *inside, after* traversing the head, and carried Hultkvist's snippet away with it as it did so. But even this solution postulates a special projectile. And though such a projectile is not, of course, impossible, it has been generally agreed that it was from the outside, and not from the inside, that the bullet struck the hat.

VIII

Holmquist's article proved to be the last shot in the long battle. The controversy came to an end; though it could not be said to have come to a conclusion. In its latter stages it had ranged over so wide a field

---

[154] Algot Key-Åberg, *Om Konung Karl XII:s banesår*, pp. 17, 31: the commission found this 'unusual', but explained it by the high momentum which the bullet still retained: *ibid.*, p. 32.

[155] Ahnlund, *Sanning och sägen*, p . 180. n. 3.

[156] If, as Hans Key-Åberg suggested, the button was originally on the left and Charles wore his hat back to front, it is hard to believe that no one noticed this highly improbable circumstance. And as to his alternative suggestion that the button had been shifted from left to right, it is enough to remark that though it might be possible to move the button, it was not possible to move the signs of wear on the hat: when the side of the hat which showed the button and the

that no one person could command the skills necessary to pass judgment on all its aspects. After 1950 nobody attempted to do so; for indeed the prospect was too discouraging. Stalemate on the ballistic front; stalemate on the medical front. No agreement, even, on the question of the most likely motive behind a possible murder. For Clason, it had become the work of 'a group of revolutionary, or rather reactionary, conspirators, who had little in common with the Swedish people',[157] by which he intended the aristocratic-constitutionalist opposition. For Lennart Thanner, who believed that 'the political conjunctures speak in favour of murder', those conjunctures seemed rather to point to the Hessians.[158] And many historians of good repute did not believe that it was murder at all. No doubt it was true that more rigorous and impartial investigation, as demanded (for instance) by Clason and Jakobsson, was possible; though one may doubt whether the results would have proved decisive. But after 1950 no one felt moved to undertake the task. Men came tacitly to accept that the problem appeared to be insoluble, and was undoubtedly becoming tiresome: there were other fields to explore, more interesting and more fruitful than this hard-tramped and arid soil. The international circumstances which had generated such heat in 1940 had passed away; old-fashioned notions of national honour could no longer raise the temperature of debate; and with the elimination of Nordstierna's button there was no need for a historian to feel the *saeva indignatio* which had moved Ahnlund. Indeed, the death of Ahnlund in 1957 can be seen as the end of an era: with his passing the last *storsvensk* historian of eminence disappeared from the scene, and with it the 'passionate personal engagement' which had prompted his intervention in this particular problem.[159] As Karl-Gustaf Hildebrand frankly said in his obituary notice, to many of the younger historians Ahnlund appeared 'totally alien'.[160] Swedish historiography was now moving in new directions. It was still overwhelmingly inward-looking: articles and books on any other country's history – except in so far as it related to Scandinavia – were (and are) still remarkably few. But there was a change in the approach of Swedish historians to the history of their own country, and a change also in the fields of interest which attracted them. The

hole had been turned round so that it was on the left rather than the right, the wear would have appeared to be on the *back* left-hand corner.

[157] Clason, *Gåtan från Fredrikshald*, p. 158.

[158] Lennart Thanner, *Revolutionen i Sverige efter Karl XII:s död* (Uppsala, 1953), p. 73.

[159] The phrase is Karl-Gustaf Hildebrand's in his obituary in *Historisk tidskrift* (1957), p. 61.

[160] *Ibid., loc. cit.* Sven Grauers's obituary in *KFÅ* (1957), p. 9, is largely devoted to Ahnlund's share in *Sanning och sägen*: Grauers judged it to 'have come as near to the truth as it is possible to get'.

growth-points of Swedish historiography shifted decisively to the nineteenth and twentieth centuries. And in all periods there was, as in other countries, a move away from personalities to social groups, to classes, movements, 'grass-roots' history, quantifiable history. This produced, as it was bound to do, an intense, continuing debate on methodology: indeed, there have been moments when, if one may judge from their historical journals, the Swedes were so preoccupied with the problem of how history ought to be written that they had little time in which to write it. *Karolinska Förbundets Årsbok* has indeed managed to reap a substantial annual harvest of the old staple grains; an attractive writer such as Frans G. Bengtsson could still produce a two-volume best-seller on Charles XII;[161] but though the new school of historians might be prepared to acknowledge the fascination of Charles's personality, they certainly felt no great urge to tackle the problem of his death: after all, as a topic for the modern historian Charles suffered from the decisive disadvantage that he was not quantifiable. They were content, therefore, to give the last word to Dr Johnson, and to leave it at that.[162] And, after surveying the tangled course of more than two centuries of controversy, we may well think that theirs was a wise decision.

[161] Frans G. Bengtsson, *Karl XII:s levnad*, I–II (Stockholm 1945): English translation, *The Life of Charles XII* (1960).
[162] Samuel Johnson, *The Vanity of Human Wishes*:
His fall was destined to a barren strand,
A petty fortress, and a dubious hand . . .